W9-COG-559

The Front Nine

Golf's All-Time Greatest Shots

Barry LeBrock

Library of Congress Cataloging-in-Publication Data
LeBrock, Barry.
  The front nine : golf's nine all-time greatest shots / Barry LeBrock.
     p. cm.
  ISBN-13: 978-1-60078-071-4
  ISBN-10: 1-60078-071-7
  1. Golf--History. I. Title.
  GV963.L43 2008
  796.352'6409--dc22

                              2008007938

This book is available in quantity at special discounts for your group or organization. For further information, contact:

> Triumph Books
> 542 South Dearborn Street
> Suite 750
> Chicago, Illinois 60605
> (312) 939-3330
> Fax (312) 663-3557

Printed in U.S.A.
ISBN: 978-1-60078-071-4
Design by Megan Dempster
Photos courtesy of Getty Images unless otherwise indicated.

To my family: 5, 15, 4

Contents

Acknowledgments

I would like to thank several people for their help as I wrote this book.

Most of all, I would like to thank my family: my wife, Susan, and my daughters, Jalyn and Keira. Time spent at the keyboard or doing research was time taken from them. A happy home makes for a productive writer, and I live for their love from now to eternity.

To my parents, Micki and Sam, my brothers, Jeff and Marc, and my in-laws, Britt and Joy; you didn't help me one bit with the book, but I sure do love you guys.

Thanks for assorted contributions to Eleanor Lanza at the World Golf Hall of Fame, Shannon Doody at the USGA, Dan Higgins at the Golf Channel, Linda McCoy-Murray of the Jim Murray Memorial Foundation, and author Brian Curtis.

I also got support from several people at FSN and Fox, including expertise from Scott Bemis, outstanding research from Brody Womer, and valuable input and editing from Elliot Harrison.

Lastly, I would like to extend a lifetime worth of thanks and gratitude to the late great William C. MacPhail, a unique man of dignity and character. It was his belief in me that has allowed me to attain many of the great things in my life. I will be forever grateful.

"Golf can best be defined as an endless series of tragedies obscured by the occasional miracle."

—Unknown

Introduction

Earliest known references to the game of golf go back to the 1400s. In all those years of play, over seven continents, on countless courses, there have been, what? A billion shots hit? A trillion?

There is no way to know the actual number, just as there is no way to know which of those were, in fact, the best. Ranking anything—from hot dogs to show dogs, from burgers to ballplayers—is an inexact science, at best. Ranking the top shots in the history of a game that has been played for six centuries is downright impossible. The list that follows is just one person's opinion.

Taken into consideration were the following factors:

Significance of Event. In which tournament was the shot hit? Yes, the shots themselves are what is being judged, but take a shot from, say, the British Open or the Ryder Cup, and duplicate it at, say, the Fill-in-the-Blank.com Invitational, and it just doesn't have quite the same impact.

Magnitude of the Moment. In the same way that a World Series home run in the late innings of Game 7 is far more memorable than one in the third inning of Game 2, a great shot on the 17th hole in the final round of a tournament is far more meaningful than one on the 6th hole of the opening round. A great shot may be forgotten. A great shot at the perfect moment will live forever.

Resulting Run. If a great shot does not lead to victory, is it truly a great shot? It can be argued either way, but for our purposes, let's just say it isn't great enough. Each of the nine shots that follow led directly to victory in a given tournament.

Persona of the Player. This was considered not quite as heavily as other factors; however, right or wrong, it is a reality of sports that greatness from an established star adds some serious rocket fuel to the engine that creates legend. An interesting question with no right answer is: were the shots featured here coincidentally hit by some of the most celebrated players in history, or are those players most celebrated because they were capable of shots like these?

The object of golf is so simple it can be stated in one sentence: hitting a ball with a club, the player tries to get the ball from the tee box into a particular cup in as few strokes as possible. That's it.

How can something so basic be so complex? To fully understand it, one must play the game. In the pages that follow, you will get a glimpse into the ups and downs, failures and successes, triumphs and tragedies of some of the greatest to ever play. With the right combination of skill, opportunity, and luck, some even pull off the occasional miracle.

Walter Hagen (left) and fellow American golfer Gene Sarazen (right), competitors for the Golf World Championship, mug for the camera on October 7, 1922.

CHAPTER ONE

1935:
He Got a *What*?!?

PRELUDE

The rhythmic, metallic click and clack of the wheels on a turn-of-the-century locomotive banged out a distant beat as the door opened and a chilling winter breeze blew through a small, run-down house shared by two families in Harrison, New York.

Upstairs, a 10-day-old infant was bundled up, sleeping next to a rickety furnace, blissfully unaware of the poverty around him. His name was Eugenio Saraceni. He was the second child and only son of an Italian immigrant named Federico Saraceni who barely made ends meet working as a carpenter. The child's mother, Adela, was a loving, supportive woman and a great cook who could work a kitchen for all it was worth.

It was standard operating procedure in the neighborhood, and in the era, for children to help their families supplement their modest incomes. As a youngster, Eugenio kicked in his share, earning money before he could even grasp its value. By the time he entered third grade, his résumé was both long and diverse. He had already worked several jobs, including selling magazines, picking fruit, scavenging scrap metal, and cleaning a woodshop, to name a few.

The extra money helped, and working the odd jobs was good experience, but his father saw one, and only one, true occupation for his son—carpentry—and the boy wanted nothing to do with it.

Eugenio first heard about golf at the age of eight. One summer night in 1910, his mother told him about the son of a neighbor who was making good money working for "the rich people who play that game with the ball and sticks." Always interested in a new way to make money, young Saraceni knocked on that neighbor's door, hooked himself up, and was soon working as a caddy at the Larchmont Country Club, a 40-minute trolley ride from Harrison. He began to literally and figuratively get a view of life on the other side of the tracks.

The lifestyle of the men who played and that certain camaraderie shared by a foursome were both very appealing aspects of golf, but it was the game itself that tugged at Eugenio's very being. From the moment he hit the first shot of his life, something just felt right about the sport, and despite all obstacles—financial and otherwise—he was determined to play. But his father, a stern and frustrated man who spoke broken English and could find little use in America for his elegant command of the Italian language, was wholly determined that his son would be a carpenter. By the time Eugenio was a teenager, most of his working hours were spent in a woodshop, learning the craft. But his mind invariably wandered, transporting him to Larchmont Country Club, where he soaked in sunshine under brilliant blue skies—systematically working every hole, strategically executing imagined shots, reading each break in every grain of the familiar greens, dropping unlikely birdies, even beating the best regulars.

In 1917, with the Great War raging, there was no work to be found in Harrison, so the Saraceni family moved to nearby Bridgeport, Connecticut, where Federico had found a job in the British Artillery Works. With his family desperate financially, Eugenio was forced to drop out of school and, with his father's guidance, began searching for full-time work. His carpentry training led him to a war-related job at a company called Remington Arms, drilling holes in the wooden racks in which ammunition shells were sent to Russia.

The next January, he caught a cold that got increasingly worse. Within a couple of weeks, he was in the hospital, unconscious for three days with a temperature of 105° F. When he awakened, there was a priest standing over his bed administering last rites.

The cold led to pneumonia, which led to pleurisy, which led to an operation in which tubes were inserted below his shoulder blades and through his rib cage to drain fluid from his lungs. For three weeks, Eugenio lay on his side with tubes protruding from his back. The operation was ultimately successful, and as he regained his strength, his discharge came with a condition. The doctor who signed his release papers insisted the young man not return to the war plant, or for that matter, any indoor job. The recipe for a complete recovery, he said, was simple: six weeks of rest followed by a life lived, in large part, outdoors in the fresh air and sunshine. Any subsequent mention by his father of a job involving carpentry was answered briefly and rather happily. Eugenio simply replied with the words, "Doctor's orders," which put an end to all conversation.

Now 16 years old, fully healthy, and sporting the reluctant carpenter's equivalent of a get-out-of-jail-free card, Saraceni was all about golf. In his earlier years, he had dreamt about a lifetime of work as a caddy, but recently that had all changed. Seeing the success of players like 1913 U.S. Open champion Francis Ouimet and the following year's winner, Walter Hagen, he realized the son of a poor man could succeed in a rich man's game. Without the funds or the connections to play any of Bridgeport's elite courses, he began hanging out at a small and simple nine-hole public course called Beardsley Park. There he approached the course pro, Al Ciuci, introducing himself and asking whether he could hit some chip shots and practice his putting. The pair quickly built a rapport and before long, Ciuci was allowing Eugenio to use empty parts of the course and encouraging him as he hit balls, one after another after another.

A few months later, Ciuci invited Eugenio to play in a foursome, which included Ciuci's brother, Joe, and a man named Art DeMane. The players stepped up to the first tee, a 145-yard par-3. Joe Ciuci hit first and stuck a short iron, at the time referred to as a *mashie*, about a foot from the pin. DeMane then ripped one even closer: about eight inches from the hole. It was then the kid's turn. He took his stance, made a compact, steady pass at the ball in prefect tempo, and sent it soaring, straight and true, headed for the green. The ball took two hops and disappeared into the cup for an ace.

The scene was almost surreal; it was as if the cup were a giant magnet and the golf balls were filled with metal. As the group celebrated Saraceni's hole in one, Al Ciuci stepped to the tee and, against all odds, dropped his ball on top of the one sitting in the cup for an ace of his own. Incredibly, the foursome had hit four golf balls from a combined total of 580 yards away and they were sitting a collective 20 inches from the hole.

The remaining eight holes were played in a far less spectacular fashion, but the talk throughout the round was of the incredible start. Returning to his pro shop, Ciuci called a friend who was a newspaper reporter and relayed the tale. The next day, in the local paper, there it was in black and white: yesterday afternoon, Al Ciuci and Eugene Saraceni scored holes in one playing together at the Beardsley Park Public Golf Course.

For Eugenio, seeing his name in the newspaper was even a bigger thrill than dropping that ace. Thirty-three years later, he would write a book about his life, which relates what happened next.

I read the write-up over and over again, sometimes to myself, sometimes out loud for a change of pace and thrill. There was only one thing wrong: I didn't like the way my name looked in print nor the way it sounded. Eugene Saraceni didn't sound at all like a golfer's name. It wasn't crisp enough. It didn't come off the tongue like Chick Evans, or Jim Barnes, or Walter Hagen. Eugene—not a bad name for a violin player or a schoolteacher, but a rotten name for an athlete. Saraceni—it was too long and everyone used to irritate me by mispronouncing it. I wanted a name that suited me and golf. A name has to be right. It's a person's trademark.

We had a small blackboard at home and at night I would sit before it chalking variations of Saraceni, experimenting with all kinds of letter substitutions. One night I added the letter z-e-n to the S-a-r-a. I tried it out several times aloud. I liked the way it sounded, rhythmic and definite. I checked the Bridgeport telephone directory. Finding no Sarazens listed, I concluded that I had invented a new name. I tried it with Gene instead of Eugene. No question about it, that was what I was looking for. From that night on I was Gene Sarazen.

With a new name and his old passion for the game, Gene Sarazen built a life and career in golf. For the next three years, he traveled through the eastern half of the United States working at golf courses and playing in tournaments. The tour card had yet to be invented, and events were mostly "opens," allowing anybody to enter.

In 1922, to avoid the feast-or-famine lifestyle of a professional golfer, Sarazen received and accepted an invitation to participate in what was known as a syndicate with several other tournament players. Any prize money won by any of them would be split equally. His first tournament after joining was the San Antonio Open, and despite finishing out of the money, he did get paid due to the success of a fellow member of his syndicate. He thought his participation in the group was a brilliant decision. The following week, he finished second at the Shreveport Open in Louisiana. As the only player in the recently formed group to collect a paycheck, he had to give up about 80 percent of his winnings and began to think the whole syndicate thing might not have been such a great idea.

The following week, the touring pros gathered at the New Orleans Country Club for the Southern Open, the most important and prestigious event on the winter circuit. In the first round of the match-play event, Sarazen was pitted against reigning U.S. Open champion Jim Barnes, an Englishman who six years earlier had won the first-ever PGA Championship. They made a strange pair; Sarazen, strong and stocky at just 5'5", 145 pounds, and Barnes, a lanky 6'4". Sarazen played a nearly flawless front nine, going out in 32. Barnes struggled to a less-than-stellar 38. Gene thought it would be a nice gesture to offer a word of encouragement, saying, "You'll do better coming in, Mr. Barnes. You'll probably get the 32 on this side."

Barnes, 16 years Sarazen's elder, did not take kindly to the comment. He stared coldly at the smaller man saying, "Listen, kid, you just play your own game. I'll take care of myself."

Sarazen learned a lesson, finished off Barnes, and went on to win the tournament, his first championship. The 1922 Southern Open paid a $1,000 first-place prize, but again Sarazen had to pay his partners. He walked away with a mere 200 bucks and promptly removed himself from the syndicate. Any future earnings would not go to others. Instead, they'd be deposited to their rightful owner, straight into the First National Bank of Sarazen.

A week later, the 20-year-old star-in-the-making fired his way to a second-place finish at the tour stop in Mobile, Alabama. With his entire chunk of prize money all in his own pocket, he walked excitedly into the tailor shop in the lobby of his hotel and was fitted for the first suit he ever bought.

A career was taking shape. Sarazen became a force among the pros and solidified his standing as one of the best golfers alive by winning two more tournaments in 1922. And they were significantly more noteworthy than the Southern Open.

That year's U.S. Open, or the "National Open" as it was called in the day, was to be played at the Skokie Country Club in Illinois. Sarazen arrived about a week before it started and developed a practice schedule that he would use throughout his career. After playing a round on the course, he would return to the driving range and devote most of his attention to the club he was hitting worst. Then he would spend hours on the putting green. Not the practice green; the actual putting greens, getting to know every element of the grain and the subtle slopes of each surface.

Sarazen would later write, "Most practice greens are a hindrance rather than a help. There are very few courses where the practice green resembles in speed, texture, and undulation the greens the player will find on the course. It is very important to get off on the right foot, and to have the first three or four greens perfectly memorized can often rescue you from bad-start jitters."

He played 36 holes of steady golf the first two days of the tournament, and after a shaky third round of 5-over-par 75, Sarazen entered play on the final day four strokes behind co-leaders Bobby Jones and Bill Mehlhorn. He turned in his best nine to start round four, going out in 33. After a bogey on the 10th hole, Sarazen birdied the 11th, banged out six straight pars, then birdied the par-5 18th for a final-round total of 2-under-par 68 and a tournament total of 288. The groups behind him made their way to 18, and news of their scores trickled in via the unofficial on-course grapevine. One-by-one, players were eliminated, either finishing with a higher score than Sarazen or still hacking away on the course out of contention. The final two players with a legitimate shot were John Black, a 43-year-old Scotsman out of California, and Bobby Jones, on his way to becoming the most revered golfer of his time, and perhaps any other. The 17th hole was the undoing of both. Jones, who needed to make up a stroke on the final two holes to tie Sarazen, bogeyed 17 after hitting his tee shot into the rough. Black needed two pars for a tie, but hooked his drive out of bounds and took a double bogey 6. Minutes later, the Open was officially closed, and the winner was a 20-year-old relative unknown, a former caddy from Harrison, New York.

Unknown no longer, about a month later, Sarazen took his improving skills and growing confidence to the PGA Championship at the Oakmont Country Club in Pennsylvania. The PGA, always considered a major tournament, was held in a match-play format from its inception in 1916 until 1957. Players would go head-to-head for 18 holes in the morning, break for lunch, then play another 18 in the afternoon. The winner of the most holes in each 36-hole match would advance to play again. From the opening day, tournament organizers paired them up, and Sarazen knocked them down. He dispatched his first three opponents handily, muscled by the next two in tight matches, and moved into the finals, where he was set to face a friendly acquaintance named Emmet French, who had survived five opponents as well.

On the final Sunday, Sarazen's game from tee to green was no more than adequate, but once on the putting surface, he was golden. In his autobiography, Sarazen recalled, "I had one of those days when the line to the hole stood out as clearly as if it had been chalked on the grass." He closed out French on the 33rd hole, winning the match 4-and-3.

Still just 20 years old, he was the youngest man to win the PGA Championship in the tournament's young history and the first player ever to win the U.S. Open and the PGA in the same season. The following year, he repeated as PGA champion, going 38 holes before finishing off one of his past heroes and future friends, Walter Hagen. Sarazen prevailed on the 2nd hole of sudden death on the strength of a miraculous approach shot from the rough to within two feet of the cup, which he dropped for a tournament-winning birdie.

While 1922 was the year Gene Sarazen established himself as a force in the golf world, it was, in retrospect, simply a good start to a great career. Over the next decade, he would become known throughout the world, winning 26 tournaments, including an astounding eight in 1930. In 1932, he flexed his championship muscle on both sides of the Atlantic Ocean, winning the U.S. and British Opens. At that U.S. Open, played in Flushing, New York, he made a finishing charge for the ages to take the title going away. The final day was a 36-hole mental marathon, in which Sarazen, after shooting par on the front nine, ripped through the morning back nine with a 3-under-par 32. In the afternoon, he put up a sizzling 4-under-par 66. All told, he shot 7-under-par on the final 27 holes on a course so difficult that his winning score was 6 over par. No less an authority than Bobby Jones would later say of Sarazen's spectacular Sunday, "It was the finest competitive round ever played."

National championships are like keys: used properly, they can open all kinds of doors. As the owner of the two prestigious titles simultaneously, Sarazen was receiving offers from all corners of the globe. The poor kid from the small town was suddenly traveling the world, playing exhibition matches, and getting paid handsomely to do it. And so it was that in the spring of 1934, he was playing in South America while most of the other pros cut the ribbon on a new tournament that had been formed stateside. The event was to be held in a small town in Georgia on land that was formerly a nursery used to grow imported trees. He missed that inaugural gathering, but in due time, Eugenio Saraceni would make his mark at the annual gathering played in a city known as Augusta.

THE TOURNAMENT

AUGUSTA NATIONAL INVITATION TOURNAMENT
AUGUSTA, GEORGIA, 1935

Not yet the most prestigious tournament in golf, and only in its second year of existence, the four-round event played in Augusta, Georgia, still attracted an all-star roster in 1935. The tournament was conceived and created by Bobby Jones, who at the time was considered the greatest golfer ever, and his business partner, stockbroker Clifford Roberts. Roberts had proposed that the event be called "the Masters," but Jones, a soft-spoken and humble gentleman, objected, insisting the name was presumptuous. Instead, the tournament was named the Augusta National Invitation Tournament.

Jones, a scholarly, well-mannered man of privilege, displayed his dominance in the golf world, winning the Grand Slam (the U.S. Open, U.S. Amateur, British Open, and British Amateur) in 1930. But golf was just a small part of the life of

Bobby Jones. A true renaissance man, he neither financially relied on nor was defined by the sport.

Born in Atlanta in 1902, Robert Tyre Jones Jr. won his first tournament at the age of six and went on to a golf career that sizzled with the electric brilliance of a passing comet. It was here, and then it was gone. He never turned professional, but he dominated a stretch of golf like no other player ever has and did so while playing competitive golf no more than three months in a year. Most of his life was dedicated to academics and the world of law. He studied mechanical engineering at Georgia Tech, graduating in three years, received a degree in English literature from Harvard, and attended law school at Emory University, withdrawing in his third semester to take and pass the bar.

After that memorable run in 1930, he retired at the tender age of 28. He would come out of retirement annually to play in the Augusta event, but clearly his best days on the course were behind him.

The adoring golf public, though, refused to let go of the legend of Bobby Jones. People so adored the man, so trusted the myth, and were so touched by the combination of his manner and accomplishments, Jones actually went into the 1935 tournament, five years after his retirement, as the betting favorite.

In a sign of the times, gambling information was a prominent element of sports stories in major newspapers. The headline of a *New York Times* article of April 3, 1935, read, "Sarazen Still Second to Jones in Betting Despite Sub-Par Golf."

The story went on to explain Gene Sarazen's dominance over other players in practice rounds leading up to the tournament. On the day before play was to begin, Jones shot a 72, which was noted as an "improvement," while Sarazen fired back-to-back 67s and was the pick of most of the pros and the press analyzing the field with their heads, not their hearts.

The article began, "Bob Jones, more successful in the part of genial Southern host than in golf, may be the magnet that has attracted so renowned a field of shotmakers to the second annual Augusta National Invitation Tournament, but his long-time rival, Gene Sarazen, is the target they all will have to worry about when the firing begins on Thursday."

With 65 golfers in the field, and $8,000 in prize money at stake—double the pot of the previous year—players teed it up on the gray, misty morning of April 4, 1935, to kick off the second annual Augusta National Invitation Tournament.

Playing out of Hershey, Pennsylvania, the same city that would be the site of Wilt Chamberlain's history-making 100-point game 27 years later, a young pro named Henry G. Picard set the course record for a competitive round. Picard went out in a slick 33, came in with a steady 34, and walked away with a first-round 67 and a one-shot lead.

Sarazen, Willie Goggin, and Ray Mangrum carded 68s. Green, a pro out of San Francisco, had the shot of the day, dealing out an ace on the 145-yard, par-3 16th. Sarazen's round was rock solid from the tee and the fairways, but he uncharacteristically missed four putts from between three and six feet. Mangrum, a professional from Los Angeles by way of Texas, stormed home with a 33 on the back nine on the strength of birdies on 12, 15, and 17.

As for Bobby Jones, the gracious host and people's choice was just not the player he used to be. Like an aging heavyweight champion realizing he's outclassed early in a fight, Jones trudged in from a practice round a few days before the tournament and all but announced his A-game was nowhere to be found. "It's difficult to recapture the old confidence," he bemoaned. "If I had any thought of making a try for the national open again, I would join the winter circuit around the first of the year and play myself into condition, but it's impossible for me to do that now."

Jones's opening round of 2-over-par 74 was not horrible, but it did leave him in a tie for 25th place, 7 strokes behind the leader. There is a romantic notion about golf, which allows for the illusion that the sport is merely a contest between a player and a course. There is a number established for each hole, and a player's score, written in black pencil on a white scorecard, is literally and figuratively black and white, with no need or want for explanation.

The idea is beautiful in its certainty and simplicity, but in tournament play, a man's measurement in relation to par is secondary. It is a player's score relative to his competition that will ultimately determine the winner and the losers.

An Associated Press story in newspapers the next morning spelled out not only Jones's seemingly hopeless pursuit of the tournament championship but also his competitors' all-out assault on his pride and joy, the course at Augusta National:

> *[The field] not only routed the one-time world champion at the outset of their second annual joust over the Augusta countryside but delivered a record-breaking attack on the bunkered battleground the great Jones helped design.*
>
> *The home folk turned out 1,000 strong in the lingering hope of seeing their favorite son come through, but Jones, no longer the golfing machine of his championship days, struggled to score as low as 74....*
>
> *On the basis of this performance, Bob will be lucky to come back as gallantly as he did last Spring, when he rallied to finish in a tie for 13th.*

ROUND 2

Round two began under the same menacing gray skies that welcomed the tournament's open. Despite reports, prevailing feeling, and sentiment of his efforts' being in vain, it was Bobby Jones who, like a rock star on stage, instantly drew the spotlight.

With his name far down the leader board, he was still the singular focus of the galleries. In a flash of greatness past, Jones lit up the front nine, again justifying the beliefs of a stubborn and faithful congregation. He holed out a chip shot on the 5th, barely missed an eagle putt and settled for a tap-in birdie on 8, and rolled home a five-footer for another birdie to close out a fabulous front nine of 33.

The magic was back. And just as quickly, it was gone again. On the back nine, his putter, a heavier successor to his once-famous flat stick nicknamed "Calamity Jane," failed him. Jones needed three putts on both the 13th and 14th greens, carding a double bogey and bogey, respectively, and came in with a 39, for a round-two total of even-par 72.

In the meantime, the first-round leader, Henry Picard, was the best of the field for the second consecutive day. The 28-year-old pro, who was inducted into the World Golf Hall of Fame in 2006, nine years after his death, fired a 4-under-par 68 for a torrid two-day total of 135. Fresh off a victory at the Atlanta Metropolitan Open, he was playing the best golf on tour and was halfway home in Augusta with a seemingly comfortable lead over the field.

Two of the players who finished one stroke behind in the opening round, Ray Mangrum and Gene Sarazen, shot identical 71s and remained Picard's closest pursuers, four strokes back at 5 under par. The only player other than Picard to break 70 was the tough and talented Walter Hagen, who stood 5 strokes behind. Five strokes is a good amount of ground to make up over 36 holes, but come the weekend, by the very force of his personality and talent, Hagen somehow always took up residence somewhere in the back of the mind of the leader, regardless of score or tournament.

Round 3

The misty and overcast conditions, which reared their ugly heads on Thursday and Friday, took a turn for the worse on Saturday. A cold and windblown third round was played mostly in rain, ranging from a drizzle to a downpour.

Like a mudder on a wet horse-racing track, a blonde bomber out of New Jersey named Craig Wood galloped from the pack and emerged with the third-round lead. Wood started the day a half-dozen strokes off the pace and didn't waste any time chipping away at Picard's lead. His 35 on the front knocked four shots from the bulge, and by the 14th hole, the eventual winner of 21 PGA tournaments had joined Picard at the top of the leader board. On the par-3 16th, the two-day leader continued to tumble, taking a double-bogey 5, while Wood continued to surge with a birdie 2, taking the lead all by himself.

Wood knew the Augusta course well. He had finished second to Horton Smith the year before in the inaugural event and understood how quickly fortunes on the difficult and delicate course could change. Checking the rearview mirror, he saw he had plenty of company, and it was full of star-power-toting titles.

In pursuit were Olin Dutra, the reigning U.S. Open champion, the very capable Picard, the always dangerous Gene Sarazen, one of the game's best in Walter Hagen, and Denny

Shute, who already had a British Open and 12 PGA tour titles to his credit.

Wood had the lead, but with 18 holes to play, had to feel somewhat like one of those mechanical rabbits at a dog track with a pack of hungry class-A greyhounds in full sprint nipping at his heels.

Darkness fell on the rain-soaked course with the leader board stacked thusly:

Craig Wood	209	-7
Olin Dutra	210	-6
Henry Picard	211	-5
Gene Sarazen	212	-4
Walter Hagen	214	-2
Denny Shute	214	-2

Bobby Jones had another respectable round, shooting 37 and 36 for a 1-over-par 73. He had not faltered the way many had predicted after the first round, but he was still far from contention, 10 strokes off the pace and tied for 16th place.

That night, as Sarazen was returning to his room at the Bon Air Hotel, he walked across the lobby and ran into an old friend named Bob Davis, a writer for the *New York Sun* newspaper. Conversation naturally turned to the tournament, and Davis asked what Gene thought of his chances. Sarazen told him he thought Wood would be tough to catch, but with a little luck he could do it. Davis then took what Sarazen would later describe as an "elaborate ring" from his finger and handed it to Gene saying he had gotten it from a dear friend in Mexico who claimed that the beloved former Mexican President Benito Juarez was wearing it at the time of his death. Davis insisted it would bring Sarazen luck if he wore it during the final round.

Sarazen thought it a bit odd and said it would interfere with his grip if he wore it, but he took the ring and promised to carry it in his pocket for the final 18 holes.

Round 4

Morning broke on April 7, 1935, with a tournament title at stake and a winner's check for $1,500 still blank and begging for ink on the "Pay To" line.

It was a rough start for leader Craig Wood, who bogeyed the 1st hole, birdied the 2nd, then hit the skids, bogeying three of the next four. Even as his own score ballooned, he took a measure of comfort seeing his closest competitor, Olin Dutra, having a miserable time of it as well, blowing up soon after he teed it up. Dutra effectively took himself out of the mix with a 6-over-par 42 on the front nine. His incredible 32 on the back was the low-nine of the entire tournament but served only to get Dutra back to third place and earn him a small piece of the financial pie. His take for four days of work was $600.

Henry Picard challenged briefly but got no closer than 1 stroke off the lead with his 38 on the front. His 37 on the back left him in fourth place, good for 500 bucks.

Shute had a consistent round, finishing fifth with a 73, and hometown favorite Bobby Jones limped home with a 78, finishing tied for 26th.

Wood eventually settled down, finishing the front with three straight pars for a 3-over 39. He went on to birdie the 14th and 15th to put him at 1 over par for the day and in great shape with just three holes to play.

A bogey at 16 followed by a par at 17 sent the leader to the 72nd and final hole with a 2-shot lead on the field.

Tournament tee times in 1935 were not determined by the leader-last system they are today, and although he came into the fourth round with the best score, Craig Wood was not playing in the final group.

Three holes behind him was the star-studded attraction of Walter Hagen and Gene Sarazen. Hagen uncharacteristically failed to get anything going on the final Sunday and was 9 shots back. Sarazen had not been at the top of the leader board at any point in the tournament but at the end of each round had been within reasonable striking distance. He went to the 485-yard, par-5 15th trailing by two strokes. His drive was solid, "exceptionally long with a tail-end hook," as he described it. The late hook sent the ball speeding toward the fairway with top-spin and propelled it forward, bouncing and rolling until it finally came to rest about 250 yards from the tee. As he and Hagen walked up the fairway approaching their golf balls, Sarazen heard a roar go up from the gallery around the 18th green. Wood had holed a birdie to finish in style, coming in with a final-round 73 for a four-day total of 282. At 6 under par, he had a 3-stroke lead on Sarazen, which seemed to be good enough to win.

THE SHOT

Sarazen remembered the scene. "As we neared the crest of the hill, I squinted at the clubhouse in the distance, where the photographers were snapping pictures of the happy winner and the newspapermen were hurrying to bat out their stories on Craig's victory."

The stocky 33-year-old was a long way from home…in more ways than one. Augusta, Georgia, is 818 miles from Harrison, New York, and his ball was 235 yards from the 15th green.

In Sarazen's book, *Thirty Years of Championship Golf*, published in 1950, he describes his thoughts upon his realization that he had suddenly lost another stroke, dropping him 3 off the lead:

> *I did some calculating. I could possibly get a birdie 4 on the 15th...maybe a birdie 2 on the 16th...and then maybe a birdie 3 on either the 17th or the 18th which would give me a tie. My high-flying optimism received a sudden jolt when I saw my lie. It was none too good. I went into a huddle with Stovepipe [his caddie] as to whether I should play a 3 wood or a 4 wood [then known as a spoon]. The 3, we decided, would never get the ball up from that close lie, being slightly deeper in the face than the 4. The 4, a new model called the Turfrider, had a hollow-back sole which enabled the club to go down after the ball. I knew that the only way I could reach the green with the 4 would be to toe the club in, to decrease the loft and so give me extra yardage.*
>
> *After it was settled that I would go with the 4, I must have been scanning the skies for some sign of approval or encouragement, for I was suddenly reminded of the lucky ring Bob Davis had given me. I extracted it from my pocket and rubbed it over Stovepipe's head to give its reputed powers every chance to work. I suppose the real contribution the ring made was that fooling with it tapered off the tension that had been building up in me. I took my stance with my 4 wood and rode into the shot with every ounce of strength and timing I could muster.*

Sarazen hit it on the screws. It was a rocket: low, long, and as straight as a flagstick. Upon impact he knew it was going to clear the water in front of the green. The question was whether it was going to run through the green, or stick.

His written description continued, "Running forward to watch its flight, I saw the ball land in the green, still dead on line. I saw it hop straight for the cup, and then, when I was straining to see how close it had finished, the small gallery behind the green let out a terrific shout and began to jump wildly in the air. I knew then that the ball had gone into the hole."

Into the hole! Into the hole for…well, there was not yet a name for what it was. Whatever it was, it was darn good. It was 3 under par on one hole. Sarazen was caught up in the moment, glancing back at Hagen as if to say, "Did ya catch that one, big guy?"

Within seconds, the competitive aspect of his nature kicked in and he began calculating again. There are many ways to make up 3 strokes over four holes of golf, but he hadn't even considered the possibility of doing it with a single shot. He had effectively chopped down a giant redwood with one perfect swing of a razor-sharp axe.

Legend has it there was a huge gallery surrounding the 15th green when the miracle shot found the cup. And as the years went by, tens of thousands of people claimed to be eyewitness to the historical shot. Truth is, Sarazen and Hagen were playing the hole at about 5:30 in the evening when there were only a few thousand spectators on the entire course. Most in attendance that day had departed when Bobby Jones finished his round, and the bulk of those who remained were either listening in as the writers interviewed Craig Wood or were at the 18th green watching each group finish.

The truth is there were about 20 people at the 15th hole, one of whom was Jones himself. And not all 20 actually saw the ball drop.

Syndicated columnist Ed Danforth wrote in his Monday story:

> *Walter Hagen, playing with Gene, had just played his second shot. It flew to the left of the green, hit a fairly tight gentleman in a yellow sweater on the shoulder and knocked him off a knoll. It was while two good Samaritans were helping up their friend and laughter was rippling out that Sarazen banged that spoon shot for the pin. The shot hit the apron of the green a few feet over the water hazard, bounced to the carpet, and took a curving path from right to left into the cup. Alas, one of my acquaintances was helping his yellow-sweatered friend regain his balance and is willing to confess he was within 20 yards of the cup and did not see it.*
>
> *Every [spectator] will tell you today he saw it, and one cannot blame them. All of them heard the hysterical scream that split the damp afternoon air when that ball rolled into the cup. It was a scream that developed slowly...started out as a murmur and swelled to a cheer, then to a wild cacophony of unbelief. The yipping and yelling continued as the swarthy-faced little powerhouse trudged down to the green to retrieve his ball. He was given a tremendous hand.*

After getting his ball out of the cup and acknowledging the cheers of the small but vocal gathering, Sarazen remembers hearing a boy whose job it was to report the scores, growing frustrated. He was talking via telephone or short-wave radio to the operator of the master scoreboard. "Yes," the boy kept insisting, it was indeed the 15th hole. "The 15th. Yes, the par-5 15th. Gene Sarazen got a 2. A 2! Like, 1–2. Yes, I am sure. A 2 on the 15th! Sarazen..."

He had miraculously pulled into a tie for the lead, but there was still work to be done.

All jazzed up with no place to go but the next tee box, Sarazen moved on. His suddenly sizzling stroke produced another beauty on the 145-yard, par-3 16th. Sarazen grooved an 8 iron to within 10 feet and marched toward the green with visions of a birdie to take the lead. His putt, though, was a bit off-line, and he had to settle for a short par putt to remain tied.

The wind was behind him on the par-4 17th, and he played it, he would later say, "without incident," taking a par and heading to 18 still tied with Wood. There, he hit a relatively weak drive into the uphill fairway, but approaching his ball, he turned to Stovepipe, not needing to say a word. His caddy pulled out the spoon—the 4 wood. Practically still vibrating from the bull's-eye on 15, it was again trustworthy and reliable. Since the final two holes at Augusta are perpendicular to each other, the wind that had been behind him on 17 was now blowing left to right across the 18th fairway. He took aim at the left edge of the green, "trusting the wind would cradle my ball into the pin." He stroked it solidly and knew immediately it was going to be good, but how good? The ball was right on target and landed about four feet past the hole. It had a good amount of backspin, but despite the wet greens, not enough spin to fully apply the breaks on a 200-plus-yard shot. Luckily, the back of the green sloped upward and the ball came to rest about 35 to 40 feet beyond the cup.

He walked with a purposeful, confident stride toward the green, like a man heading to an important business meeting just quickly enough to arrive exactly on time.

A make wins it. Down in 2 ties it. Three-putt, and, well, the shot he would minutes later call "the greatest thrill I have ever had on a golf course" would be rendered essentially meaningless.

Or worse yet, reduced to a mere footnote, a fancy prologue to a missed opportunity.

In his book, Sarazen wrote, "A great many expert putters, Ben Hogan for one, have 3-putted the wickedly contoured home green at Augusta. It is a terror, and particularly when you have to gauge the delicate speed for a lengthy downhill putt. Hagen putted out while I studied the rolls and examined the grain. I stroked my approach putt gently and it trickled slowly down the rolls and died a slow death three feet short of the cup. Too much analysis would be a bad thing in that spot, I decided. I stepped up and hit the three-footer instantly. It dropped, and I had tied Wood."

An article written in *Golf Digest* in 2000 states that members of the press huddled together after speaking with Sarazen and collectively tried to come up with a name for a shot resulting in a score of 3 under par. The common term in Europe is *albatross*, but that had either yet to be coined, or was unbeknownst to the scribes at Augusta. The writers kicked around several ideas, including the likes of *twin dodo*, but ultimately settled on *double eagle*.

Regardless of what the shot was called, what it meant was 72 holes were not enough to determine a winner of the 1935 Augusta Invitational. Tournament rules dictated a head-to-head, 36-hole playoff would be held the following day.

Augusta National Invitation Tournament
Round 4, April 7, 1935

HOLE	1	2	3	4	5	6	7	8	9	OUT	10	11	12	13	14	15	16	17	18	IN	TOTAL
PAR	4	5	4	3	4	3	4	5	4	36	4	4	3	5	4	5	3	4	4	36	72
Sarazen	4	4	4	4	4	3	4	5	5	37	5	4	3	4	4	(2)	3	4	4	33	70

THE PLAYOFF

The Masters playoff would later be downsized to 18 holes and then, in 1976, changed to the modern-day, sudden-death format. But on the morning of April 8, 1935, two men played two rounds for the tournament title. It was another wet one in Augusta, and on this day, a bitter cold accompanied the now familiar rain. But "semi-freezing temperatures," as they were described in the next day's newspaper, could not put a chill over the steady, workmanlike exhibition put on by a true champion.

Craig Wood and Gene Sarazen, two of the era's best, set out to play 36 with only their respective competitive fires to keep them warm. Wood carded birdies on the 1st and 6th holes to give him his only two leads of the match. Sarazen responded to each of those deficits immediately with birdies of his own to even the match and never trailed for longer than a single hole. They each fired even-par 36s on the front nine of the first round, but from there, Sarazen seized control and never let go.

The powerful, compact right-hander gained a stroke on each of the first four holes of the back nine and held a lead of at least 4 strokes for the rest of the day. His cerebral approach, perfect course management, and ultraconsistent effort gave Wood no opening. Sarazen completed perhaps the steadiest weeklong stretch in his career with a tournament-winning playoff total of even-par 144, good for a 5-stroke victory, sending Wood to a second-place finish for the second year in a row.

The new champion was over par only after the first of the 36 holes, and after going under par on number 10, didn't fall back to even until the 71st hole, long after the end result was already determined. Most impressively, under the pressure of a one-on-one match, and with the championship at stake, Sarazen never flinched. Impervious to the many perils of the dangerous course, he was not in a single sand trap, 3-putted just three of the 36 wet, undulating greens, and at one stretch recorded 24 consecutive pars.

It was a performance *The New York Times* referred to as "one of the most flawless exhibitions of shot-making ever witnessed....His golf was so consistently perfect it was monotonous."

AP sports editor Alan Gould saw it as a "frost-bitten, cold-blooded playoff."

The extra rounds, though, were merely a continuation of what had started the previous week as players prepared for the tournament with the then-standard four practice rounds. In all, Sarazen played 10 rock-solid, surgeon-steady rounds of golf: 180 holes over nine days on one of the trickiest courses in the world, and never carded anything higher than a five.

AUGUSTA NATIONAL INVITATION PLAYOFF
April 8, 1935
Morning Round

HOLE	1	2	3	4	5	6	7	8	9	OUT	10	11	12	13	14	15	16	17	18	IN	TOTAL
PAR	4	5	4	3	4	3	4	5	4	36	4	4	3	5	4	5	3	4	4	36	72
Sarazen	5	4	4	3	4	4	3	5	4	36	3	4	3	5	4	5	3	4	4	35	71
Wood	4	5	4	3	4	3	4	5	4	36	4	5	4	6	4	5	3	4	4	39	75

Afternoon Round

HOLE	1	2	3	4	5	6	7	8	9	OUT	10	11	12	13	14	15	16	17	18	IN	TOTAL	PLAYOFF TOTAL
PAR	4	5	4	3	4	3	4	5	4	36	4	4	3	5	4	5	3	4	4	36	72	144
Sarazen	4	5	4	3	4	3	4	5	4	36	4	4	3	5	4	5	3	5	4	37	73	144
Wood	5	5	5	3	5	3	5	5	4	39	4	4	3	4	4	5	2	4	4	34	74	149

TOURNAMENT TOTALS

1. Sarazen	68	71	73	70	282	-6
2. Wood	69	72	68	73	282	-6
3. Dutra	70	70	70	74	284	-4
4. Picard	67	68	76	75	286	-2
5. Shute	73	71	70	73	287	-1
…						
9t. Nelson	71	74	72	74	291	+3
15t. Hagen	73	69	72	79	293	+5
26t. Jones	74	72	73	78	297	+9

POSTSCRIPT

Rare is the moment that lasts a lifetime. Even more rare is an instant in time that takes on a life of its own and spans generations. Sarazen's daughter, Mary Ann, lives in Florida and in 2007 spoke with pride of her father's shot 72 years earlier. "People always associate the double-eagle with Dad," she says.

Her two sons golf, as do her four grandsons, all very much aware of their links legacy. One of the boys, in fact, was assigned as part of a state proficiency test in Virginia to write about a famous American he would put on a coin. He wrote eloquently about his great grandfather, Gene Sarazen, and received an advanced grade.

• • •

Craig Wood's heartbreak in Augusta was, in a fitting metaphor, par for the course. The capable and likable Lake Placid, New York, native was becoming known not for his great skills, but instead for his propensity to finish second. His playoff loss at Augusta perpetuated a stretch of bothersome near misses in which Wood was just good enough to be not good enough. Two years earlier, he had lost a 36-hole playoff to Denny Shute in the British Open at St. Andrews and, in 1934, lost to Paul Runyan on the 2nd hole of sudden death in the match-play final of the PGA Championship.

By all measures, Wood had an excellent career and was one of the better players on tour in the '30s and '40s. Yet he simply could not break through in any of the sport's most important tournaments. In 1939, he birdied the 72nd hole of the U.S. Open, forcing a playoff with Byron Nelson. Once again, though, Wood came up short, making him the first player ever to lose all four major championships in extra holes.

His determination and resolve finally paid off two years later when he won both the Masters and the U.S. Open. The victories were doubly sweet because he got a measure of revenge in each, by beating men who had previously beaten him. The Masters win was the first wire-to-wire victory in tournament history and it came by 3 shots over Nelson. A couple of months later, he took the U.S. Open, winning by 3 over Shute. He was the first player ever to record victories in each of the first two majors of a season and retired in the mid-'60s having won 21 PGA tournaments.

As for Bobby Jones, although tournament golf had lost its allure years earlier, he continued to play in the tournament that would become part of his shining legacy. In 12 appearances at Augusta, he never finished better than 13th, but his very presence on the course brought elements of stature, cachet, and distinction not found in any other sporting event.

With the $1,500 in first-place prize money from Augusta burning a hole in his pocket, Sarazen hit the road heading north. About a week after the tournament he was in New York when, once again, he ran into his writer friend Bob Davis, the man who had given him that magical ring the night before the playoff. The old pals shared an embrace and a laugh, and before parting ways, Davis said, "One more thing Gene…about that ring. I'm afraid I have a little confession to make. Juarez never even saw that ring. It was just a trinket I picked up from a vendor one day while I was waiting to get my shoes shined." •

With or without the legend of the ring, tales of the incredible series of events that unfolded in Augusta on that cold April day circulated throughout the golf world, giving the new tournament an air of mystery and a degree of publicity money could not buy. The annual competition, which was officially named the Masters in 1939, has become the most dignified and prestigious gathering in golf, perhaps in all of sports. It is a tournament that makes careers. Successes at Augusta are exaggerated and failures are magnified. It is a tournament that can indisputably put a player on the map. And the event itself was put on the map in a matter of moments by one swing of that fateful 4 wood, a stroke that would come to be known as golf's "Shot Heard 'Round the World."

With the famous shot in his rearview mirror, Sarazen continued to shine as one of golf's elite. Heck, the man *invented* the sand wedge. According to the World Golf Hall of Fame, Sarazen was

taking flying lessons from Howard Hughes in 1931. He noticed
how an airplane's tail adjusted during takeoff, and applied the
principle to a golf club that could scoop a ball out of a sand trap.
He spent months perfecting the concept and later called the
advent of the club his greatest contribution to the sport.

Even though the Augusta National Invitation was not yet a
major tournament in 1935, by winning it, and having previously
won the U.S. Open, the British Open, and the PGA Championship, Sarazen is retroactively credited as the first player in
history to win the modern Grand Slam.

He won more than 50 tournaments around the world,
including 39 PGA events and seven majors. He was a member
of six American Ryder Cup teams and went on to become a
radio commentator and the television host of *Shell's Wonderful
World of Golf.*

Although his on-course brilliance faded, Sarazen remained
a fixture in the golf world while most of his contemporaries
retired. In 1950, the great Bobby Jones wrote about his old foe:

> *Sarazen has lasted longer as a player than any one of
> us who were at or near the top during the
> '20s.... This, of course, is one the hallmarks of his
> greatness as a player, his ability to carry on with a new
> generation of stars.*
>
> *But the explanation of this seeming agelessness is a
> frequent subject of speculation.*
>
> *I think I know the answer, and it lies in one of
> Sarazen's qualities that has made him such an interest-
> ing player to watch. It is his unconcealed and undi-
> minished zest for the game, and for competition. Most
> of the others who have quit competition have done so
> long before any physical deterioration could have*

impaired their effectiveness. They were unwilling to take the punishment any longer. But Gene loves to get in the middle of a good tussle.

In 1956, at the age of 54, Sarazen finished tied for fifth in the PGA Championship. In 1973, a full 23 years after Jones marveled at his longevity, Sarazen was still swinging 'em as a senior citizen. It was then, at 71 years young, that he put an exclamation point on his long list of on-course accomplishments with an ace at the 8th hole at Royal Troon while competing in the British Open. He was inducted into the World Golf Hall of Fame as a charter member the following year, and in 1996, when the PGA Tour established its Lifetime Achievement Award, Sarazen was its first recipient.

In 1992, his golf life came full circle when he was presented the Bob Jones Award from the United States Golf Association. The award, bearing the name of his old friend and confidant who witnessed that great shot 57 years earlier, is the USGA's highest honor, given in recognition of distinguished sportsmanship. It is presented annually to the person within the sport who best emulates Jones's spirit, his personal qualities, and his attitude toward the game and its players.

Sarazen earned his nickname, "the Squire," after buying a farm for his family in upstate New York, but he always considered Augusta, Georgia, his second home. Every spring beginning in 1981, he, Byron Nelson, and Sam Snead stepped to the 1st tee to signify the beginning of the Masters. In a spectacular collision of golf's past and present, the legendary threesome ceremonially teed off in front of an adoring gallery and starstruck modern-day players, with understated fanfare to polite applause.

A 1995 *Sports Illustrated* article told of the then 93-year-old Sarazen's humorous but begrudging acceptance of the aging process. He was quoted as saying, "I don't wish 93 on anybody. You can't play golf. You see a beautiful woman and look at her and you say, 'What the hell, you might as well look at a tree.' But my doctor says, 'As long as you still *think* they're beautiful, you're all right.'"

Asked about his famous shot and the 60 years in between, he said simply, "God, it's gone by fast."

With arthritis in his shoulders and a backswing that reached only waist-high, Sarazen took his final swing in April of 1999. At age 97, he ripped a 140-yard winner down the left side of the 1st fairway at Augusta, and another Masters was officially under way.

He soon said his annual good-byes to the friendly and now-familiar faces around the course and to the tournament that had gone through so many changes, yet somehow, over the better part of a century, remained very much the same. A month later, after a short battle with pneumonia, the man who had been born Eugenio Saraceni to immigrant parents in a small town in New York and went on to achieve worldwide fame playing a game he loved, died in Naples, Florida, survived by his two children.

Tributes poured in from all corners of the golf world, most notably from competitors who spanned the eras. Byron Nelson said sadly, "He will be remembered for as long as golf is played." Jack Nicklaus remarked, "When you discuss or research the history of golf, the name Gene Sarazen is unavoidable. He was the cornerstone of the game we all enjoy today."

Double Eagles at Augusta National

1935—Gene Sarazen, 4th round, 15th hole (4 wood, 235 yards)
1967—Bruce Devlin, 1st round, 8th hole (4 wood, 248 yards)
1994—Jeff Maggert, 4th round, 13th hole (3 iron, 222 yards)

Ben Hogan, in classic form, making his approach shot on the 72nd hole of the 1950 U.S. Open.

CHAPTER TWO

1950:
Hogan's a Hero

PRELUDE

JANUARY 31, 1949

The Arizona sun that had burned brilliantly all day disappeared behind the mountains as longtime buddies Ben Hogan and Jimmy Demaret finished off a couple of stiff postround drinks. Demaret's glass was empty first. Spirits have a way of going down a bit easier and tasting a bit sweeter following a victory than they do after defeat. Seven days after Hogan had beaten Demaret in an 18-hole playoff to take the Long Beach Open, Demaret returned the favor by downing Hogan in an extra 18 to win the Phoenix Open.

The pair had played hundreds of rounds together and had even won together, claiming first place as teammates in multiple four-ball tournaments and, more significantly, in Ryder Cup play. But the past two Mondays, the old friends were new foes, going head-to-head for PGA tournament titles.

Demaret mused aloud about himself and Hogan taking their two-man minitour to Tucson for the following week's event and making their recent stretch of dominance an unofficial best-of-three format. Hogan, though, had other plans. He had been on the road and on the move nonstop since New Year's Day. He had crisscrossed the western United States in his new Cadillac to play in four tournaments (winning two), banked more money than any other player on tour (nearly four grand), put on several clinics and exhibitions, and had even gone a bit Hollywood, making an instructional golf film. .

Tucson? No thank you. Hogan and his wife, Valerie, were headed to their home in Fort Worth, Texas.

The first day on the road, they drove about 550 miles and stopped in the small West Texas panhandle town of Van Horn. The entire town takes up a little bit less than three square miles, but Hogan, never one to forget a spot with clean rooms and great home cooking, passed through often and was a regular at the El Capitan Motel. The next day, with nearly 500 more miles in front of them, they got an early start and headed east down a two-lane highway to Fort Worth. Despite bright morning sunshine, there was a biting chill to the air, and a thick ground fog, which made driving conditions so hazardous that Hogan reduced his speed to about 20 miles per hour—in his words, "practically nothing."

About 45 minutes into the trip, at precisely 8:30 AM, Hogan saw a huge, dark object emerge from the haze about 200 yards in front of him. It was big, it was fast, and it was closing quickly. A Greyhound bus, trying to pass a westbound truck, was bearing down on the new Cadillac, leaving Hogan few options, and no good ones. Swerving left would get him a face-to-face meeting with the oncoming truck. Cutting the wheel to the right would bounce the vehicle off the solid steel guardrail and send it careening back into his lane and into the oncoming bus. Out of choices and out of time, he cut the wheel slightly to the right to get as close to the rail as possible, let go of the steering wheel, and selflessly dove to his right to shield Valerie from the inevitable impact.

The last thing he saw was the terror on his wife's face. The last thing he heard was the horrifying sound of crunching metal and breaking glass. The last thing he felt was a crushing blow to his midsection and what remained of his two-ton automobile lifted off the pavement, propelled backward. And then everything went black.

There is no way to know what images are conjured by the unconscious mind, but as Hogan lay in peril amid the twisted wreckage of an automobile on a Texas highway, significant moments of his life were possibly racing through his brain.

• • •

He was born William Ben Hogan on August 13, 1912, in Dublin, Texas, a tiny town in the center of the state. When he was nine years old, his father put a .38-caliber pistol to his own heart, pulled the trigger, and was gone forever, taking with him any certainty about the reasons for his actions.

Much like Gene Sarazen a decade earlier, Hogan came from very modest means, was reeled in by the game of golf, to some degree between fascinated and obsessed, and got his start in the game as a caddie. At just 5'7", and about 140 pounds in his prime, Hogan was given the nickname "Bantam Ben," a moniker against which he seemed to wage war early in his career with every vicious swing of his then wild driver. He turned pro at age 17 and joined the tour at 19, but had little success and earned a minuscule portion of the still-small purses available in tournaments. Twice in the 1930s his financial struggles became so great he stashed the clubs and returned to his adopted home of Fort Worth to take steady jobs, including mopping floors, carrying luggage, and working a stick as a croupier in a gaming house. But as soon as he scraped enough money together, either by saving slowly or convincing friends and relatives to back him, he returned to the tour, hopeful of turning his passion into a paycheck.

A well-circulated story is told about Hogan's arrival in December of 1931 at the Pasadena Open with a mere 15¢ in his pocket. He maintained his energy throughout another California event by eating oranges he picked from trees in a grove parallel to some of the fairways. As determined as he was to make it on the tour, his game simply was not as good as it needed to be to finish in the money—often the top five, sometimes six. By the end of 1937, he was ready to pack it in again and move on to whatever might be next, this time for good. In fact, what to do next was the topic on the table as he and Valerie were having lunch at the Blackstone Hotel on a late December day in Fort Worth.

Passing through town and fatefully stopping at the same hotel was Henry Picard, the man who had been in contention in 1935 when Gene Sarazen won at Augusta. Picard had come into his own and surged to the top of the golf world by winning a dozen tournaments in the three seasons since that near miss, and was just a few months away from taking a Masters of his own. He was convinced that Hogan had what it took to be a champion and told him so. Picard backed his words by making an offer that the Hogans could not refuse, saying if Ben would make one more go of it by playing the winter tour, he was willing to take care of them financially if the need arose.

Feeling a bit more comfortable about life on the road, a couple of weeks later the Hogans arrived in California. Ben proceeded to enter three consecutive tournaments but finished no better than eighth, pocketing a grand total of $140. Next up was the Oakland Open at the Sequoyah Country Club, and as they drove up the California coast, Ben and Valerie made a decision. If he did not play well enough to win a significant amount of money in Oakland, they would sell the car, buy train tickets, and return to Texas. A golf career was hanging in the balance.

The headline from the final round in Oakland was that Harry Cooper, a pro from Britain, rallied from 4 shots back, dropping an eagle on the final hole to win the tournament by a single stroke. There was no mention of anyone named Ben Hogan in the next day's *Oakland Tribune* tournament article, but a fifth-place finish netted Hogan his largest paycheck to date: $285. He remembered the moment more than four decades later in a televised interview, emotionally telling Ken Venturi, "That was the biggest check I had ever seen."

The Hogans felt like the Rockefellers. And there was more where that came from. The next week, Ben finished third in Sacramento, banking another $350. It was a good start to the year, but Hogan still had not won a tournament. He knew his game had to become more consistent, so he settled into a practice routine that would serve him well for the remainder of his career and, like the golfer himself, become something of legend.

Several writers over the years have penned biographies on Hogan, but none more completely than author James Dodson. In the supremely comprehensive book, *Ben Hogan: An American Life* (2004), Dodson explains:

> *Everything he managed to learn about the golf swing—which was apparently twice as much as anybody ever had before him—he dug out of the dirt by practicing until his hands bled. When the skin of his palms blistered and cracked open, he soaked his hands in pickle brine to toughen them for the long haul. After almost nine years of unrelenting effort and disappointment, he cured his tendency to hook the ball under pressure and finally won his first golf tournament, transforming himself into a precision golfing machine and the most feared competitor of his day, almost as if he had discovered a formula for golfing perfection, a "secret" of some sort for playing the game better than anyone had before him.*

In his book, Dodson quotes an old Hogan friend and rival named Tommy Bolt—a sometimes friendly, sometimes moody, but always competitive golfer from Arkansas.

Bolt recalled, "Before Ben started doing it, nobody in their right mind regularly went to Misery Hill. That was our nickname for the practice range, see, because that was where guys went to try and figure out what the hell was wrong with their swings. Hogan, on the other hand, went there to figure out what was right about his golf swing. Take it from me, brother. That was revolutionary! And by practicing as much as Ben did, which I swear was twice as much as anybody I ever saw, he basically reduced the margin for human error to damn near nothing. There was no shot he hadn't already hit a thousand times already out on Misery Hill. Nothing was ever a surprise to Ben Hogan in a golf tournament. That's the first thing that set him apart."

Hogan's first tournament victory came in the fall of 1938 at the Hershey Four-Ball, a tournament in which players were divided into eight two-man teams. Hogan had originally been paired with the famous Tommy Armour, but Armour broke a bone in his hand just prior to the tournament and withdrew. Hogan's newly assigned partner was a 27-year-old pro out of New Jersey named Vic Ghezzi, a winner of five lifetime tournaments coming into that season but none yet of any significance. With the field made up of the top 16 players on tour, the Hogan/Ghezzi entry was among the least intimidating on the grouping sheet, but they led from the beginning and easily beat out the team of reigning PGA champ Paul Runyon and the venerable Sam Snead to win the championship and pocket $550 apiece.

As the 1930s were turning into the 1940s, Hogan went on an impressive yet maddening run of second- and third-place finishes. The closer he came to winning, the more he would practice. There was, he felt, a perfect golf swing. It was in there somewhere, and he was determined to find it. There were stretches in which he would practically live on the driving range, hitting three balls every minute for a three-and-one-half-hour stretch each morning and evening. Seven hours per day, 180 balls per hour. His goal was to ingrain the proper movements into his muscle-memory. When the pressure mounted in tournament play, he wouldn't have to think about his swing. He'd just have to swing as he'd done hundreds of thousands of times before. In those marathon sessions, he cured a nasty hook that had plagued him for much of his career, settling on a consistent fade. The change cost him a bit of distance, but it served him quite well and ultimately became his trademark.

•••

The whirring siren of the ambulance startled him back to consciousness. It had been 90 minutes since the crash.

The steering wheel on Hogan's Cadillac had rocketed through the front seat. The impact to his body almost certainly would have killed him had he not vacated the spot to shield Valerie. For fear that his car would explode, passengers on the bus had moved him to the backseat of another car where he remained until he was placed in the ambulance. His vital signs were fluctuating and his blood pressure was irregular. Medical personnel saw he was obviously injured, but how badly? The decision was made to stop at the nearest medical facility, a small clinic a few miles away where X-rays were taken to assess the damage. Physicians called ahead to a hospital in El Paso, telling doctors there to expect a seriously injured patient. Hogan was lifted back into the ambulance for the nearly 100-mile ride and blacked out again.

•••

His first solo tournament victory came at an event called the North and South Open in 1940, one of the most prestigious tournaments of the first half of the 20th century. The event, played at Pinehurst Resort in North Carolina, was established in 1902 and played annually until 1951, when tour players insisted on a bigger pot of prize money to bring the awards more in line with other tournaments.

The week prior to the tournament, Hogan, now a known commodity on tour despite an increasingly haunting, large-type, boldface "0" in the victory column of the mind, canceled two scheduled exhibition matches that would have netted him $500. He passed on the easy money and instead drove straight to Pinehurst and checked in a week early. He proceeded to learn the club's elegant number-two course as well as possible, studying each hole as if it were his personal road map to success.

By the time the rest of the players arrived, Hogan had already spent the better part of eight days on the course that many of the others would see for the first time when they stepped to the tee to start tournament play. He came out smoking (and not just his ever-present cigarettes) with a birdie on the 1st hole, then the 2nd, and then the 4th.

Author James Dodson summarized the first round this way:

> *Striking shots and walking briskly, leaving a trail of burnt Chesterfields behind him, head up and chin thrust forward in an attitude Valerie could have recognized from 300 yards, he tore a smoldering hole through the crisp spring morning, didn't miss a fairway all day, compiled a 6-under 66, and tied the competitive course record set just one year before by robot man Harry Cooper.*

The next day, Hogan's assault on the course continued as he fired a 67. Halfway home, he led the star-studded field by a whopping 7 strokes. Sam Snead and Johnny Revolta were his nearest competitors, and all the big names of the day—Nelson,

Sarazen, Picard, Wood, and Horton Smith, to name a few—were even further behind.

Despite some of his competition's predictions that Hogan would choke away the lead as he had done many times before, rounds three and four were merely a continuation of his dominance. Hogan hit the ball so well and so consistently, there simply was no opportunity for anybody to gain any significant ground. He played it safe on the final nine and won it easily, taking his first solo title by 3 strokes over Sam Snead to win the $1,000 first-place prize.

Dodson reports that sportswriter John Derr of the *Greensboro Daily News* put together his story for the morning paper and sent it down to the printing room to be typeset. Derr was shocked to see the headline in the early morning editions screaming, "Hagen's 277 Leaves Snead Three Strokes Back."

Horrified at the mistake, Derr says he quickly phoned the copy desk and told them they had gotten it wrong. "It was Ben Hogan," who won the tournament, "Ben Hogan, not Walter Hagen!"

The reply from the typesetter was, "Hogan? Who the hell is Hogan?"

Never again would anybody have to ask that question. Hogan's victory at Pinehurst was just the first of 15 titles he accumulated from 1940 to 1942.

Starting in March of 1943, Hogan spent about two years in the Air Corps. While he was gone from the game, he was very well aware of the elite status being attained by fellow Texan and one-time friend Byron Nelson. Although Hogan never spoke of his obvious grudge against Nelson, wide speculation holds that Hogan found it galling that Byron, who was categorized as a hemophiliac, was exempt from serving in World War II. With Hogan and many other players serving in the military in 1944 and 1945, Nelson dominated the sport with an incredible total of 26 wins, including a still-standing record of victories in 11 consecutive tournaments. To the golfing public, Nelson became a national hero. To sportswriters, he became "Mr. Golf," a moniker that Hogan clearly resented.

Years of frustration, though, were wiped away upon Hogan's return from the war. In four brilliant days on a golf course at the 1945 Portland Open, Hogan fired rounds of 65, 69, 63, and 64 for a mind-bending total of 27-under-par 261. The score was an all-time record low, and perhaps more important to Hogan, it was 14 strokes better than Byron Nelson's second-place finish of 275. After accepting the trophy, Hogan said to a friend, "I guess this takes care of that 'Mr. Golf' business."

Including the victory in Portland, Hogan won five times in 1945, and he reestablished himself as a true force in 1946, bringing home 13 titles, including his first major, the PGA Championship, a 6-and-4 final-round match-play romp over Ed Oliver.

The next two years yielded 17 more victories, another PGA Championship, and the 1948 U.S. Open. His skill, determination, and mental toughness were qualities to be admired. His public reputation and apparent disdain for outsiders was another story.

William Ben Hogan was a private man with a very small inner circle. Those who knew him best spoke glowingly of a kind, polite, and loving man forever and completely dedicated to his wife. Those who did not know him well saw an uncaring loner with an icy exterior and no need for, or interest in, anybody who did not serve a purpose in his life. On the course he was focused to a fault. His image was not that of a man who didn't acknowledge galleries, but of a man who didn't even *see* the galleries. Even his playing partners got the Hogan treatment, sometimes going through an entire round without so much as a "nice shot" from the man's mouth.

One player with whom Hogan did have a substantial relationship was the friendly and colorful Jimmy Demaret, who got a ton of mileage out of a wisecrack he counted on for decades. The routine would invariably be pulled out on an unsuspecting audience at a bar over postround drinks, or at dinner following a tournament. It went something like this:

Demaret: "You won't believe this, but old Ben was talking up a storm on the golf course today."

Surprised response: "Really? What was he saying?"

Demaret: "You're away."

• • •

As the ambulance carrying Hogan arrived at the hospital in El Paso, word erroneously went out over initial wire reports that said he had been killed in the crash. Doctors found him mangled, but alive. He had suffered several deep lacerations and bruises around his left eye, a fractured collarbone, a double ring-fracture of the pelvis, a cracked rib, and a broken left ankle.

Common belief years after the accident—and the story that circulates to this very day—is that the injuries were certain to end Hogan's golf career. However, a *New York Times* story, printed the following day, reports, "The physicians expressed confidence that Hogan would be able to play golf again, but would not venture a guess as to when."

The *Los Angeles Times* reported similarly, saying, "Three physicians who examined Hogan said he had received 'numerous fractures' but will recover. 'In all probability,' it was agreed, Hogan will be able to play again 'after a long period of recuperation.'" But the worst was yet to come.

A month later, still in a large cast but ready to go home from the hospital, Hogan had a pair of large blood clots making their way from his injured left leg toward his upper body. The clots settled in his stomach and posed a far greater risk to his long-term health than any of his injuries. Renowned doctor Alton Ochsner, a progressive and inventive surgeon, flew in from New Orleans to assess the issue and decided to operate immediately. He acknowledged afterward that the star golfer had been in critical condition the night before the operation, but with the blood clot removed, he would be feeling better within a week, and up and around within a couple of months. However, because Hogan's inferior vena cava veins, which return blood from the lower body to the heart, were tied off, most demanding physical activity would be trying. Merely walking, doctors warned, could be extremely painful, and it was unrealistic to think he would be as mobile as he always had been. The most hopeful prognosis was that he would be able to walk for short stretches—maybe a couple hundred yards at a time—without assistance. His legs would be thick, heavy, and swollen for the better part of a year. Competitive professional golf anytime soon was out of the question. Ever returning to the tour was a long shot.

While Ben Hogan's body was recovering from the trauma, Ben Hogan the person was undergoing a bit of a change. So touched by all the cards and letters wishing him a speedy recovery, Hogan began to take note of the people around him. Those same human beings that he just did not see, did not want to see while he was on the golf course, expressed love and support in thousands of letters from all over the country. He made it his mission to answer every single one of them, thanking them for the good wishes, and he emerged from the hospital, in part, at least, a changed man. For the remainder of his life, he was more sympathetic. He developed a soft spot for people who had been through various trials and tribulations, unfortunate victims of random bad luck.

Two months to the day after he hightailed it out of Phoenix following that playoff loss to Demaret, Hogan left the hospital in El Paso and resumed the trip that had been stopped cold by a 10-ton bus. He finally made it home to Fort Worth with a newfound compassion in his heart, fresh scars on his body, and the old game on his mind.

Getting back on a golf course motivated Hogan more than anybody around him could have known. He immediately began to work his weakened legs to build strength. He pushed himself to the limit and sometimes beyond with daily walks that left him in tremendous pain. At first, he'd walk around his house. Then around his yard. He added distance every day until he could make his way around his entire Westover Hills neighborhood. There were times he overextended himself and wound up sitting on a curb in excruciating pain, trying to massage the cramps out of his tired muscles. Eventually, he was strong enough to hit balls on a driving range, and by November he was looking at the tournament schedule, plotting his return.

In mid-December, he and Valerie made their way to California with Ben's eye on the Los Angeles Open in early January. He wasn't certain he could withstand the demands of Riviera Golf Club in Pacific Palisades, but he knew there was only one way to find out. After he played in practice rounds on consecutive days, Hogan was quoted in a December 30 *L.A. Times* article written by Jack Curnow as saying, "Except for my legs I feel great. I'll probably decide the day before the open…whether I play or not."

On January 6, 1950, in the afterglow of the turn of a new half-century, and a strong 3 iron away from the magic of Hollywood, Hogan's golf career resumed. With his legs wrapped in elastic bandages from above his knees down to his ankles, Hogan stepped to the first tee. A record first-day Los Angeles Open crowd of 9,000 spectators packed Riviera, and they weren't there to see Ed Furgol, who played his way into the first-round lead. Hogan finished with an unspectacular 73, good for 1 over par, 5 shots off the pace.

As the tournament went on, Hogan settled down. Although he battled fatigue daily, he finished his fourth round with his third consecutive 69 and the tournament lead. A few holes behind him, Sam Snead was taking aim at the flags and the leading score, and he tied Hogan's 280 total on the strength of birdies on five of the final seven holes to force a playoff. It was exactly what the tired and weary Hogan didn't need—another 18 holes the following day.

After a good night's sleep, Ben and Valerie woke up at the Beverly Wilshire Hotel to the beautiful and welcome sounds of rain and thunder. Ten minutes before the scheduled tee time, the playoff was called off. Since the second round of the tournament had also been rained out, forcing the final round to be played on Monday, the playoff couldn't be held until Wednesday, at the earliest. With the three-day, four-round Bing Crosby Pro-Am scheduled to start the next day at Cypress Point on the Monterey Peninsula, an agreement was made to postpone the Hogan/Snead playoff an entire week.

Snead was a crafty guy who had every shot in the book, and some that weren't. An old story goes that Ernest "Dutch" Harrison, the famous hustler, was at a Los Angeles course in 1937, waiting for his next mark to come along. Soon a young player Harrison had never seen came by and asked, in speech littered with country slang and twang, whether Dutch would like to play with him. Harrison, barely able to control himself, said he'd love to play, provided the kid was willing to make it interesting along the way.

Before long, the pair was out on the course betting on just about every shot. Regardless of what proposition Harrison threw out there, his new competitor was equal to it. At the end of the day, thoroughly beaten, Dutch was paying his debt when the kid asked what time Harrison would be at the course the next day. "Uh-uh," Harrison replied. "I'm workin' this course tomorrow, you go work someplace else."

Dutch recalled years later, "That was the first time I ever met Sam Snead."

When Snead and Hogan finally got together back at Riviera, Ben was no match for the rock-steady Slammer. Snead led the playoff from the beginning and won rather easily, by 4 strokes. However, it was interesting to note the choice of the masses. Most of those in attendance were pulling for the once-vilified Bantam Ben. In Charles Curtis's *L.A. Times* article, he pointed out, "The gallery was for Hogan, remembering that just four weeks ago Hogan was considered a name for the history books. Even in defeat, his return to golf is one of 1950's greatest sports stories…. Anyone who apologizes for Hogan's showing is off his rocker. It's amazing to realize that the man whose golf career was called at an end two months ago has now played nine tournament rounds since Jan. 6 and he's done pretty well."

Hogan played a handful of tournaments in the early part of 1950 without much success. His shot-making ability had reverted to its old glorious form, but his legs were still giving him trouble, especially in the latter stages of tournaments. In April, after playing the first three rounds of the Masters in a total of 4 under par, he literally and figuratively limped home with a final-round 76 and finished 5 strokes behind. He packed his bags, left Augusta, and set his sights on the next major, the U.S. Open, two months later, in Ardmore, Pennsylvania.

THE TOURNAMENT

U.S. Open, Merion Golf Club, Ardmore, Pennsylvania June 8–10, 1950

Everybody loves a winner. Everybody loves an underdog. Ben Hogan was both; a paradox in spikes. He had the skills and experience of a champion, mixed in among the misfortune and handicap of an also-ran. The owner of 53 tournament titles checked in to the sophisticated and elegant Barclay Hotel a week prior to the start of play at the 50th edition of the United States Open, held at Merion Golf Club's east course just outside of Philadelphia.

Hosting the tournament 42 years before being designated a National Historic Landmark, Merion was already well established as one of the premier courses in existence. In 2005, *Golf Digest* ranked the layout number seven in its "100 Greatest Golf Courses" edition, and no less an authority than Jack Nicklaus has said, "Acre for acre, it may be the best test of golf in the world."

Merion was originally a cricket club built in the late 1800s, redesigned in 1911 by 32-year-old Hugh Wilson, a prominent member of the club sent to study courses in England and Scotland, specifically to gain insight into the elements that made a grand and challenging course. Despite its relatively small size of just 126 acres, Merion's east course is peppered with 120 steep-face, Scottish-style bunkers, a trait that would, in later years, influence scores of course architects. It was a fair, but difficult, course with ultrafirm, undulating greens and a very low risk-reward ratio on potential stroke-saving gambles. Until 1950, it was perhaps best known as the site where Bobby Jones finished off his Grand Slam of 1930 by winning the U.S. Amateur Championship.

Players arrived in Ardmore for the golden anniversary version of the national championship, with Sam Snead as the acknowledged favorite and the winning score expected to be par or worse. Hogan was considered a possible challenger, but a major obstacle loomed large in the distance. U.S. Open format dictated the opening round would be played on Thursday, round two on Friday, and the final two rounds on Saturday. Since his return from the accident, Hogan had not played two competitive rounds in a single day. Those who had watched him closely on the course knew his legs were still in bad shape, and he often had trouble making it through 18 holes, let alone 36.

Having played Merion's east course several times before other players even got to town, Ben made a strategic decision prior to the start of the first round. Only allowed to carry 14 clubs, he ditched his 7 iron in favor of a 1 iron. Any golfer on any level knows that the 7 is a valuable tool often relied upon heavily, while the 1 is extremely difficult to hit, with a 4 or 5 wood a viable substitute. Asked why he made the curious move, he replied simply, "There are no 7-iron shots on this course."

The opening day yielded a shocking surprise. With well-known names like Snead, Hogan, Sarazen, Boros, Fazio, Picard, and others in the field, it was the previously unknown Lee Mackey Jr., an unemployed golf pro out of Birmingham, who strolled out to a comfortable lead. Mackey beat up the other players, the course, and the record books with a U.S. Open record score of 6-under-par 64. Mackey was particularly good with the flat stick, amazingly needing just one putt on 10 of the 18 greens, as he walked away with a 3-stroke lead over Long Island champ Al Brosch. Of the 165 players who finished, only six broke par. A group at 2 over included Hogan, Sarazen, and Lloyd Mangrum, with Snead coming in at 3 over. The headline on *The New York Times* sports page screamed of Mackey's low round, but the sub-headline read,

"Hogan Attracts Big Gallery in Open Golf Play." The accompanying picture showed, the new fan favorite, finishing his swing in perfect form on the 14th tee with hundreds, if not a thousand, of spectators surrounding the tee box.

ROUND 2

The next day was Exhibit A in the demonstration of why tournament golf is more than an 18-hole event. Everything that had gone perfectly for the leader in the opening round suddenly went against him as Mackey carded a bulky 11-over-par 81, tumbling from the top of the leader board to off of it completely.

Meanwhile, the colorful Dutch Harrison—the eventual winner of 18 pro tournaments—was playing Merion to near perfection. He took over the lead by following his opening-day 72 with a second-round 67. Harrison started his career as a left-hander but switched to the far more common right-handed swing (a myth that has been perpetuated about Hogan himself over the years, but is not true). He had the well-deserved reputation as a hustler, gambling on just about anything on a golf course, picking up spending money winning nassaus and assorted side bets in noncompetitive rounds. Sam Snead recalled the day that Harrison lost a $20 bet to a player he thought was an easy mark. The man, well aware of his opponent's reputation, said, "Dutch, taking your money is truly an honor. In fact, I am going to frame this bill and mount it in my office."

"In that case," Harrison replied, "can I write you a check?"

Harrison's two-day total of 139 was a stroke better than the threesome of Austalian-born Jim Ferrier; Julius Boros, who had just recently turned pro; and Johnny Bulla, a former commercial airline pilot who fired the day's low round with a 66. Hogan's 69 was good for a two-day total of 141, leaving him very much within striking distance just 2 shots behind. Ten more players were within 4 shots of the lead with Gene Sarazen 5 back and pre-tournament choice Sam Snead 9 back after a second round of 5-over-par 75.

As he returned to his hotel that evening, Hogan's legs were shot. He unwrapped the now familiar bandages and went through his nightly routine of soaking in a tub of Epsom salts. As he rewalked the course in his mind, he wondered to himself and then to his wife if he could even make it through the 36-hole finish the following day.

Rounds 3 and 4

Saturday, June 10, 1950, started out warm and by high noon had become a steamy summer day in southeast Pennsylvania, the kind of day on which golfers might enjoy playing one round, but not two. Blue skies and a lazy breeze welcomed an estimated 14,000 spectators to the course for nearly eight hours of golf designed to decide the 50th U.S. Open championship.

Players were paired up, with each group assigned two tee times four hours apart. The first group went off at 8:00 AM sharp, and the final group started at 10:30. Like boxers feeling each other out in the opening rounds of a fight, most players near the top of the leader board took a safe, cautious approach to the opening 18, looking to remain in good position to make a tournament-winning charge in the afternoon. Lloyd Mangrum, who came into the day trailing by 3 shots, posted the low score of the morning—a smooth 65, which gave him the lead with 18 pressure-packed holes to play.

Two shots behind Mangrum was the trio of Ben Hogan; Dr. Cary Middlecoff, a former dentist; and Johnny Palmer, an eventual seven-time tour winner out of North Carolina.

Players rolled in from the heat into the cool comfort of the clubhouse, but for Hogan nothing felt very comfortable. His legs had swollen badly over the last hour of his morning round, and playing another full 18 seemed like torture. Newspaper reports stated he could barely get his shoes back over his bloated feet to return to the course. His front nine was a balancing act between preserving energy, walking gingerly, and staying alive in the tournament. He went out with eight pars and a bogey, good for a 1-over-par 37. Amongst those in contention, it was the best score for the afternoon's front nine. Of those who had a legitimate shot at winning, Mangrum, Harrison, Palmer, and Bulla all registered identical 41s. Middlecoff put up a 39. As Hogan forged on to the 10th, he had moved to the top of the leader board.

THROUGH 63 HOLES

Ben Hogan	250	+4
Lloyd Mangrum	252	+6
Cary Middlecoff	252	+6
Joe Kirkwood Jr.	253	+7
Dutch Harrison	253	+7
Johnny Palmer	254	+8
George Fazio	254	+8

It was a 2-stroke lead with nine to play, but with or without failing legs, the hardest stretch of the course still lay ahead.

Hogan got off to a good start with pars on both the 10th and 11th. Watching from the 11th green was golf writer Jim Finegan, a former collegiate golfer and Philadelphia-based student of the game, who saw a great champion struggling. He later wrote, "Every step had become agony. Hogan was managing to put one foot in front of the other…but here, obviously, was a man whose legs were near to buckling under him."

And then they actually did. As he followed through on his tee shot on the 400-yard, par-4 12th hole, his legs stiffened up. Hogan began to stumble and likely would have gone to the ground but grabbed the arm of playing partner Cary Middlecoff, who later admitted he thought Ben was going to collapse. Middlecoff, a Memphis-bred gentleman, subsequently marked Hogan's ball on the remaining greens to save Ben the pain of bending over. Hogan's caddie would then retrieve the ball out of the cup after each hole. Hogan's drive on number 12 was good, but his approach was not. Although he was relatively close—within 12 feet—he had uncharacteristically left himself a steep downhill putt. He barely tapped his ball but still rolled it about five feet past the cup and missed the comebacker to wind up with a bogey 5.

The 13th at Merion is a sweet and simple par 3. Posing a bigger problem for Hogan than the hole itself was merely getting to the tee box. Just 133 yards long, the 13th is played from an elevated tee down to a smallish, hilly green. He slowly climbed the incline, was handed a short iron, and made a smooth pass at the ball that had been teed up by his caddie. The shot was on line the entire way, hit the green, checked, and came to rest about 10 feet from the cup. He took 2 putts, bagged his ninth par in a 10-hole stretch, and slowly but surely moved on. Stories told around Merion to this day insist that by the time he got to the 14th tee, his legs were convulsing again. Doubled over in agony, Hogan reportedly said he had had enough. The legend goes that his caddie was adamant that he continue on, and after a brief bit of rest, he did.

A par on 14 brought Hogan to the 15th hole with a 2-stroke lead, although, without on-course scoreboards, it is not certain whether or not he knew it at the time. George Fazio, who had the day's first tee time, saved his best for last. He had birdied the 13th and 15th holes, shot 33 on the grueling back nine, and was in the clubhouse with a four-round total of 7-over-par 287. Lloyd Mangrum shot 35 on the back and had finished with the same score. Middlecoff had double-bogeyed the 10th and was 3 shots behind. Kirkwood and Harrison were not challenging. Hogan could play the final four holes in 1 over par and win the tournament.

On the 395-yard, par-4 15th, he hit a solid drive and a great approach. He putted to within two feet, maybe closer to one foot. His next stroke sent the ball toward the outside of the cup, where it rode on the lip for an instant and continued a couple of inches past for a tap-in bogey. Like a sprinkling of water, the margin for error had disappeared into 18 inches of short grass, vanished in a maddening moment. He had three holes left and needed to par all of them for the victory.

After a par at 16 to keep the 1-shot edge, Hogan stepped up to one of the longest par-3s in tournament golf then or now, the 230-yard 17th. The hole was later lengthened even further to 246 yards, a move that caused Lee Trevino to jokingly refer to it as "the shortest par-4 in Open history." It is known as the "quarry" hole because the tee shot is over a deep quarry. The green is deep, but narrow, and surrounded by a half-dozen bunkers. Hogan's tee shot found one of those bunkers, but his shot from the trap was a beauty, as he blasted out to within six feet of the cup. With thousands watching from around the green and back on the elevated tee, he studied the green. He walked from behind his ball in an arc to the hole, then back to the ball. And then he did it again. And again. When he finally felt certain he had the line, he drew back the putter and sent the white sphere rolling smoothly. His read was dead on. He had the line perfectly, but the speed fooled him. The ball stopped about an inch short of the cup, forcing him to tap in for a 4. Just like that, the lead was gone. Two bogeys in a span of four holes, and it was suddenly a three-way tie for the lead. Mangrum remained in the clubhouse, while Fazio joined the gallery as Hogan forged ahead to 18 in a three-way tie.

THE SHOT

The home hole is a 458-yard uphill par-4, where many a good round had disintegrated into shambles. By Merion's own hand-icapping system, number 18 ranked as the highest-scoring par-4 on the course. Going in the opposite direction of the previous hole, the drive required a blind shot that had to carry 220 yards over the quarry. Hogan focused squarely on his already-teed-up ball, blocked out the pain in his legs, and fired a smoking line drive. Seeing that the ball was hit well, the thousands in the gallery sent up a roar that continued as the ball cleared the solid rock lip of the quarry and settled into a healthy spot of the fairway. Businesslike, he began the slow uphill walk to his ball. His body was traveling about a mile per hour, but his mind was racing a mile a minute calculating the possibilities of what to do next. It was both complex and simple at the same time. The complexity lay in the different ways he could approach the remainder of the hole; the simplicity was in the fact that, regardless of what he did, he needed par to tie and birdie to win.

He found his ball sitting up nicely and, like a judge pondering a fair sentence, ran through all the factors—a perfect lie for either a long iron or a fairway wood. A shade over 200 yards to the green. Slight downhill lie to a partially upward-sloping green beyond an uphill run of fairway. One medium-deep bunker protecting the green, front right; another shallower one to capture mistakes, back left. Flag about three-fifths of the way toward the right side of the green, slightly back. Light breeze coming at him, maybe a bit left-to-right. Sun kind of low in the sky, shining directly toward him at address. A 4 wood would certainly get it there, but holding the green could be a problem. If he ran it through, there was thick rough, harrowing and hungry, lying in wait immediately beyond the putting surface. No, he thought, not the wood. The 1 iron.

There's an old golf crack that says, if you are ever playing in the rain and there is lightning in the area, just use your 1 iron, because even God himself can't accurately hit a 1 iron.

At that moment, though, that sparkling thin blade that Hogan had, prior to the tournament, almost prophetically placed in his bag instead of a 7 iron, practically called out to the smooth swinger from Texas. The 1 iron was his choice, and there was no wavering.

He took his stance and settled his aching feet. He picked up his head and stared confidently at the waving flag in the distance. Spectators, three and four deep, silently stacked like a forest of small trees along the entire contour of the fairway and circling the green, looked on, captivated by both the man and the moment. Hogan inhaled deeply, then exhaled as he turned his eyes toward his ball. A slight breeze blew the smell of summer across the grass. A chirping bird in the distance went quiet. Time stood still.

Moments later, he drew the club back in that familiar arc and, at the top of his backswing, uncoiled. His head remained motionless as he brought his hands down with that sweet, sinewy, silky swing and made perfect contact.

Hogan held his follow-through for a brief instant, but long enough for photographer Hy Peskin to hold it for all time. In one of the most famous sports pictures ever taken, and perhaps the most well-known golf picture, a man who came out of the mangled wreckage of a fierce collision is frozen in visual grace forever. The follow-through is so technically perfect, it looks as if Hogan might have been posing.

The ball came off low and then, as if forced upward by a blast of air, began to rise. At its highest point, the spinning sphere seemed to float for a couple of seconds, defying gravity and heading toward the green like a heat-seeking missile. He knew it was going to be good, but how good? It landed on the front portion of the green, skipped forward and to the left, then rolled up the slope. As the ball slowed, the cheers rose. The gallery roared its approval as the rock came to rest about pin-high, 40 feet to the left of the cup. It was one of the most clutch shots of a career defined by calm under pressure. He chose the toughest club in the bag and hit it to perfection. It was the kind of shot today's commentators would call "gutsy," but to Hogan that was simply the way he played. A U.S. Open championship was a stroke away. Birdie was possible, par was probable, bogey was unlikely. Perfect.

Again the trek began. It was just 200 yards, but like a marathoner with the tape in sight, for Hogan each step was like a beating in itself. He had been on his feet for the better part of eight hours and walked at least five miles. Fans yelled encouragement and cheered as he passed, but there was still work to be done. Once on the green, he surveyed the situation and stroked a solid putt toward the cup. Like a bell-shaped curve, the murmurs from the gallery escalated slowly, reached an apex as the ball approached the cup, held for an instant, and then tapered off as the ball passed the hole and rolled three and a half feet by. Hogan made his way over, studied the variables briefly, and then rolled home a par putt to finish at 287, deadlocked with Fazio and Mangrum and headed for a three-way, 18-hole playoff the following day.

The others had played two rounds of golf. Hogan had battled his own body and severe pain. And now, 20 hours later, a threesome would start all over again, playing 18 more for one of the most prestigious championships in the land.

After a long bath and more than one martini, Hogan went to sleep that night a mess. He woke up a new man. Pennsylvania law stipulated that no Sunday sporting event could begin before the last scheduled church service ended, so the playoff was scheduled for 1:00 PM, allowing him a few extra hours of sleep, which, according to his wife, he used soundly.

As Hogan made his way through the hotel lobby the next day, looking rested and healthy, he bid the assembled press corps a pleasant good morning. At the same time, morning editions of the *Los Angeles Times* were hitting breakfast tables out west. The sports page told a tale of national interest, a heroic effort a country away.

> *Bantam Ben Hogan battled pain and par to a standstill today and his fighting heart conquered faltering legs to carry him into a three-way tie at 287 with Lloyd Mangrum and George Fazio for the National Golf Open Championship. His trembling legs tormenting him in every throbbing tendon, the tight-lipped little man from the Lone Star State staggered home through the heat that blanketed Merion Golf Club with a 4-over-par last round....*
>
> *Out there under the blazing sun, fighting pain and heat and hazards, came Hogan. For a time it looked like the tiny Texan might take it all, but it was just too much to ask of this little man who captured America's most coveted golfing prize in 1948 and then almost lost his life in an automobile accident in February of 1949.*

U.S. Open
Round 4, June 10, 1950

HOLE	1	2	3	4	5	6	7	8	9	OUT	10	11	12	13	14	15	16	17	18	IN	TOTAL
PAR	4	5	3	5	4	4	4	4	3	36	4	4	4	3	4	4	4	3	4	34	70
Mangrum	5	6	2	6	5	5	5	4	3	41	4	4	4	3	4	5	4	3	4	35	76
Fazio	4	4	4	5	4	4	5	4	3	37	4	4	4	2	5	3	4	3	4	33	70
Hogan	4	5	4	5	4	4	4	4	3	37	4	4	5	3	4	5	4	4	(4)	37	74

THE PLAYOFF

With the survival of Saturday's competition and conditions behind them, a far more pleasant day greeted the threesome at Merion on Sunday. The skies were just as blue, but the oppressive heat that had beaten down most of the field the day before was mostly gone, replaced by a comfortable warmth.

On the tee stood the three men. George Fazio was born three months after Hogan in 1912 and was the winner of two PGA tournaments. His most lasting achievements came after his playing days as he would go on to become one of the sport's premier course architects. Along with his nephew, the more well-known Tom Fazio, he designed two of the five courses at PGA National in Palm Beach Gardens, Florida, and Devil's Elbow South in Hilton Head, South Carolina.

Lloyd Mangrum was two years younger than Hogan and Fazio. He won 36 tournaments in an outstanding golf career that was interrupted by World War II. It is unlikely that Mangrum was rattled by the pressure of that day's playoff, given that he was a well-respected American service veteran injured in the Battle of the Bulge and the recipient of two purple hearts.

The front nine yielded little clue as to the eventual winner. Hogan and Mangrum each went out with one birdie and one bogey for even-par 36, while Fazio's more aggressive play yielded three bogeys and two birdies for a 1-over-par 37.

Through 15 holes of the second round, Hogan had a 1-stroke lead on Mangrum, and a 2-stroke edge on Fazio. On 16, facing a par putt from about 10 feet, Mangrum marked his ball and waited for Hogan to putt out. Mangrum then put his ball back down and took his practice swings. As he moved into position to putt, he noticed a bug crawling on his ball, so he marked his spot with the toe of his putter, picked the ball up, blew the bug off, and replaced the ball on the green. He then went through his routine again, knocked in the 10-footer for par, and proceeded to the par-3 17th.

As Mangrum got ready to tee off, Ike Grainger, the USGA president, who was serving as a marshal for the match, intervened, saying Mangrum would be assessed a 2-stroke penalty for marking his ball twice, which was a rules infraction. Incredulous, the former war hero stared at Grainger. Hogan's precarious 1-shot lead over Mangrum was suddenly 3. Fazio had fallen back with bogeys on each of the last three holes and trailed by 4. Eighty-eight holes after it had started, the U.S. Open was all but decided.

Hogan now had honors on 17 and played safely to a flat part of the green well below the hole. As if to make the point that he needed no help from an opponent's blunder, Hogan marched up to the very green that swallowed up what had remained of his lead the day before and rolled a gorgeous, uphill, 50-foot monster dead-center for a birdie 2.

Back at the clubhouse, with the 18th hole now a mere formality, word got to Valerie that her husband had done it, had won the U.S. Open. She broke down in tears and wept with joy.

Ben finished with a par on 18 to wrap up a pristine round of 1-under-par 69. Amazingly, it was just the 15th sub-par round of the 437 that were played in the tournament. He won it by 4 strokes over Mangrum and by 6 over Fazio. Afterward, to the cheers of the gathered throngs, Hogan graciously accepted the championship trophy and the accompanying $4,000 check.

The day after the playoff, Arthur Daley of *The New York Times* wrote:

> *If Battling Ben had lost this play-off, no one could have blamed him. After all, he had done miraculously well in dragging his wearied legs this far. Yet this was such a gushily romantic setting, and he was such an overwhelmingly sentimental favorite, that it would have been cruel indeed for him to have wavered. So the little Texas bulldog, who had defied the doctors, took it upon himself to defy the laws of probabilities and to defy Merion's constantly outrageous challenge.*
>
> *He beat Lloyd Mangrum. He beat George Fazio. And as a final flourish he also beat Merion's par.*
>
> *This is a sport success story without parallel. All hail Ben Hogan, a champion amongst champions!*

Most in attendance on that serendipitous Sunday had been witness to four days of struggle, ultimately resulting in victory by a great champion. Weeping silently, Valerie considered it more the culmination of 16 months of mentally draining uncertainty, a return from the depths of despair where the precarious razor-thin line between life and death defined their very existence. Where a life once hung in the balance a trophy now stood, far less a gauge of the greatness of a golfer than a measure of the man himself.

U.S. OPEN PLAYOFF
Sunday, June 11, 1950

HOLE	1	2	3	4	5	6	7	8	9	OUT	10	11	12	13	14	15	16	17	18	IN	TOTAL
Par	4	5	3	5	4	4	4	4	3	36	4	4	4	3	4	4	4	3	4	34	70
Hogan	4	5	3	5	4	4	3	5	3	36	4	4	4	3	4	4	4	2	4	33	69
Mangrum	4	4	4	5	4	4	4	4	3	36	5	3	5	3	5	3	6	3	4	37	73
Fazio	5	4	3	5	4	5	5	3	3	37	4	4	4	3	5	5	5	3	5	38	75

POSTSCRIPT

Athletic achievement is wildly celebrated in this country, perhaps disproportionately so. The words *heroic*, *gallant*, and *superhuman* are used often to describe exploits on the field, but rarely does the action do justice to the true meaning of those terms. There have been numerous memorable and valiant efforts through the years, though, attained against all odds, which to a great extent legitimize the adulation heaped upon their performers. We all remember Michael Jordan willing his way through 44 excruciating minutes, dropping 38 flu-ridden points on Utah in a Game 5 victory in the 1997 NBA Finals. Emmitt Smith endured more pain and pressure and pounding than could be reasonably expected of a running back as he racked up 229 yards of offense, mostly with a separated shoulder, in the bitter cold of a New Jersey winter to lead his Cowboys to a division-clinching win over the Giants in the 1993 regular-season finale. And perhaps the most incomprehensible of them all, in 1973 Muhammad Ali courageously fought 10 violent and brutal rounds with a broken jaw against the fierce and powerful Ken Norton. Immediately after the fight, Ali, who lost a split decision, had the jaw operated on in a procedure that took nearly two hours. The bones that connected his upper and lower jaw were separated by a quarter of an inch, prompting the surgeon to say in awe, "I can't fathom how he could possibly fight like this."

Ben Hogan's return from the depths he reached in 1949 to the heights he attained in 1950 rank among the most incredible performances in any sport and any era. His battle through the pain and trauma of his accident and subsequent rehabilitation is a return to glory deserving of superlatives that have yet to be invented. But his career achievements did not end that summer day in Pennsylvania.

Always bothered by the inadequate blood flow in his legs, Hogan limited his play to a maximum of seven tournaments per year for the remainder of his career. The majors, though, rarely went off without his celebrated presence. In 1951, he defended his amazing championship at Merion with a win at the U.S. Open at Oakland Hills in Michigan, posting a sizzling 32 on the final nine. Two years later, he won the Open again at Oakmont Country Club in Pennsylvania as he put together one of the most efficient, if not productive, years in sports history. He played in just six events and won five of them, including that U.S. Open, the Masters, and the only British Open in which he ever played, to complete a career Grand Slam.

Competing in the U.S. Open 10 times in an 11-year stretch beginning in 1946, Hogan compiled an extraordinary record of four firsts, two seconds, and a third, while never finishing lower than sixth.

Late in his career, he developed what is known as "the yips," an inexplicable problem with his putting that, despite his immaculate ball-striking ability, hampered his chances to win. The putting woes bothered him so much, he actually campaigned for an increase in the size of the golf cup—in part to reconfigure the relative importance of putting to the rest of the skills needed to get from tee to green. He had supporters for the idea, but not enough of the game's power brokers were behind it to make it a reality.

He retired with 63 tournament victories, including nine majors: four U.S. Opens, two Masters, two PGA Championships, and a British Open. He played on two Ryder Cup teams, captained three of them, and was elected to the World Golf Hall of Fame in 1974, three years after his retirement. Perhaps most amazingly, he finished in the top three in 47.6 percent of the 292 PGA Tour events in which he played, and finished in the top 10 in 241 of them.

In his later years, Hogan had surgery for colon cancer and developed Alzheimer's disease. On July 25, 1997, William Benjamin Hogan passed away in Fort Worth, Texas, at the age of 84.

Upon Hogan's death, the great Pulitzer Prize–winning *L.A. Times* columnist Jim Murray wrote:

> *My late wife used to say, "If Jim ever gets to heaven and Ben Hogan isn't there, he ain't staying." We all laughed. But you know something? I hope today they have in heaven this little 18-hole golf course with trouble on the right, narrow fairways, maybe a par-3 with this sand trap in the middle of the green, a long par-5 or two that requires a 1-iron second, and a finishing uphill hole against a sloping fairway to weed out the ribbon clerks and identify the champions....*
>
> *The Lord will say, "We'll play at full handicap, play it as it lies and I'll promise no miracles."*
>
> *But Hogan will say, "Wait a minute! No disrespect, but you may need a couple miracles, Sir. I'm really on*

my game.... How about [you get] 3 shots and two mir-
acles a side, and we'll adjust at the turn?"...

Hogan left us the other day for greener fairways.
Good-bye to a man who was part of our youth, a
source of our pride. A man whose friendship was as
rare as rubies.

For what Hogan meant, it's the old story. For those
who know golf, no explanation is necessary. For those
who don't, no explanation is possible.

Ben Hogan lives on in the world of golf, partly in history books but mostly in how-to books. His swing, a thing of graceful beauty until the day he walked away from the game, is to this day the basis for much of what is taught by pros on golf courses throughout the world. Hogan's book, *Five Lessons: The Modern Fundamentals of Golf*, which was not ghostwritten but eloquently penned by the man himself in 1957, has sold more copies than any instruction book in the history of his, or any other, sport.

Tommy Bolt, a contemporary of Hogan's, was asked whether Nicklaus or Hogan was the best player ever. He thought about it a minute and said, "Well, I've seen Jack watch Ben practice on many occasions, but I've never seen Hogan on the range watching Nicklaus. Does that answer your question?"

The Golden Bear himself had the utmost respect for Hogan, saying, "The argument of 'greatest ever' will never be settled, but Ben Hogan remains the most ruthlessly accurate shotmaker the world has ever known."

Just as Hogan's legacy is figuratively etched in stone, the marking of the now-famous 1-iron shot at Merion is literally. On the 18th fairway of Merion's east course, where the U.S. Open could very well be decided when it returns in 2013, a flat slate of light gray rock commemorates the spot from which the ball was hit, launching Hogan into that playoff more than a half century ago. It is the rare golfer who plays the course who does not drop a ball and take a whack to measure himself against one of the game's all-time greats. The stone reads:

> *JUNE 11, 1950*
> *U.S. OPEN*
> *FOURTH ROUND*
> *BEN HOGAN*
> *ONE IRON*

Although the shot will live on as a testament to a great champion, the question of what happened to the actual golf club Hogan used to hit it is of great debate. The 1 iron now resides in the USGA Hall of Fame in Far Hills, New Jersey, but how the club got from point A to point B is an interesting and convoluted tale.

According to Hogan himself, the "butter knife," as a 1 iron was often called, was stolen out of his bag sometime after the round. Whether it was five minutes or five hours after he played that fateful 18th hole is uncertain, but in a response to questions he received in a letter from Merion club members, Hogan wrote, "After hitting my shot, my 1 iron was stolen. I haven't seen it since. Also, that night my shoes were stolen out of my locker and I haven't seen them either."

For the next 32 years, the club was a ghost, presumed destroyed, sitting in someone's garage gathering dust like an old tool box, or worse yet, not thought of at all. Then in 1982, respected golf memorabilia collector and owner of American Golf Classics, Bob Farino, was invited to sell refinished clubs to pros before the Tournament Players Championship at Sawgrass in Florida. "All of the guys would come looking for clubs that weren't made anymore," he says. "The 8802 Wilson blade putter, classic irons, persimmon drivers…this is the early '80s back when pros actually paid for their clubs! They loved something about the metal used in making the old clubs. Some people say they were made from scrap metal left over from the war—very soft forgings—great clubs that were all made in the U.S.A."

It was there, Farino says, an elderly man he had never previously met, offered him a bag of old Ben Hogan signature MacGregor clubs. Farino liked what he saw and paid the man $150.

Like finding a rare coin in the change cup of a vending machine, or a valuable stamp on a Christmas card, upon further inspection Farino made an amazing discovery. Realizing the 1 iron in the bag did not match the other clubs in the set, he looked at it more closely. On it, the words "personal model" were inscribed. His mind started to race. He began to wonder to himself, Could this be Ben Hogan's actual 1 iron? The inscription was Exhibit A, but he needed more evidence. Farino looked down the shaft and was struck by what he saw on the clubface. Exhibit B: a worn spot about the size of a quarter. Whoever owned this club was a pretty damn consistent ball striker. "Either Hogan or somebody incredible," Farino remembers thinking.

Farino vaguely remembered hearing some kind of tale about that stolen butter knife from 1950, put two and two together, and called Hogan's equipment company to relay the story of the club suddenly in his possession. He was told that Ben Hogan himself would be willing to verify the club's authenticity. Farino got the club to Jack Murdoch, a fellow collector who would be hosting Lanny Wadkins in North Carolina when Wadkins came through to play at the Greater Greensboro

Open. Soon after, Wadkins was headed to the Colonial in Fort Worth, where he would certainly come in contact with Hogan, who was the tournament's unofficial grand marshal.

Wadkins, says Farino, happened upon Hogan at the driving range the day before the Colonial started in 1983 and explained the story of this old 1 iron. Thirty-three years after hitting it for the last time, Ben Hogan gave the club a quick once-over, gripped it, walked over to an open spot on the range, and stroked a few balls. Hogan nodded and said without a doubt it was the genuine article.

Instead of returning the club to Wadkins, though, who would have presumably given it back to Murdoch and in turn to its latest owner Farino, Hogan held on to the club and had his people present it to the United States Golf Association Hall of Fame in Far Hills, New Jersey.

Looking back in early 2007, Farino says, "I never got anything for that 1 iron. There's no telling what it was really worth. Thing is, though, even though I bought it, I never actually considered it mine. The club was stolen from Hogan—it was his. For me, it was just awesome to be part of golf history."

Sports memorabilia has recently reached an almost insane level, invoking the phrase, "Something is worth only what somebody is willing to pay for it." In 2000, a Honus Wagner baseball card sold on eBay for $1.26 million, so putting a modern-day value on Hogan's 1 iron is impossible. When reminded that John F. Kennedy's sets of woods and irons sold at auction in 1996 for a combined $1.15 million, Farino considered the magnitude of Hogan and said of the purchase of JFK's clubs, "Yeah, and he was merely the president."

Arnold Palmer points to his name on the scoreboard, showing his 4 under-par total in the 1960 U.S. Open.

CHAPTER THREE

1960:
A Saturday Drive

PRELUDE

Jackie Gleason suddenly had company, and away he went. As televised sports made its way into more and more of America's living rooms in the 1950s, Gleason, Dinah Shore, Ed Sullivan, and other small-screen stars of the day moved over to make way for a new star. With golf becoming popular over the airwaves, it became increasingly difficult for fans to take their eyes off an emerging supernova named Arnold Palmer.

Born in a suburb of Pittsburgh in 1929, Palmer learned golf from his father, Deacon, who was the pro at the Latrobe Country Club. The course there was a par-34, nine-hole track with little quirks and challenges best overcome with a healthy helping of local knowledge. Even as a young boy, Arnold had plenty of that.

Never allowed to play on the actual course when members were present, he would hang around hitting balls whenever and wherever he could. He would hack balls out of the rough—into more rough, putt on greens when nobody was looking, and sometimes play a complete nine either just as the sun rose or just after it set when the course was empty.

He eventually became a caddie at the club—more for the access to the course it allowed him than to actually make money. The best days, though, were Mondays when the course was closed and he and the other caddies would have the run of the place. Although only 11 years old, Arnold took those rounds seriously, and after playing 9 or 18 or 27, he'd stay out on the course and practice until dark. As his game took shape, he was introduced to another aspect of the game that would become ingrained in his personality and serve him well for half a century.

It was the summer of 1943, and while world war raged overseas, peaceful and proud Latrobe, in the foothills of the

Allegheny Mountains, was getting a visit from one of the greatest athletes who ever lived. Still seven years away from sweeping all three events considered the women's golf Grand Slam, Babe Didrikson Zaharias, who won three medals in track-and-field at the 1932 Olympics, was in town to put on an exhibition. As impressed as Arnold was with her golf skills, it was more her showmanship that attracted him.

With a substantial crowd around her, Babe stepped to the first tee box, set up her ball, and turned to the gallery. "Okay, ladies and gentlemen," she bellowed, "hold on while I loosen my girdle!"

The crowd roared with laughter. Arnold was transfixed. Babe turned back to her ball and with a flawless, compact swing, sent it sailing straight and true down the fairway. Palmer later wrote in his book, *A Golfer's Life,* "The crowd ate it up. I think I became aware of my own budding desire to show off and please people in that manner. Babe had a flair for the spectacular and the talent and flair to pull it off. Though no one but me realized it then, so did I. Prior to that, the only people I aimed to please with my golf shots were my father and mother…but watching Babe do her thing, it occurred to me how great it would be to make lots of people—complete strangers at that—ooh and aah over a golf shot…. Something in me was clearly drawn to the kind of public admiration I witnessed that day Babe Didrikson Zaharias came to Latrobe."

Through the 1940s, Palmer's knowledge of the game grew, as did his body. By the time he was in high school, he was a thick, strapping teenager hitting the ball a mile and swinging as if he wanted to hit it two. He won his share of amateur tournaments and attended Wake Forest long enough to win an Atlantic Coast Conference championship. After a brief stint in the Coast Guard, it was back to the golf course to play as often as possible for as long as possible. He took a job as a rep for an industrial paint company, allowing him to meet with prospective customers on weekday mornings and tend to the real business in his life in the afternoons and on weekends.

In 1954 Arnie crept into the lower tier of the golf world's consciousness with a victory at the United States Amateur tournament in Detroit. Nearly half a century later, his precious memories of that August day are focused more on his father's acknowledgment of the victory and the praise that followed than on the accomplishment itself.

Shortly after the win, he was asked by a newspaper about his future plans and answered by saying, "I like selling paint. I have no intention of turning professional." At the time, the PGA Tour required new members to go through a six-month apprenticeship in which they could play in the tour's events but, regardless of finish, collect no prize money. What's a paint salesman to do?

Real-world practicalities, though, would begin to make decisions for him. With a new bride and an uncertain future, Palmer met with the Wilson Sporting Goods Company in Chicago. With a $2,000 signing bonus and a $5,000 annual contract doing the talking, Arnold agreed to join a long line of amateur and professional champions such as Byron Nelson and Sam Snead as representatives of Wilson. Paint was out, golf was in. The PGA Tour players had a new member, and it wasn't long before he'd shake up the whole lot of 'em.

His first win came at the 1955 Canadian Open, beginning a streak in which Palmer won at least one pro tournament for 17 consecutive years. He won twice in 1956 and four times the following year with an untamed, swashbuckling style that often hurt him more than it helped. On the heels of blowing final-round leads in multiple events in 1957, he won the Oklahoma City Open in 1959, protecting his 54-hole lead by finishing with a solid final 18. Afterward he was asked which golfer he feared the most going into the last round and he answered, "Myself."

Palmer's career and following hit new heights in 1958 with his first major victory at the Masters. He won the event again in 1960 and, with the help of television and ever-increasing media coverage, left Augusta with more national hype and hyperbole swirling around him than any golfer before him. Even though he was probably not the most talented player on tour, his style was like a magnet to the masses. His appeal was undeniable. He was 30 years old, blessed with supreme confidence and rugged good looks, and skyrocketing to the top of his profession. He couldn't possibly have known it at the time, but he was also a few months away from his first meaningful on-course battle with an up-and-coming kid who would become a lifetime nemesis and impact the sport forever.

•••

Jack Nicklaus was not the anti-Palmer, but in some ways, he was close. Where Arnie was loud and boisterous, willing to share his talent with the world, Jack was quiet and self-assured, happy to go unnoticed as he crept up a leader board. Where Arnie was willing to make bold declarations about his intentions, Jack simply let his clubs speak for him. Arnold was a grown man, muscular and strong, while Jack was still a chubby 20-year-old kid with a bright sweater and a bad haircut.

Born more than 10 years after Palmer, Nicklaus played his first round of golf at age 10, and shot 51 for nine holes. He racked up a ton of tournament wins through his teenage years, including five consecutive Ohio State Junior titles, and qualified for the U.S. Open at age 17. In 1959, he won the same event Palmer had won five years earlier, taking the U.S. Amateur as the youngest player to win the title in 50 years. He played in the 1960 Masters, and even though he did make the cut, saying he competed against the eventual champion Palmer is a bit of a stretch. Jack shared low-amateur honors, but wasn't even a blip on the Palmer radar screen, finishing 11 strokes back. As that summer's U.S. Open rolled around, Jack had already made a bit of a name for himself, but winning in a field of amateurs was one thing; mounting a challenge against a group of pros was something else entirely. Coming into the tournament, Palmer was the clear-cut favorite. Nicklaus was a trivial footnote, if he was even mentioned at all.

THE TOURNAMENT

U.S. Open, Cherry Hills Country Club Cherry Hills Village, Colorado June 16–18, 1960

A record 2,472 golfers across the country registered to qualify for the 1960 U.S. Open. All but 150 of them were eliminated in the weeks leading up to the event, which was to be played at beautiful and spacious Cherry Hills Country Club just outside of Denver. The par-71 course measured 7,004 yards, which was the fifth longest layout in Open history. Because of the high altitude and resulting extra distance balls would travel, though, Ben Hogan remarked that the length was deceptive and would need to be around 8,000 yards to make it a true test.

Coming off his win at the Masters, Arnold Palmer had already racked up more than $52,000 in season winnings and was listed as a 4-to-1 favorite to take home the $14,400 winner's check. Palmer knew the course pretty well because one of his many high-profile playing partners was a member of Cherry Hills named Dwight D. Eisenhower. Reacquainting himself with the course during two practice rounds, Palmer pulled out his driver on the opening hole, a downhill par-4 of 346 yards. He drove the green on successive days and decided that he would employ the same strategy during the tournament and go for the putting surface to try to collect a quick birdie to get him started.

Sam Snead, who had finished second in his first U.S. Open in 1937 but was still looking for his first Open championship 23 years later, was listed with defending champ Billy Casper as a 5-to-1 pick. Ben Hogan and Ken Venturi were next on the odds board at 6-to-1, and Gene Littler and big hitter Mike Souchak were given strong consideration at 7-to-1.

Down in the cold, lonely bowels of the Las Vegas kennel, where the underdogs sleep, was the name of Jack Nicklaus at 35-to-1. In the mid-1990s, Nicklaus confirmed a well-traveled story that was said to have taken place during the week prior to the tournament in which his father informed him of the odds and asked whether he'd like to make a bet on himself.

"That's true," said Jack. "I said, 'You're damned right I would—I'll have 20 bucks of that.'" Because of Nicklaus's amateur status at the time, even if he had pulled off an incredibly unlikely victory, he would not have received a penny in prize money. Betting on himself was his only way to cash in. "I was about to get married," he remembers, "and I needed the money!"

The tournament opened on June 16, 1960, in the disappearing chill of a typical Colorado June morning. Under a brilliant blue sky, they began play at 8:00 AM sharp, and golfers going off early had the distinct advantage of playing before many of the greens hardened under the unrelenting glare of the Rocky Mountain summer sun.

Like the early laps of a 500-mile race or the first quarter of a basketball game, the opening round of a golf tournament is a lot about feel. Players try to get a sense of the course, the surroundings, and their opponents. Often an opening day at an event goes by without major incident, but that was certainly not the case at Cherry Hills, where several bizarre happenings made up what the *Los Angeles Times* referred to as "the wackiest day in U.S. golf."

It started with Ben Hogan, whose putting problems had, by this time, become the defining characteristic of his otherwise still strong game. Hogan snap-hooked his drive on the 9th hole, hitting a spectator square in the stomach. On the 17th hole, Sam Snead hit a shot that was either too short to clear a lagoon or too long to lay up. His ball skipped across a 12-foot moat, bounced onto the green, and minutes later turned into one of the most fortunate birdies in history. "The most amazing thing I've ever seen," according to Snead's playing partner, reigning British Open champion Gary Player.

Another golfer, Doug Sanders, went to 18 needing a par to tie for the lead, but badly mishit his tee shot when a loud splash in the lake next to the tee box unnerved him in the middle of his swing. "That fish was big enough to be a whale," he said of the jumper. "I thought for a minute someone was unloading a truckload of empty beer cans." Sanders managed to stop his swing after hearing the splash, but said at that point, his concentration was shot. He reset and hooked his ball into the lake, double-bogeyed the hole, and finished the round 2 strokes off the lead. Lastly, Tommy "Thunder" Bolt, a fiery and temperamental player from Oklahoma, who had won the U.S. Open two years earlier, was one of the final arrivals to Cherry Hills and was in one of his bad moods from the beginning. He hit town late on Tuesday complaining of a cold, the bothersome high altitude, and swollen hands. He fired his caddie midway through a practice round on Wednesday and then, on Thursday, had trouble avoiding the water. He hit his tee shot into the drink on the par-3 12th, ending up with a triple-bogey 6. He arrived at the par-4 8th hole already

5 over, and proceeded to hit not one, but two tee shots into the lake. As soon as the second one died its watery death, Bolt teed up a third ball, which he promptly sent soaring into the thick rough. That was the last straw. He was so irate, he drew back his driver with both hands, looking like a baseball batter in a stance at home plate, lunged forward, and flung the club as hard as he could. The driver sailed end over end, flying about 50 yards into the lake, where it played temporarily as an underwater threesome with the misguided golf balls that had just flown errantly off its face. A young boy eventually retrieved the club and was talked into giving it back to Bolt, with a $10 "tip" for his troubles.

Bolt angrily finished the hole, taking a quadruple-bogey 8 to finish off a sloppy and maddening opening round of 80. He marched straight off the green toward the clubhouse, withdrew from the tournament citing illness, got into his car, and drove out of the parking lot barking at a few inquiring reporters on his way. His playing partner, Claude Harmon, later said the wayward driver had missed his head by about 18 inches, and insisted that had he gotten hit, he would have gotten the best of Bolt because, at that point, Harmon would have been the only one of the two with a club in his hand. True enough. And newspaper reports from coast to coast supported Harmon's story of a near-death-by-driver experience, but a snapshot of the moment of madness suggests otherwise. In the picture, Harmon, who was making his way onto the tee box, is actually about six feet behind Bolt, recoiling in stunned surprise as Bolt, hands held high by his right ear, begins to fling the club forward.

On top of the leader board was Mike Souchak, a 33-year-old, solidly built, former Duke University football player with 10 PGA wins to his credit prior to 1960. Playing in a group with his former Ryder Cup partner Bob Rosburg and the following year's Open champ Gene Littler, Souchak finished with a 1-stroke lead at 3-under-par 68. Most notably, Souchak needed a mere 10 putts to cruise through the opening nine in 31 and didn't have to duck out of the way of a single thrown driver.

Jerry Barber and Harry Ransom both shot 69s to tie for second, and eight others were bunched up at 70 in a tie for third on a day when only 11 of the 150 golfers were able to break par. In a group at 71 stood Nicklaus, who offset his three bogeys with three birdies. Following the Ohio State star in the gallery that day was legendary Buckeyes coach Woody Hayes, who was in town to put on a football clinic in nearby Boulder. Hayes was wildly impressed with Jack, who was the latest in a long line of amateurs who had started a U.S. Open impressively to wind up near the top of a leader board. Most of those players faded like a Ben Hogan tee shot, but according to Nicklaus's playing partner that day, who just happened to be the defending champion, this 20-year-old kid was a different story. "He will definitely be in contention all the way through the tournament," proclaimed Billy Casper, who also checked in with a 71.

Arnold Palmer's plan of attack blew up almost before he could implement it. Gripping and ripping on the 1st hole, intending to drive the green, he instead drove the creek to the right of the fairway. He was forced to take a drop with a 1-stroke penalty and then hit his next shot off of a tree branch. Laying 3, he hit a wedge completely over the green, chipped back on, and sunk a five-footer for a double-bogey 6. Palmer recalled years later, "You could have fried an egg on my forehead at that moment. I was so furious with myself for blowing a hole I clearly should have birdied." Yet, his love/hate relationship with the 1st hole at Cherry Hills was merely in its infancy.

Palmer was paired with Cary Middlecoff and Jack Fleck, who had two things in common. First, they had both won the Open previously, and second, they were two of the slower players on tour. Arnold, a "hit it, chase it, and hit it again" kind of player was bothered all day by their pace of play, made even worse by the thin air that caused most of the field to move more slowly than usual. After the double bogey on 1, Palmer got around the rest of the course in even par to finish with a 2-over 72, 4 shots off the pace.

Three shots behind Arnie was Ben Hogan, who, since his fourth Open victory in 1953, had made no secret of how badly he wanted to break his career tie with Bobby Jones and Willie Anderson to win an unprecedented fifth. Hogan, still considered the tour's preeminent ball-striker, fought through an unthinkable stretch in which he bogeyed four consecutive holes to finish with a 75. The absurdly un-Hogan-like run began on number 7 and didn't get put to bed until the nightmare ended with a streak-snapping par on the 11th. He actually still could have salvaged the round with a strong finish, but he ripped his 4-iron approach over the 18th green and disgustedly settled for a bogey 6 to close the day 7 full shots behind.

Eighteen holes down, 54 to play, and the board sported a clear-cut leader at the top.

Mike Souchak	31–37	68	-3
Jerry Barber	35–34	69	-2
Henry Ransom	32–37	69	-2
Bruce Crampton	36–34	70	-1
Jack Fleck	36–34	70	-1
Huston La Clair	34–36	70	-1
Gary Player	33–37	70	-1
Doug Sanders	32–38	70	-1
Dick Stranahan	34–36	70	-1
Joe Taylor	36–34	70	-1
Don Cherry*	32–38	70	-1

Seven others tied 71 E

* = Low Amateur

ROUND 2

There was no club throwing, but the flying fish did make another appearance on a hot Friday just south of Denver. "But he jumped this time, after I had driven," said Doug Sanders, who caught a quick glimpse of his old airborne nemesis at the 18th tee. Sanders double-bogeyed the hole in round one thanks, in part to that distracting splash, but with a great tee shot and a better approach, he knocked down a birdie to finish round two. Sanders, a fun-loving, hard-partying playboy from Georgia who was once quoted as saying, "If I died today and could come back as anybody, I'd come back as me," came in with a polished 68 and a two-day record-tying total of 138.

His mark did not last long, though, as the 18-hole leader Mike Souchak continued to shine. His putter wasn't quite as hot as it was the previous day, but how could it be? He was still ultraefficient on the greens, needing just 26 putts to finish off another fantastic round. Souchak racked up eight 3s en route to a sweet 67, which gave him a two-day total of 135, smashing the previous 36-hole U.S. Open record tied an hour earlier by Sanders. Souchak's score was a full 3 shots better than the mark set by Sanders and three other players, including two of the game's all-time greats, Sam Snead and Ben Hogan.

Two months shy of his 48th birthday, and seven years removed from his record-tying two-round stretch, Hogan made his presence felt again. For years "the Hawk" had fueled his reputation for gamesmanship by either boldly stating his intentions to win a given tournament or working the other end of the spectrum by downplaying his chances. With that in mind, nobody really knew exactly what to make of his postround statement: "I can't get accustomed to judging distances here.

Sometimes it goes a mile, sometimes it doesn't. My game isn't sharp." He uttered those words minutes after putting together his best U.S. Open round in seven years with a 4-under-par 67, leaving him within striking distance halfway home. The irony was that the part of his game that was the strongest was really the only part in which he needed to be precise with his distance. Hogan's driving was erratic and his putting was shaky. What saved him was the skill with which he hit his deadly accurate approach shots. In fact, after the round, playing partner Dow Finsterwald, a longtime tour veteran, said that Hogan had put together "the finest exhibition of iron play" he'd ever seen. The fact that Ben had missed five birdie putts of between four and 15 feet on the back nine alone is what prevented a good score from being a great score. He didn't 3-putt any greens, but that was mostly a function of his propensity to stick the ball close to the pin on his approach. Still a powerful drawing card, *The Denver Post* estimated Hogan's gallery at about 6,000 people. Witnessing the mental aspect of Ben's putting problems, they often watched in painful, anticipatory silence as he would stand over his ball for as long as 30 seconds before drawing back his putter to start his stroke.

With a two-day total of 142, Hogan was tied with Jack Nicklaus, who put together another consistent round. Nicklaus had shown no signs of nerves, or of folding under the pressure of the professionals surrounding him, and hit the midway point having posted back-to-back 71s. His day started with an errant drive into the creek bordering the first fairway, but he shook it off, took a drop, and got up and down for par.

Palmer, still sticking to his plan, attacked the opening hole a bit more ferociously than Nicklaus, and hit a far better shot than he did the day before. Again ripping his driver with the intention of reaching the green, Arnold kept the ball straight, but came up short. He left himself a little chip shot that he hit beautifully to set up the first of his five birdies. Palmer walked away with a round of even-par 71 and later said he felt he deserved better, but many observers thought he was lucky not to have done worse. He was in the rough several times but bailed himself out with a combination of pure strength and daring iron shots. His approaches left him several lengthy or testy putts, but he saved par numerous times with magic from the flat stick. Most notably, after driving out of bounds on 14, he nailed a tricky 30-footer for bogey to minimize the damage. He finished with four straight pars and headed to Saturday's 36-hole finale tied with seven others for 15th place, at 1-over-par 143.

ROUND 2 LEADER BOARD

Mike Souchak	68–67	135
Doug Sanders	70–68	138
Jerry Barber	69–71	140
Dow Finsterwald	71–69	140
Jack Fleck	70–70	140
Billy Casper	71–70	141
Bruce Crampton	70–71	141
Ted Kroll	72–69	141
Sam Snead	72–69	141
Don Cherry*	70–71	141
Boros, Hogan, Nicklaus, and Player		142
Palmer and 6 others		143

* = Low Amateur

ROUND 3

Players with scores of 146 or better survived the cut and arrived at the course to play 36 holes on another warm and sunny Colorado morning. The two rounds on the final day of U.S. Open action were a test of mental toughness and physical stamina nearly as much as they were a challenge of the golfers' respective skills.

A galactic collision of the sport's recent past and near future took place either clairvoyantly or by happenstance with the pairing of two of the four players at 142. With the playing field cut by about two-thirds, the intriguing twosome of Ben Hogan and Jack Nicklaus teed off together at 9:00 AM sharp.

Once upon a time, the icy, stoic Hogan might have made the day rather uncomfortable for the young amateur who was 27 years his junior. The Hogan of 1960, though, was no longer that man. "Several golfers I knew had previously told me that Hogan was hard to play with," Nicklaus wrote in his 1969 book, *The Greatest Game of All*. "This, I discovered early in the day, was absolutely wrong. I have never been partnered in a championship with a man who was in a contending position, as Ben was at Cherry Hills, who was so enjoyable to play with."

Maybe it was Hogan's company that was enjoyable, but perhaps Nicklaus's own play contributed to his satisfaction with the round. Unfazed by the enormous Hogan-watching gallery around him, Jack started the day 7 strokes behind the leader but played as if he had no thoughts of anyone or anything other than the course itself. He chopped 2 strokes off of par, coming in with a rock-steady 69, leaving him with a three-round total of 211 and very much alive with 18 to play.

As strong as his own round was, afterward, Nicklaus could speak of nothing but the way his partner had played. He was taken not only by Hogan's demeanor, but also by his legendary ball-striking ability. Ben followed his 67 on Friday with a 69 on Saturday morning, hitting every green in regulation; every single one of 'em. He managed two birdies, but had he been a bit more accurate with his increasingly vexing putter, it would have been several more. Even with the missed opportunities, Hogan had, like Nicklaus, played himself into contention with a three-round total of 2-under-par 211.

Only one player scored better than Nicklaus and Hogan in the early round, and his name was Julius Boros. The 6' tall, 215-pounder out of Connecticut would go on to win 18 PGA tournaments including three majors, play on four U.S. Ryder Cup teams, and be instrumental in helping put together the Senior Tour in the late '70s. Paired with Gary Player, Boros tore it up for a 3-under-par 68, leaving him a stroke ahead of Nicklaus and Hogan. Player's even-par 71 left him at 213.

Arnold Palmer woke up on Saturday "telling myself that if I was going to lose the Open, I'd do it kicking and screaming." As he had promised himself before the tournament started, Arnie whipped out the driver on the 1st tee and once again took a mighty cut hoping to reach the green. As in round two, his ball stayed straight, but as in both round one and round two, he did not wind up on the green. The ball came up short and was entangled in the rough in front of the green, causing Palmer to chip poorly. He took 3 putts, angrily stuffed the disappointing bogey in his pocket, and moved on to the 2nd hole yet another stroke behind. He played the rest of the round in even par despite five birdies. Palmer's 72 gave him a three-round total of 215. The pretournament favorite had become a major long shot, wallowing in a ridiculous logjam with nine other golfers tied for 15th place, a whopping 7 strokes off the pace. Kicking and screaming, indeed.

Mike Souchak could not possibly have hoped to continue the blistering record-setting pace he had put together over the first half of the tournament. Instead, the leader was looking to limit mistakes, minimize potential damage, and shorten the distance between himself and the winner's trophy with a long string of pars. It wasn't that he was going to play safe, but he certainly was not going to take any unnecessary chances; as the day progressed, if he needed to put together a few birdies, then so be it. Talking to a *Greensboro Daily News* reporter by telephone on Friday night, Souchak said simply, "I'm going out there with just one thing in mind, and that's to bring that big trophy back home to North Carolina."

Though he didn't play particularly well, Souchak milked an up-and-down round to even par through 17 holes. Sanders, his playing partner, was stumbling, and everybody who managed to shave shots off of par in round three had started at least 7 strokes behind him, so Souchak remained in good position. On the 18th tee, though, it began to fall apart. As he started to descend from the top of his backswing, a nearby spectator snapped a picture with an old-fashioned box-style camera. The loud pop of the shutter stunned Souchak, causing him to badly mishit the shot and pull it out of bounds.

He ended up with a double-bogey 6 to finish the morning round at 2 over par. As he headed toward the locker room after the hole, Souchak told reporters, "It's over and done with. There's nothing I can do about it now, and this afternoon is a new day."

Inside, though, the man was burning.

In 2008, 80-year-old Mike Souchak began his 35th year as a partner of Golf Car Systems, a preventive maintenance company in Clearwater, Florida. "I work a day job now, nine-to-five," he chuckles. He is the father of four, grandfather of four more, and plays golf infrequently because of carpal tunnel syndrome he developed in both hands "from hitting too many balls." He was so bothered by the camera incident that, to this day, more than 46 years later, he remembers it as if it were yesterday. "Unfortunately, on the 54th hole, some idiot had a big camera, and he caught me right in the middle of my swing," he says. "I flinched and over-cut the ball, and hit it out of bounds by about a foot and wound up making a 6 instead of a 4. It upset me for the rest of the day." He laughs as he hears the emotion in his own voice and continues, "I've gotten past it, but every now and then I think about it. I would like to get my hands on that guy and kick him from here to downtown."

"Can you actually remember all these details from 46 years ago?" he was asked. "Of course I can," he answered, surprised at the question. "I know where I was, what club it was, everything."

Souchak, a Pennsylvanian who competed against Palmer in high school and still remains friends with him, also remembers having a lead in the final round of the Open the previous year, 1959, and again the following year, 1961. In those tournaments, he finished in a tie for third and a tie for fourth, respectively. In 1960, he went to the practice green between rounds with his suddenly shrinking lead down to 2 strokes with 18 holes to play.

ROUND 3 LEADER BOARD

Mike Souchak	68–67–73	208
Jerry Barber	69–71–70	210
Julius Boros	73-69–68	210
Dow Finsterwald	71–69–70	210
Ben Hogan	75–67–69	211
Jack Nicklaus*	71–71–69	211
Don Cherry	70–71–71	212
Jack Fleck	70–70–72	212
Johnny Pott	75–68–69	212
Gary Player	70–72–71	213
4 others		214
Palmer and 8 others		215

* = Low Amateur

ROUND 4

As Souchak was regrouping, Arnold Palmer was refueling. Seven strokes and 13 players away from the top of the board, he ordered a hamburger and a Coke and tried to figure out how he managed to turn 12 birdies in 54 holes into a score of 2 over par.

Palmer ate his lunch at a table with old friend Bob Drum of the *Pittsburgh Press*, golf writer Dan Jenkins, and fellow golfer Ken Venturi. "What if I shot 65?" Arnold asked them. "That would put me at 280. Two-eighty always wins the Open."

Palmer recalled in his book, *A Golfer's Life*, "They all looked at me as if I'd grown a second head, and Drum responded, 'Two-eighty won't do you one damn bit of good.'"

Palmer continues:

> *I'd only taken a couple of bites of my burger, but I stopped chewing, ready to explode with anger at his remark. I'd come looking for support and encouragement from a man I considered a friend...and essentially he'd dumped a bucket of cold water over my head. 'Oh yeah?' I said. 'Watch and see.'*
>
> *I put down my sandwich, turned, and left, yanked my driver out of my bag as I marched to the practice tee, teed up a ball, and slammed it to the back of the range. Still seething mad, I hit maybe one or two more such monster drives before I heard my name being paged, the official summons to the 1st tee.*

The pairings were not reshuffled for the afternoon round, and because groups in PGA tournaments were still not yet sent out in reverse order of score, the Hogan/Nicklaus twosome was already on the course before Palmer and his partner, Paul Harney, teed off. Hogan continued his masterful tee-to-green march, hitting all nine greens to bring his streak to 27 straight in regulation. Again, though, he only managed a single birdie among eight pars, bringing him to 3 under par with nine holes left.

Nicklaus not only kept up with Hogan but did him one better. Actually, two better. Jack eagled the 5th and birdied the 9th to move to 5 under par. With nine holes to play, the 20-year-old, baby-faced amateur was in a tie for the lead. Meanwhile, behind him, all hell was breaking loose.

THE SHOT

At 1:42 PM, with the taste of both hamburger and anger still in his mouth, Arnold Palmer had stepped to the 1st tee with attitude to match the altitude. Even without his pretournament plan to use his driver on the opening hole, he surely would have pulled out the Big Dog now that he was staring down the barrel of a 7-stroke deficit. In his current state of mind, he was certain to hit the ball a long way, but in which direction?

After Harney hit, Palmer teed the ball low, as was his MO in those days, and stepped back from the ball. The gathered gallery wasn't at the 1st hole to specifically see Palmer, but their attention was certainly grabbed as the reigning Masters' champ stepped up to take his always-impressive cut. He noted the almost nonexistent breeze, set his feet a bit more than shoulder-width apart, worked his hands into a firm, familiar grip, and looked up to pick out a spot for his target. He chose the flag, 346 yards away.

With silence around him, he lowered his head to focus on the ball and waggled the extrastiff shaft before going still. His takeaway was low, long, and smooth. He reached the top of his exaggerated backswing, the clubhead wrapped all the way around his body and pointed toward the fairway, and uncoiled like a spinning corkscrew. The ball exploded off the clubface with a deep resonant thud and took off at mach speed into the distance, spinning perfectly and sizzling as it flew. It was hit well—very well—and it was dead straight, so it had a chance. He held that vintage Palmer follow-through with his arms stiff and his head moving slightly from side-to-side with a grimace still on his face as he watched the ball's flight. It landed in the thick rough in front of the green where he had gotten caught about four and a half hours earlier. But this time, it had enough steam to fight through the grass, up a slight incline, to roll softly and sweetly, coming slowly to a stop, pin-high, about 25 feet to the right of the cup.

The gallery surrounding the green roared, and an instant later, the group around the tee joined them. The applause seemed to seep through Arnie's pores into his very soul. There was suddenly a bounce in his step as his hitched up his pants and marched up the fairway.

"As I reached the green, all the anger melted away," Palmer wrote in *Golf Magazine* in the mid-'80s. "As I waited to putt, I began to feel very, very nervous. To this day I don't know why. It was as if I were anticipating something that I wanted to happen."

Always an aggressive putter, Palmer's try for eagle rolled by the cup. Though it was close enough "to make people gasp," he says, it went five or six feet past the hole, leaving him a tester for birdie. What a shame it would be to waste the tee shot for which he had waited all tournament long. He didn't. The birdie putt dropped, and he was off and running, playing a final 18 for the ages.

On the 2nd hole, he chipped in from the fringe for another birdie. On 3, he stuck his approach to within a foot for a tap-in tweeter, and on 4, he dropped a 17-footer for yet another birdie and another raucous ovation. Four holes, four birdies, and four megajolts of electricity drawing increasingly strong waves of reaction from the gallery growing quickly around him. With each shot, with each grunt, Palmer was giving the crowd something to cheer, and as their reactions became more passionate, he became more determined. Good shots led to adoring eruptions, which led to great shots. It was symbiosis at work in the Rockies.

On the 5th hole, a 538-yard par-5, with adrenaline pumping through his veins and thoughts of a historic comeback swirling through his brain, Palmer took a mighty cut and pushed his tee shot into the right rough. He got out with a 3 wood but landed in a green-side bunker. From there, he blasted out onto the green but needed 2 putts to get down for a deflating par. That is what it had come to: par was suddenly a bad score.

By this time, word had filtered out and encircled Cherry Hills like a smoke cloud. As the course grapevine crackled with word of Arnold's run, fans from all over the course vacated either their stationary spots or the players they had been following and descended on the Palmer/Harney twosome. At the 6th hole, the briefly interrupted streak continued, as Palmer stroked a gorgeous curling 25-footer that found the bottom of the cup for a 5th birdie. On the next hole, he followed a good tee shot with a great chip shot and a tap-in putt for a birdie 3. The ever-growing crowd went wild. The great Palmer was on a rampage, collecting an astounding six birdies in seven holes. He was building his own personal Audubon Society.

Players at all reaches of the course didn't need the leader boards to tell them something was happening—the frequent roar spoke to that. One glance at the list, though, made it clear exactly what it was. Each time they looked up, the name *Arnold Palmer* was higher on the board, climbing like Sir Edmund Hillary.

Arnie's thoughts of an unheard-of 29 on the front disappeared with a bogey at the 8th hole, but after a par on 9, he was in with a red-hot 30 and suddenly very much in contention at 3 under par.

Both Nicklaus and Hogan parred the first three holes on the back nine, temporarily giving Jack the lead in the tournament, but on the 13th, Nicklaus's youth and inexperience hurt him. On the 385-yard par-4, he ran a birdie putt about 18 inches past the hole. As he set up for his come-backer, Jack noticed a small indentation on the green. Unsure whether he was allowed to repair the mark, he could have taken the quite common step of checking with a USGA official. But, with the legendary and dead-serious Hogan looking on and the pressure mounting,

Jack was embarrassed to ask. Ignoring the mark, he made a soft, smooth stroke and sent his putt rolling toward the hole. The ball caught the ridge of the indentation, veered slightly off course, and slid by the edge of the cup, forcing Nicklaus to tap in for bogey. He also bogeyed the next hole, and with Hogan stringing together five more greens in regulation and five straight pars, the pair stood tied at minus-3. With four holes to play, like Palmer, they had moved to within 1 shot of the lead.

Five groups behind them, Mike Souchak was finishing his front nine well aware that players all over the course were going low and threatening his lead, which had been shrinking since the disconcerting camera pop. Souchak went out in 36, bringing his 63-hole total to 4 under par. His edge had been a relatively comfortable 4 strokes just 10 holes earlier, and as the leader board got more crowded, he had to feel like a caged mouse among hungry snakes.

While Souchak was making the turn, Palmer was making another birdie with a 4 at the par-5 11th. He followed that with a par on 12, and at the moment the top of the board looked like this:

Player	Score	Through
Souchak	-4	9
Fleck	-4	10
Palmer	-4	12
Hogan	-3	14
Nicklaus	-3	14
Boros	-2	13

From there, Fleck fell away with three back-nine bogeys to close at 1-under-par 283. Souchak offset a bogey on the 10th with a birdie on the 11th, but then sealed his own frustrating fate with a double bogey at number 12. He had led for three of the four rounds, but not the one that counted, and walked off the final hole with a 283 total, wondering what might have been. Nicklaus finished the last four holes in 1 over, and exited with a good, but not good enough, final round of 71, and a 2-under-par total of 282. Hogan, desperately seeking that fifth U.S. Open championship, made a fatal mistake on the par-5 17th.

Laying 50 yards from the green in 2, and thinking he needed a birdie, Hogan made the rare choice to shoot for the flag. The man who made a career of firing for the fat part of greens was instead trying to knock one stiff despite an incredibly difficult hole location. For the final round, the cup on 17 was cut a mere 12 feet from the front edge of the green. Leading up to the green was a steep slope. If a shot came up even a couple of inches short of the putting surface, it would surely roll down the slope into the shallow water of a moat that surrounded the island green. If it landed pin-high, especially this late in the day when the greens were hard and dry, it would roll significantly past the cup. Perfect execution would be to land the ball on the front edge of the green with enough backspin to make it stick or allow it to roll slowly toward the hole. It was as delicate a shot as there was on the course.

With a remarkable streak of 34 straight greens in regulation intact, Hogan put a crisp and smooth quarter of a swing on a wedge and sent the ball flying softly toward the flag. It landed just on front of the green, took a bite out of the short grass, and spun backward. Either six inches short of perfect, or perhaps with a touch too much spin, the sphere hung on the crest for an instant, then trickled down the hill. Making a taunting trek, the ball didn't stop until it was wet, coming to rest in the moat with the top part of the ball sticking out of the water. The crowd groaned outwardly. Hogan groaned inwardly. "I find myself waking up at night thinking about that shot right today,"

Hogan said in a television interview 23 years later. "There isn't a month that goes by that it doesn't cut my guts out."

The Hawk made his way slowly over a bridge and down to the bank of the slope. He examined the situation, considered his score and the damage that would be done by taking a drop, and knew what he had to do. He sat down and began to remove his right shoe. A murmur started to roll through the gallery and quickly turned to applause. The 47-year-old living legend was pulling out all the stops. He planted his left foot on the edge of the bank and stepped into the water with his bare right foot. Finding it hard to get a solid stance on the slippery underwater surface, he stepped back out and replaced his shoe, leaving his sock on the grass.

He once again stepped into the water, got comfortable, and blasted out in spectacular fireworks of mud, water, and dimpled polyurethane. All considered, it was a great shot. Problem was, without any meaningful spin, the wet ball skipped and then rolled significantly past the cup, leaving Hogan about 15 feet to save par. He didn't.

The pair of Nicklaus and Hogan dejectedly left the 17th green, each feeling that he had blown it. Two groups back, fierce and focused, Palmer continued as steady as a rock.

With a string of five straight pars and a back-nine total of 1 under, Arnold stepped to the 17th tee with, unbeknownst to him, the lead all to himself. There was no leader board in sight, and he had not yet heard of Hogan's bogey, but he knew at minimum that he was in the discussion. His tee shot was straight and true, leading to an easy 2nd shot with which he laid up, leaving him about 60 yards to the pin. While he was deciding whether to shoot for the flag like Hogan had done with devastating results minutes earlier, he was informed of Ben's bogey and Jack's par, and realized that pars of his own on the final two holes would bring him in with the lead. Yes, there were still golfers playing behind him, but to catch him, they each had ground to make up on a very difficult stretch of the course. With the knowledge that Hogan and Nicklaus were now both a stroke back, Palmer's decision regarding his next shot was made for him. Wanting no part of any liquid danger, he cracked a rigid pitching wedge that landed about 30 feet beyond the hole and rolled almost to the back of the green. He took his 2-putt, another par, and got out of Dodge. Now to 18—the 72nd hole of a tournament he had always dreamed of winning, and which suddenly seemed well within his grasp.

The Hogan/Nicklaus group left the final green moments before the Palmer/Harney group got to the tee. Discouraged with his bogey on 17, Ben hit his drive into the water and ended up with a triple bogey, while Jack played sloppily for a tournament-ending bogey. Hogan was in at 284 and would never again come so close to fulfilling his goal of winning a fifth Open championship. As he sat in the locker room, sweaty and spent, he undoubtedly realized that the pudgy, unseasoned 20-year-old with whom he had just played, possessed the sheer power and raw skills that would soon make him the brightest shining star in the golf galaxy. He was a bit less impressed, though, with his playing partner's mental game. "I played 36 holes today with a kid who, if he had a brain in his head," the aging champion insisted, "should have won this thing by 10 strokes."

Instead, dragged down with three bogeys in the final six holes, Nicklaus finished with a 2-under-par total of 282. He was the leader among the players who had finished but had to know, against all hope, it would never stand up.

"One more par," Arnold Palmer recalls telling himself as he walked to the final tee box. "Concentrate, don't get ahead of yourself, stay calm, keep your head down." Item of business number one: avoid the water. He thought about the driver but, with the lake on the right running parallel to the entire length of the fairway, instead pulled out his 1 iron. Although the 468-yard 18th hole was two yards shy of the longest par-4 on the course, he gladly gave up some distance to reduce the risk of a slice. For a player with the ultimate go-for-it approach to the game, this was over-the-top conservatism in all its glory. The 1 iron was straight and true, but the 4 iron that followed drifted a bit left, leaving him about 80 feet from the cup in the always-thick U.S. Open rough to the side of the green.

Up and down for par would bring him home in 280, the exact score he talked about (fantasized about?) before the round. He considered the lie and felt the magnitude of the situation. "You could wait your entire life for a moment like this," Palmer wrote 39 years later. He took out his wedge and made a firm but delicate swing, popping the ball onto the green and rolling, beautifully toward the cup. He left himself about two feet, but they "looked more like two miles," he would say. With his hands moist and throat dry, he took a steady swing and dropped his putt for par. The gallery erupted in the last of who knows how many ovations Palmer received in a final round that became instant legend. Swept up in the emotion of the moment, Arnold pulled his ball from the cup, turned, removed his visor, and flung it as high as he could toward the cheering masses. The move was a bit unusual, given that others on the course still had a chance to catch him, but the display was more a celebration of his round than it was an exclamation point on a tournament victory. He wasn't the only one carried away by the finish—an announcer for NBC saw the putt drop and yelled, "Palmer has won! Palmer has won!"

Arnie walked through the crowd like a gladiator through a gauntlet. He accepted congratulations and pats on the back as he headed to the scorer's tent to sign his scorecard. He looked at the numbers, almost detachedly so, as if he were reading a fictional tale of an impressive and unlikely accomplishment. He added 'em up: 65. He re-added: 65 again. And, convinced, finally signed.

Out on the course, the few remaining players still with a shot to win or tie could not find the necessary tools. In fact, nobody even came close. On a day Arnold Palmer charismatically and confidently stared down the monster that is the U.S. Open—the mental and physical fatigue, thick unruly rough, daunting final-round pin placements, and intense pressure that is inherent to a national championship—all others faltered to one or more of the passively wielded weapons of the grand event.

He racked up an amazing seven birdies against just one bogey. The stretch that will be remembered forever is the sequence of six birdies in the first seven holes, but the run that ultimately won him the tournament was his ultrasteady, bogey-free jaunt through a nerve-racking, potentially tormenting back nine. He came in with a 1-under-par 35, the low score for the day, which was equaled only by Ted Kroll. By comparison, all the other contenders were merely pretenders. Dutch Harrison and Dow Finsterwald both came in at 37. Barber, Boros, and Cherry shot 38s, and the megatalented foursome of Hogan, Nicklaus, Fleck, and the tournament-long leader, Souchak, could manage no better than 3-over-par 39s.

With his name being inscribed on a first-place check of more than $14,000, Palmer accepted congratulations in the press tent and bathed in the contentment of his accomplishment. To him, the "65" was only the second most important number he called on that memorable Saturday in the Rockies. He took a deep breath, grabbed the phone, and dialed his wife, Winnie. His heart thumped in his chest as he heard her voice on the end of the line. "Guess what?" he asked rhetorically. "We won!"

Round 4, Saturday, June 18, 1960

HOLE	1	2	3	4	5	6	7	8	9	OUT	10	11	12	13	14	15	16	17	18	IN	TOTAL
PAR	4	4	4	4	5	3	4	3	4	35	4	5	3	4	4	3	4	5	4	36	71
Palmer	③	3	3	3	5	2	3	4	4	30	4	4	3	4	4	3	4	5	4	35	65

1960 U.S. Open Scores

1.	Arnold Palmer	72	71	72	65	280
2.	Jack Nicklaus*	71	71	69	71	282
3t.	Julius Boros	73	69	68	73	283
	Dow Finsterwald	71	69	70	73	283
	Jack Fleck	70	70	72	71	283
	Dutch Harrison	74	70	70	69	283
	Ted Kroll	72	69	75	67	283
	Mike Souchak	68	67	73	75	283
9t.	Jerry Barber	69	71	70	74	284
	Don Cherry*	70	71	71	72	284
	Ben Hogan	75	67	69	73	284

* = Amateur

Arnold Palmer had been on top of the golf world as he arrived in Denver a week earlier. As he left, he was the sport's newly crowned king. Just 30 years old, he was undoubtedly the best of the new guard of golf.

Hogan, Snead, Sarazen—great champions all—had had their best days behind them. Now if only Palmer could find another player, a capable and worthy opponent, that would challenge him and push him to attain new heights in the weeks, years, and decades ahead...

POSTSCRIPT

The immediate paths of the 1960 U.S. Open champion and the tournament's runner-up diverged dramatically. With the $14,400 winner's check in his pocket, Arnold Palmer left Denver and headed for Ireland to compete in the Canada Cup, a prestigious international competition. In contrast, second-place finisher Jack Nicklaus, whose amateur status rendered him ineligible for the $5,000 in second-place earnings, left Denver and drove to Colorado Springs to play in the NCAA Championships. The pro flew first class. The college kid drove a rental car. Their parting was temporary.

The one-two finish of Palmer and Nicklaus at the 1960 U.S. Open marked the unofficial beginning of the greatest rivalry in the history of sports. Considering there are only four major tournaments played each year, the pair's total of 125 majors in which they competed against each other is astounding. Nineteen of those 125 times—about 15 percent—both players finished in the top 10, and five times they finished first and second.

Other rivalries might be in the discussion of "greatest ever," but none holds up like that of the King and the Bear, who went at each other in one way or another for longer than a reasonably expected athletic lifetime. Wilt Chamberlain and Bill Russell had epic battles as the two elite players in the NBA during the 1960s, but teammates and coaching often played a large role in determining winner and loser. Same for Larry Bird and Magic Johnson in the 1980s. Muhammad Ali and Joe Frazier beat the spit, the spirit, and skill out of each other in three colossal showdowns in the 1970s, but how can their two and a half hours in the ring be compared to nearly four decades of Palmer versus Nicklaus?

Yankees versus Red Sox? A great team rivalry, but over the years, there are just different players playing in the same uniforms. Ohio State–Michigan? Unequaled pageantry and tradition, but the participants themselves change every four years. Connors-McEnroe, Evert-Navratilova, Dempsey-Tunney? All good. Great, in fact, but Palmer-Nicklaus they are not.

Jack's first memory of Arnold goes all the way back to 1954 at the Ohio Amateur event in Sylvania, Ohio, when Nicklaus was just 14 years old. Jack's great future in golf may have already been loosely plotted out in the map of his mind, but to Palmer, Jack was just some kid watching him hit balls, if he even saw him at all.

"It was pouring rain," remembered Nicklaus in the summer of 2000. "When I came off the course, there was a guy all alone on the driving range. He was drilling one ball after another, lining them about waist-high. I didn't know who he was at the time, but I stood there for about an hour just watching him. Someone said, 'That's the defending champ, Arnold Palmer.' And I said, 'Man, oh, man, he's so strong!'"

Arnie's earliest memory of Jack came about four years later at an exhibition in honor of Dow Finsterwald, a pro from Athens, Ohio, who won 11 PGA events, including the 1958 PGA Championship. "We had a driving contest, and I beat him by a bit," Palmer recounted to the *Orlando Sentinel*. "After that, I kept an eye on him and was aware of what he was doing in golf. You never know how someone's game will develop, but with Jack I figured it was just a matter of time."

That time arrived in 1962. Palmer, known as "the King," added a couple more jewels to his crown, winning the Masters after storming from behind to wedge himself into a three-way playoff, and then captured the British Open for the second consecutive year. A month before the next British Open was the

U.S. Open, held essentially in Arnold's backyard, at Oakmont Country Club in Western Pennsylvania. Nicklaus, in his first year as a professional, was paired with Palmer in the first two rounds, and got a taste of what was to come from a clearly partisan and boisterous pro-Palmer gallery. Jack shot a final-round 69, while Arnie fired a 71, leaving the two men tied atop the leader board and forcing an 18-hole playoff the following day.

Arnie's Army was out in full force, and despite their heckling of Jack and holding up signs that read, "Nicklaus Is a Pig!" among other things, the 22-year-old kid displayed the poise and concentration that would become legendary. Most in attendance were shocked at Nicklaus's length off the tee as he bashed one monstrous drive after another, almost always finding the fairway. The difference, though, as it usually is, was ultimately on Oakmont's challenging greens, where Nicklaus 3-putted just a single green over the course of his 90 holes, while Palmer 3-putted 10 times. Jack won the playoff by 3 strokes, in what might be considered a rather noteworthy first professional victory.

Afterward, a gracious Palmer cracked, "I'm sorry to say, he'll be around for a long time."

They both were.

Playing in the 1960 U.S. Open, when Palmer took the title with that amazing final round, was a determined pro out of North Carolina named Davis Love Jr. Love didn't register very high on the relative talent scale for professionals, but he passed his passion and knowledge of the game on to his son, who went on to a stellar career, winning 19 tournaments, including the 1997 PGA Championship.

Asked in 2007 about the impact of Palmer and Nicklaus, Davis Love III says, "My father told stories about that era. Dad was the kind of player who had two towels on the bag when he practiced. One was to clean the clubs, the other was to wipe the blood from his hands because he hit so many balls." Regarding the long and storied rivalry of the sport's two preeminent players from his father's day, Davis nods in acknowledgment. "It certainly made the game popular," he says, "and this whole tour is really built on what Arnie and Jack did both on and off the golf course."

Of course, with two competitive fires burning so powerfully for so long, there have been times when the heat of one seemed to flare up and strike at the other. The Nicklaus-Palmer rivalry has, like any passionate relationship, undoubtedly gone chilly at times. There have been decades-long assumptions of jealousies from both camps: Arnold because of Jack's seemingly effortless rise to the top, and Jack because of Arnie's unmistakable stranglehold on the hearts of fans worldwide. Both men acknowledge they have had their differences, but details have been scarce, and by now, are perhaps irrelevant.

With the gentlemanly principles of golf so ingrained in each one's personality, neither man has ever gone on record with specific negative comments about the other. As a result, the degree to which bad blood has existed between the two, although widely speculated over the years, can be nothing but pure conjecture. Confidants of each are undoubtedly aware of the minutiae behind the madness, but they wouldn't be confidants without possessing a great deal of discretion, and they remain silent on the topic.

In his 1997 book, *Jack Nicklaus: My Story*, written with Ken Bowden, Nicklaus explains, "I'm happy to say that, after drifting apart for a long time after our playing careers and other interests took different paths, the deeper we have gotten into our senior years the more we have found ourselves renewing the old friendship. The rivalry between us will surely exist as long as we live.... But if Arnold ever were to need anything, I'd be there for him in a flash, both as a friend and as an admirer of the great contributions he has made, not just to golf, but to the advancement and elevation of true sportsmanship. I'm proud to call him my friend."

In Palmer's book, penned with James Dodson two years later, he writes of Nicklaus: "Behind the scenes of those celebrated Arnie-versus-Jack years we traveled together quite a lot, dined together, privately discussed at great depth issues of the Tour and family life, agreed philosophically on far more things than we disagreed on, and ruthlessly pounced on any opportunity to needle each other in private about beating the other at his own game.... The simple truth is, I like Jack and I admire him in more ways than I can probably express."

With their competitive rivalry having moved from playing golf courses to building them, the subject of their relationship was addressed in a television interview with CBS's Jim Nantz in 2006. The ease and warmth with which the men interacted in the studio was notable. If there is any discord or ill will between the two, it is disguised so well that you figure, despite being wildly successful in their chosen field, they would have been even better off going into acting.

About rumors of disharmony, Nicklaus said, "I think that comes from the press.... Never let the facts interfere with a good story. Arnold and I have been friends." Jack went on to say that despite being an established star, Arnold was kind and gracious to Nicklaus in Jack's early years on tour and equated the rumors of issues between he and Palmer to those about trouble between today's top stars, Phil Mickelson and Tiger Woods.

"When I was Presidents Cup captain [in 2005], I heard there was bad blood between Phil and Tiger. The first day I get there, Tiger and Phil say, 'Hey, come on, let's play some Ping-Pong.' Two guys playing Ping-Pong and having a good time, laughing, kidding each other. Is that bad blood?"

As Palmer looked back, he recalled the intensity of the rivalry. "It got so heavy sometimes. People don't know this—Jack and I both know it. There were a number of tournaments...major tournaments...we got to playing each other, and of course both of us know the rules—you don't play each other in a medal play tournament—you play to win the golf tournament. But we got to playing each other so hard that we blew the tournament. Someone else came right by and beat us both."

And like an old couple finishing each other's sentences, Nicklaus chimed in, "And that happened more than once!"

In a 1994 interview for *Golf Magazine*, Jack was asked about that bet he reportedly made on himself at 35-to-1 to win the 1960 U.S. Open. He acknowledged the wager and remembered the details. He thought about it for a few seconds and said, "I was about to get married, and I needed the money. Arnie, you were the only one that kept me from winning that $700." Without looking up at the multimillionaire sitting next to him, Palmer responded, "You have my apologies."

Chi Chi Rodriguez once said, "Every professional golfer should say a prayer every day and thank God for Arnold Palmer. He has made us all rich and famous." That is just part of the reason that the PGA Tour's leading money winner each year receives the Arnold Palmer Award. Incidentally, the Player of the Year receives the Jack Nicklaus Award.

In his illustrious career, Palmer won 62 PGA tournaments, including seven majors. Nicklaus won 73 events with 18 majors—a mark that stands today as the most ever, even as Tiger Woods has distant sights set on the prestigious record.

The years have been friendly to both of them. Sure, they've aged, but that is a lot better than the alternative. In December of 2006, they competed in the Father-Son challenge in Florida. The 77-year-old Palmer played with his grandson, Sam

Saunders, who plays for Clemson, and the 67-year-old Nicklaus played with his son, Jackie.

The round was full of jokes and laughs between the two old superstars who both, long ago, officially reached living-legend status. The wisecracks about each other's age had the galleries howling, and the smallest mishit from one would draw a mocking stare or mock laughter from the other. It was all in good fun. And then, as they got late in the round, hole 16 or so, something remarkable happened. The joking stopped; they each fell silent and focused on the business at hand. Moments of truth and instants of intensity transported the players and those watching to another place and time. The Palmer-Nicklaus rivalry will live for as long as the men themselves. And in some ways, longer.

On the final hole, Jack watched his putt fall and raised his club skyward as he had done so many times before. He fished his ball out of the cup, shook hands with everybody in the group, and then locked eyes with his old friend, Arnold. They shook hands, put their arms around each other, and walked off the green, as if they were strolling right back to the 1960s.

Gary Player blasts out of a greenside bunker in the final round of the 1972 PGA Championship.

CHAPTER FOUR

1972:
Taking Aim in the Rain

PRELUDE

The decade that warmly welcomed the new age of golf with Arnold Palmer's ascent in 1960, came to a close amid years of political turmoil that sent a chill through every element of society. The United States battled on many fronts throughout the '60s, plodding through assassinations, civil unrest, a controversial war, and the unofficial end of a nation's innocence.

The final PGA Championship of the decade took place at the NCR Country Club in Dayton, Ohio, a typical midwestern city with its share of racial problems and economic strife. In the days leading up to the tournament, a civil rights group calling itself the Dayton Organization let it be known that, with the national press in attendance at the tournament, they would be heard.

Unhappy with the racial and economic inequalities of the city, the group presented tournament directors with a list of demands, which called for 2,000 free tickets for the PGA Championship, a promise that all profits from the tournament would be donated to the city's poor people, and a guarantee that time and effort equal to that spent on the tournament would be devoted to Dayton's underprivileged community. With the city unwilling to meet those demands, tournament organizers braced for possible danger.

•••

Hearing news of the potential trouble stemming from racial and economic inequities struck an all-too-familiar chord with one of the golfers in the field. Gary Player, who won the PGA Championship seven years earlier, grew up in Johannesburg, South Africa, and experienced the demonic and destructive forces of apartheid for most of his life.

Born in 1935, Player lost his mother at age eight and saw his father earn a tough living, sweating out his days 12,000 feet underground working the South African gold mines. Gary didn't take up golf until the age of 14 but was a quick study, turning pro just four years later in 1953. Player won some tournaments in Europe and Australia, but he dreamed of America. The world's greatest golfers played in the United States and were making a far better living than golfers abroad. In 1957, with a passport in one hand and his golf bag in the other, Player took off for America.

Impressed by the PGA professionals' length off the tee, Player set out to make his drives longer by making himself stronger. At just 5'7", the diminutive Player was cut from the same physical mold as Gene Sarazen and Ben Hogan, but what he lacked in size, he made up for in desire and an insatiable appetite for something previously of no interest to golfers—weightlifting and fitness. At a time most professional athletes, even those who would benefit from some extra bulk, such as football players, worried that weight training would make them musclebound and stiff, Player was a firm believer in its benefits. Combining weights, stretching, and proper diet to enhance his athletic performance, he was dedicated to fitness principles that were three decades ahead of their time.

The first sign of Player's greatness to come in the United States was his second-place showing at his first U.S. Open in 1958. At just 22 years old, in the intense heat and wind of the Oklahoma summer, only tournament champion Tommy Bolt posted a better score than the newcomer. According to the World Golf Hall of Fame, Player's idol Ben Hogan approached him after the final round of the event and said, "Son, you are going to be a great player."

From there, with supreme confidence in his ability to compete with the world's best, Player began collecting majors like some people collect shot glasses; seems everywhere he went, he'd pick one up. He won the 1959 British Open at Muirfield, took the green jacket at the 1961 Masters, and then claimed victory at the 1962 PGA Championship at Aronimink Golf Club in Pennsylvania. Three years later, he chalked up the last of the remaining majors, the U.S. Open. After blowing a 3-stroke lead on the final three holes at the Bellerive Country Club in St. Louis, Player regrouped the following day to beat Kel Nagle in an 18-hole playoff. The kid who turned pro at 18 suddenly, amazingly, had a career Grand Slam at the tender age of 29.

Perhaps more amazingly, the moment he collected his winner's check, the money was gone—but not in the way the modern athlete might spend it. At the awards ceremony, Player announced that he would return $25,000 of his $26,000 prize to the USGA, asking that $5,000 be earmarked for cancer relief work and $20,000 to promote junior golf. It was a generous gesture five years in the making.

In 1960 he had contended to the end of the U.S. Open, and before the final round, he told the executive director of the USGA that, if he won, he would donate his earnings. "I am doing this because I made a promise to [USGA executive director] Joe Dey five years ago," said Player at the ceremony in 1965. "I am doing this to repay America for its many kindnesses to me over the past few years."

The charitable gift cost him $25,000, but the overall response to the donation ultimately paid him back in countless ways and incalculable amounts. The move endeared him to the mass American golfing public, which was collectively taken by Player's generosity. He was suddenly not so much a foreigner as he was a cowboy in a white hat.

And a black shirt.

During that U.S. Open, Player continued a tradition that

lasted a golfing lifetime. Thirty years before Tiger Woods made the Sunday Red famous, one of the brightest shining lights on the PGA tour opted for dark. "I remember wearing the same black shirt every day and washing it myself every night and hanging it over the shower rail to dry," Player recalled. "It was a silly superstition, perhaps, but it gave me a certain level of mental karma." The man who became known as "the Black Knight" regularly dressed for the course in black, usually from head to toe. Always looking for a competitive edge, the dark garb absorbed and held sunlight, which, he said, kept his muscles warm.

Over the next four years, Player won two PGA events, including the 1968 British Open, and was well aware of the planned protests in Dayton as he prepared for the 1969 PGA Championship.

•••

The first two rounds went off without a hitch. Raymond Floyd led the tournament at the halfway point with rounds of 69 and 66 for a 7-under-par total of 135. Player was alone in second place, 1 shot behind, and several others were within 4 strokes of the lead, including Jack Nicklaus, who was 3 back.

On Saturday, August 16, Player and Nicklaus were paired together in the second-to-last group, and it was obvious early in the round their day was going to be difficult. On the 4th tee, Gary was addressing his ball when a spectator threw a tournament program at him. The bulky book, all 278 pages of it, missed Player, who stepped back from his ball and watched as security located the man who threw it and led him away.

On the 9th green, a man in the gallery shouted, "Hey!" as Nicklaus was in the middle of his putting stroke, and as the golfers walked to the 10th hole, a spectator ran up to Player, forcefully threw a cup full of ice in his face, and yelled, "Racist!" After the round, a man marveled over Player's calm reaction to the heckler, saying, "Gary will be a hero after this one." Commissioner Joe Dey responded, "He should be. Do you know what Player said to that man? He just asked him, 'What have I done to you, sir?'"

The real fireworks, though, came on the 10th green. As Nicklaus and Player were lining up their respective putts, a group of people ran under the fairway ropes and began to rush the green. "I saw this big, mean-looking guy bearing down on Jack, and I didn't know what might happen—it was a harrowing experience," said Player.

Nicklaus added, "I saw this guy come running through the trap. He didn't say anything. He didn't have to. He was about 6'4" and 280 pounds. I said to myself, 'If he keeps coming, he's going to get it,' and I had my putter drawn back. I wasn't worried so much about myself, I was worried that my boy, Jackie, who was in the gallery, had to see it."

Security, on high alert because of the earlier incidents, jumped into action, knocking down one of the demonstrators and grabbing another who had picked up Nicklaus's ball and thrown it toward a sand bunker. The security staff corralled five other demonstrators, and all seven were led away and arrested. As "harrowing" of an experience as it might have been for Player, he seemed unfazed a minute later as he rolled in a 10-footer for birdie. Nicklaus missed an eagle putt but shaved a stroke from a par with a birdie of his own.

As Player was preparing to putt on the 13th hole, a woman threw a ball onto the green, breaking his routine. Again, though, he reset, blocked out everything but the ball and the cup, and knocked down a birdie on his way to a round of even-par 71. There were no further disturbances, but as word spread of the day's events, the Player-Nicklaus gallery grew. With the golf course equivalent of traffic-accident rubberneckers packing the fairways, Gary and Jack got extended ovations as they made their way around the course.

After the round, Player told the gathered press that one of the protesters, as he was being led away by security, looked at him and said, "Nothing against you or your country, Gary, this is against the PGA tournament." What gnawed at him, though, was the protestor who shouted "Racist!" Player looked vulnerably at the media and insisted, "Just because you are from South Africa doesn't make you a racist."

As dawn broke the following day, 125 special security officers, 90 uniformed policemen, and several plainclothes officers were assigned duties and stations around the golf course. With picket lines outside the club and the massive police presence seemingly everywhere, there was a palpable nervous tension in the players' locker room. *The New York Times* reported Gary Player asked an attendant, "Does it look bad out there?" The answer came back, "Yeah, it's cloudy. It might rain."

Player responded bluntly, "Rain is the least of my worries," and he walked out, flanked by a sheriff's deputy, heading for the practice range.

Alas, the final round was played without incident. Leader Raymond Floyd was paired with Player, and before the round started, the men were instructed not to leave the greens without a police escort. After each hole, a surreal scene played out with six to eight armed officers surrounding them as they walked to the next tee box. What might be the most peaceful game ever invented looked as if it were playing out on a battlefield.

Floyd, who came into the day with a comfortable 5-stroke bulge, saw his lead slowly dwindle most of the day. When he bogeyed the 15th hole, Player was suddenly within a single stroke. On 16, with Player six feet away from a par, Floyd hit the green in regulation but was 35 feet from the cup, staring at a nasty side-hill bender that had "3-putt" written all over it. Instead, he struck it perfectly and watched as the ball tracked toward the cup and dropped in as if pulled by a magnet. The sensational birdie putt increased the 26-year-old's lead back to 2 strokes. A moment later, Player missed his par putt, and Floyd's lead was 3 with two to play.

"I swear to God," Floyd said of his clutch birdie afterward, "I was trying to 2-putt!"

With Floyd playing cautiously the rest of the way, Player made up a stroke on each of the final two holes, but it wasn't enough. Raymond Floyd won it by 1 shot to take the first and, for many of the wrong reasons, most memorable of his four career majors.

For Player, the event was just another ugly example of the reality that is racism. He saw evidence of it throughout his significant travels and believed it to exist all over the world. Back in South Africa, apartheid remained a constant, cruel way of life that both outwardly and silently tore at the very fabric of the country. Half a world away, on a golf course in Dayton, Ohio, Player's South African citizenship, in part, led to his own condemnation.

Anger directed at him, though, was not entirely a function of guilt by association. In his book *Grand Slam Golf*, published in 1966, Player wrote, "I am South African. And I must say now, and clearly, that I am of the South Africa of Verwoerd and apartheid." That sentence in itself, supporting the ideals of former South African Prime Minister Henrik Verwoerd, was reason enough for many people to label Player as a racist. Verwoerd, who reigned from 1958 until his assassination in 1966, established divisive policies in which races were segregated and black people were inhumanely treated as inferior. Had Player made his declaration in a television interview or in a newspaper article written by a columnist, it might not have had nearly the same impact. Because he was the author of the book and so strongly and unambiguously stated his position, he became the target he did.

As time went on, Gary Player's inward feelings on the race issue seemed to soften. His outward stance definitely did, eventually turning around completely. As a result, his modern-day reputation is strong, and some of the world's most celebrated humanitarians have embraced him based on his subsequent words and actions. But as the 1960s came to an end amidst the racial turmoil in the United States, Player moved into the '70s as a controversial figure whose beliefs were protested and led to death threats on numerous occasions.

•••

To a golfer who has won five majors in 10 seasons, going four years without one can be considered a drought. Player's second-place showing at the 1969 PGA Championship was his only top-20 finish since his U.S. Open victory a year earlier, and the years ahead were littered with near misses and failed opportunities. In 1970 he finished 1 stroke behind at the Masters and, beginning the next year, went on a streak in which he finished in the top 10 five times in the span of seven major tournaments leading up to the last of the prestigious events of 1972.

THE TOURNAMENT

PGA CHAMPIONSHIP
OAKLAND HILLS COUNTRY CLUB
BIRMINGHAM, ALABAMA
AUGUST 4–7, 1972

As in 1969, the 1972 PGA Championship was awarded to a city in the Midwest. Oakland Hills Country Club in Birmingham, Michigan, hosted the event and was soaked by a downpour during the Wednesday practice round. "It will be an entirely different game now," predicted Arnold Palmer. "Some of the course was under water and they won't be able to cut the fairways. Generally, scores should be higher."

That was a sobering thought considering the already daunting reputation of Oakland Hills—a track about which John Daly would say decades later, "My first wife was nicer than this course."

The day before the tournament, Jack Nicklaus went on record saying the layout at Oakland Hills was tougher than the sites of each of the past three majors. The statement spoke volumes given the relatively high scores posted at those events by the respective fields. Nicklaus had won earlier in the year at Augusta as the only player under par; he took the U.S. Open at Pebble Beach with a total of 2 over par and was one of only six golfers to finish under par at the British Open at Muirfield, coming in second to Lee Trevino.

A week removed from a minor surgery to curtail an infection on his right index finger, Nicklaus opened with an unspectacular round of 2-over-par 72. With all of the sport's big names in the field, including Palmer, Player, Trevino, Floyd, and Snead, to name a few, it was a pair of unlikely unknowns taking the first-round lead. The bothersome conditions apparently didn't have much of a negative impact on 27-year-old Vietnam veteran Bud Allin or 44-year-old Kansas native Stan Thirsk.

Moving in unison to the previously uncharted territory of the top of the leader board, the pair might have attributed their stellar opening rounds of 2-under-par 68 to a lack of gallery-inspired nervousness. In fact, the crowds around the guys were so sparse, if they hadn't had their playing partners, they might have been lonely. So shocking was their vault into the lead, the headline on the *L.A. Times*'s sports page read, "Allin, Thirsk—Honest! Share Lead in PGA."

One stroke behind the surprise leaders was a group of five players led by Palmer and Floyd. Two back, at even par, were a half-dozen others, including 60-year-old Sam Snead. Gary Player and Chi Chi Rodriguez were in a group of eight who were 3 behind.

Round 2

A bright sunny day dawned in Michigan, but the course itself seemed to be in a nasty, unforgiving mood. Oakland Hills, about which Ben Hogan said, "I brought the monster to her knees," after firing a final round 67 at the 1951 U.S. Open, flashed its fangs and stood tall against all assaults. Only one player, Jerry Heard, survived with a two-day score in the red. Heard's second-round 70 left him with a 1-under-par total of 139. A 27-year-old, former all–Big 8 Conference defensive back from the University of Colorado named Hale Irwin, who would go on to win three U.S. Opens, was tied with Raymond Floyd, 1 stroke behind.

Seven others, including Lanny Wadkins and Gary Player, were within 3 shots, but most of the guys who received the bulk of pretournament hype had struggled. Arnold Palmer—who said afterward, "I'm sick of the way I'm chipping and putting, it's just awful!"—was 5 shots back along with Snead and Trevino. Future tour commissioner Deane Beaman and Jack Nicklaus were 8 back at 7 over.

Nicklaus minced no words in summing up his round, "I didn't drive well. I didn't hit my irons well. I didn't chip well. I didn't putt well. I didn't think well." He then added, unnecessarily, "The whole thing was pretty bad."

The thrill ride enjoyed by the first-round leaders was short-lived as Bud Allin followed his opening-day 68 with a round of 77. Yet he was far better than Stan Thirsk, who clumsily parlayed his 2-under-par start into a 10-over-par total. Thirsk made a mess of the second round to finish at 12-over-par 82, surviving the cut by a single stroke.

Round 2 Leader Board

Jerry Heard	69–70	139
Ray Floyd	69–71	140
Hale Irwin	71–69	140
Gay Brewer	71–70	141
Jim Jamieson	69–72	141
Bob E. Smith	72–69	141
Tommy Aaron	71–71	142
Gary Player	71–71	142
Dan Sikes	70–72	142
Lanny Wadkins	74–68	142

Round 3

Jerry Heard's professional golf career was off to an incredible start with two tournament victories in 1972 and one the year before. Going into the PGA Championship, he had collected more money by age 25 than any player in golf history not named Jack Nicklaus. With the lead heading into Saturday's third round, however, Heard was entering new territory. His best showing in a major came earlier in 1972 when he finished in a fifth-place tie at the Masters, but at the midpoint in Augusta, he was already 5 strokes behind Nicklaus, who went on to win it by 3.

On the 9th hole at Oakland Hills, Heard still had the lead when, just as had happened to Mike Souchak in 1960, his concentration was broken by the clicking of a camera. Heard mishit his tee shot when a photographer snapped several quick pictures of him as he was set in his stance. Heard admitted later, "I should have backed up and not hit the ball, but I went ahead and hit it, and I hit a bad shot." He walked off the tee box without a word and bottled his anger until he reached the green. There, unable to remain silent any longer, he got into a heated verbal exchange with the photographer before missing a putt for par. Heard bogeyed the hole, did not hold the lead from that point forward, and finished the round with a 2-over-par 72.

Having a far more enjoyable day, Gary Player used a safety-first strategy to roll in with a 3-under-par 67. The fairways at Oakland Hills are so infamously narrow that Cary Middlecoff once cracked, "People have to walk down those things single-file." Knowing there was little room for error, Player decided to mostly leave the driver in the bag, opting instead for a 3 wood or 2 iron off the tee. He gladly sacrificed some length to stay out of the unruly rough that seemed to be growing thicker and meaner by the hour. Shorter tee shots, though, lead to longer approach shots, which often make for longer putts. On this day, that was no problem for the determined South African who 1-putted seven greens, including four on which he rolled in birdie putts of 25 feet or longer.

"I wanted a 66 so bad I could taste it," he'd say afterward, but he lost the chance on the final hole—a 459-yard devilish dogleg right with a fairway that slopes to the left. Needing a par, Player had little choice but to opt for his driver. Trying to get some extra length, he pulled his shot into a fairway bunker leading to a bogey 5, and an 18-hole total of 67. Despite the late disappointment, he still tied for the low round of the day and walked to the clubhouse with a 1-stroke lead on the field.

Also shooting 67 was Billy Casper, a man whose golf career is considered good but could have been great had he sustained a longer period of elite-level play. A quirky, determined player,

Casper was known for several unusual characteristics, including scores of allergies, his conversion to Mormonism, and on-course experimentation with self-hypnosis. He would often force himself into a trancelike state of focus, which he said was a tribute to Ben Hogan's legendary level of concentration.

Casper fathered five children, adopted six others, and is widely accepted as one of the true good guys of the tour, and among the game's all-time great putters. His career peaked during an epic stretch from 1964 to 1970, in which he was as consistent and successful as any player on tour. Most famously, he captured the 1966 U.S. Open in which he stormed back on Arnold Palmer, making up 7 strokes on the final nine holes to force a playoff, which he won the next day. Through 1972, he had won three majors, but would not win another until 1983, when he took the U.S. Senior Open.

The steady round of 3 under par put Casper a stroke behind Player, all alone in second place with the start of Sunday's finale about 15 hours away.

Round 3 Leader Board

Gary Player	71–71–67	209	-1
Billy Casper	73–70–67	210	E
Jerry Heard	69–70–72	211	+1
Phil Rodgers	71–72–68	211	+1
Gay Brewer	71–70–70	211	+1
Doug Sanders	72–72–68	212	+2
Jim Wiechers	70–73–69	212	+2
Tommy Aaron	71–71–70	212	+2
Larry Wise	74–71–67	212	+2
Jim Jamieson	69–72–72	213	+3
Floyd and 3 others		214	+4
Irwin, Snead, Trevino, Nicklaus, and four others		215	+5
Palmer and J. Miller		216	+6

Round 4

Gary Player dressed in his familiar black outfit for the final round, and not even the almost constant, chilly drizzle falling from ominous gray skies could dampen his spirits. Earlier that morning, Player spoke by telephone to his 73-year-old father in South Africa. He acknowledged afterward that his dad, so proud of Gary's success, had gotten choked up during the conversation, urging, "Son, please win it for me."

With his father's words practically still echoing in his head, Player proceeded to promptly lose his lead by racking up bogeys on three of the first four holes. The saving grace was a 20-foot birdie putt on number 2, effectively canceling out one of the bogeys and leaving him 2 over for the day though four holes. From there, Player settled down and strung together five straight pars to close out the front nine, leaving him with a tournament total of 1 over, with nine holes remaining.

Gary's playing partner in the final group, Billy Casper, started the day a stroke behind, and at several points on the front nine, was tied for the lead. As twosomes in front of them played the course, three others—Doug Sanders, Jerry Heard, and Jim Jamieson—also moved into a tie atop the board at one point or another. But not long after each stepped up, the pressure of the tournament and the punch of the course knocked them right back down. Sanders bogeyed four straight holes; Casper bogeyed three of four on the back nine; and Heard eventually hacked his way home with a final round of 4 over par to finish 4 strokes back.

The only man in contention who was able to slay that "Oakland Hills Monster," or more accurately, keep the monster from slaying him, was likable 29-year-old pro Jim Jamieson.

The Michigan native played in 180 career PGA events in 10 seasons on tour, with just one victory. Nineteen seventy-two, however, was a great year as he put together eight top-10 finishes, a fifth-place tie in the Masters, a second-place tie at the U.S. Open, and a victory at the Western Open.

As much as Gary Player was the poster boy for physical fitness, Jamieson was the opposite. Although he liked to refer to himself as "cherubic," the fact of the matter is that Jim was simply out of shape. In the size spectrum, he fell somewhere between the moderately overweight Craig Stadler of the early 1990s and the ever-expanding John Daly of 2008.

Coming into the day 3 shots over par, Jamieson brought his best and played flawlessly for most of the round despite using a bag of mixed-brand clubs and a $17 department-store putter. His patient approach to the course and a refusal to shrink against the magnitude of the situation combined to put him in great position. When he had birdie opportunities, he went for them, and in fact, recorded three in the first 15 holes, against no bogeys. As he stood on the 16th tee, he was all alone in first place, a shot ahead of Player and a mere three holes away from his first major championship.

"I was thinking about how a win would change my life," Jamieson later said, no longer able to block out the enormity of what stood before him. On the par-4 16th, his approach shot did not hold the green, and he walked away with a bogey 5. He bogeyed the 17th, as well, and on 18, faced a two-and-a-half-foot putt for par. Thirty inches never looked so long.

What could be classified as a "gimme"—for any pro playing without the pressure inherent to major championship golf—would give Jamieson a decent shot at getting into a playoff. On this day, though, there was pressure, and a lot of it. He missed the putt and left the green dejectedly with a round of even-par 70, finishing the tournament with a 3-over-par total of 283.

"I was really feeling the pressure on that putt," he admitted after the round. "But that's okay, I'm leaving with more money than I came with." Like a game-show contestant accepting a parting gift, he walked away with a check for $20,850, leaving the grand prize for someone else.

At the same time Jamieson started his final and fatal stretch of the last three holes, Gary Player was playing the 12th, having broken a six-hole par streak in style with a birdie on the 11th.

Two more pars followed at the 12th and 13th, and Player was back on top by 2 strokes. But typical of a major tournament played on a difficult golf course, fates changed in a matter of minutes when he gave the strokes back with bogeys on back-to-back par-4s. His tee shot on the 14th never had a chance to land in the fairway, and he was lucky to escape with a 5. On 15, he missed a putt shorter than the one Jamieson had missed on 18. Player's game was suddenly nowhere to be found, and with three holes remaining, he held a 1-stroke lead, thanks mostly to scores in the black from players ahead of him.

THE SHOT

At just 409 yards, the 16th hole at Oakland Hills is not terribly long, but it is tricky to navigate, and an inaccurate tee shot likely means disaster. The landing area is of average width for the course, which is to say it's pretty darn narrow, and the fairway doglegs severely, at about a 60-degree angle to the right. The green is protected in front by a pond and in back by a series of bunkers.

Because of two huge weeping willows lurking ominously to the right of the angle in the fairway, the ideal spot off the tee— the only spot, really—is to the left. With back-to-back bogeys chopping his lead down to a single stroke, Player desperately needed to stop the bleeding. Aiming left, he sliced his tee shot badly to the right. His eyes darted back and forth, alternating between the ball and its probable landing area. With each millisecond that went by, the likelihood of favorable outcome seemed to decrease immensely until finally the ball disappeared into the thick, greedy rough.

Player shook his head, ditched his club, and began to make his way up the fairway like a man heading into a doctor's office to get the bad news. The only question was, how bad is it?

The lie itself was not horrible. With rough that thick, Player knew it could have been buried completely, but it wasn't. He was, he would later say, "exactly 150 yards from the hole," but those large trees were directly between him and the green and blocked his view of the flagstick. Player surveyed the situation. One option was to punch out to the fairway, then hope to get up and down for par, but more likely take a third straight bogey.

No good.

As the mental wheels turned, he walked forward between the trees to take a look at the green. Directly beyond the flag, atop a hill, he noticed a spectator sitting in a chair, which was visible from the spot where his ball lay. Problem number one was solved as he decided to use one of the chair legs as his target line.

Problem number two was how to get the ball out of the rough with enough loft to clear the trees, yet enough distance to reach the green. The distance called for a 7 iron, but the old pro knew he could not get a 7 high enough quickly enough to get over the treetops. Instead, he walked back to his bag and pulled out the 9 iron.

Under the ostensibly portending doom of the unshakably dreary Sunday, the man in black set his feet, gripped the club, and lowered his head. Unsure about his footing, he took a practice swing, bringing the club back in a wide arc, pausing for an instant at the top, and swinging the club at half speed over the top of his ball. He knew he'd have to swing harder than normal to coax an extra 15 to 20 yards out of his 9 iron but had to make sure the additional length did not come at the cost of lesser loft. Too short, he'd be in the water. Too low, he'd be in the trees.

Ready to hit, he exaggerated all of the elements to a swing that had long since been burned into his muscle memory by a hundred thousand repetitions. He felt his left shoulder wind back, tight under his chin, then with his powerful arms, mightily pulled the club head down into the lettuce-like rough and through the back of his ball. The thwack was not the pure, clean sound of a well-struck golf shot, but instead more of a drawn-out *thump!* as the ball took flight and a hefty divot of dirt, leaves, and grass flew in every direction as if a portion of the ground had been blown up by a stick of dynamite.

The contact was perfect, and upward the ball sailed. Player heard the sweet sound of silence as the ball cleared the trees without so much as a scrape. He leaned back and turned his head upward, but the ball had already disappeared beyond the uppermost branches. He began quickly moving to his left and toward the fairway, looking up and to his right to try to pick up the flying white speck against the light gray sky. As he moved, so too did the spectators who had been lined along the fairway closer to the green than he. It was as if he had to race the entire gallery to the fairway just to get a glimpse of his ball. The crowd began to murmur and then broke into a full cheer as the ball sped downward toward the flag and dropped with a thud.

Player caught sight of the ball just as it was coming to a stop, cuddling up to the pin as cozy as a kid at a campfire. It was a classic make-or-break situation, and Player came through in a huge way, turning near disaster into a golden opportunity, as his ball sat gloriously four feet from the cup. Top-tier professional golfers could take a hundred cracks at that shot from that spot and would likely not get a single ball closer to the pin. He had essentially written the great American novel without the luxury of a second draft. Or even an eraser. The author himself said afterward, "That must rank as the greatest shot I ever hit."

Associated Press reports called it "the shot that was heard around the golfing world."

With a bit more than 407 yards behind him, a mere four feet lay ahead for the payoff. Player stepped up and calmly dropped his putt softly in the center of the cup for a phenomenal birdie 3. His lead was back to 2 strokes with just two holes to play.

He missed the green on the par-3 17th, but a good chip led to a converted par putt. With a stroke to spare, he played the par-4 18th the way they draw it up in the how-to books—a long, accurate drive, an approach on the green, and down in 2 putts for par.

The only foreign-born player to ever win the PGA Championship had won it again. Player's up-and-down final round consisted of three birdies, 10 pars, and five bogeys. His 2-over-par 72 was not the day's best, but his four-round total of 281 was, by 2 strokes.

Jamieson's short miss on 18 ended up not costing him the tournament, but there is no way to know how Player would have played the final hole with a lead of 1 stroke instead of 2. Tommy Aaron tied Jamieson for second place, 2 shots back.

An interesting group of three players finished at 284: Ray Floyd, who had beaten Player in that infamous tournament with the disturbances three years earlier; Billy Casper, who had started the back nine tied with Player; and 60-year-old Sam Snead, who brought back a bit of magic from the past, tying for the day's best with a 69 to close it out. Asked afterward how long he would keep playing, Snead needed no reminder that it was on this very course in 1937—35 years earlier—that he tied for second in the U.S. Open. He smiled and answered, "I guess I'm just too dumb to quit."

As for the first-round coleaders, well, they learned the valuable lesson that in major tournament golf, Thursdays are to Sundays what community theater is to Broadway. Bud Allin finished with a four-day total of 298, 18 over par. Stan Thirsk stumbled home at 306, a full 25 strokes behind the leader. Both men collected prize money in the amount of $333.

Second-round leader Jerry Heard fared significantly better, collecting more than $6,000 as he finished 4 shots back in a tie for seventh place. Despite a career in which he posted nearly 60 top-10 finishes, Heard is best known for being in the wrong place at the wrong time. Playing in the rain at the 1975 Western Open, he and his playing partners, Lee Trevino and Bobby Nichols, were struck by lightning. Heard, one of the bright young stars on tour, never fully regained his form after the strike, and retired in 1980, at age 33, with five PGA victories to his credit.

Basking in the glow of his victory, Player called Oakland Hills the "toughest course in America." In a postround newspaper interview, he said, "This is a humbling course, a great one. And Hogan wasn't kidding when he said it was a monster."

After collecting the highly coveted Wanamaker Trophy and the prize money, in true Player form, he celebrated by reconnecting with the two things that mattered most to him—family and fitness. Gary spent a healthy chunk of the $45,000 first-place check on a lengthy call to his father, wife, and kids back in South Africa. And then, in the collecting darkness of a damp Michigan evening, with the afterglow of the grit, greatness, and glory of a major championship victory hugging him like a dear friend, he hit the pavement for a nighttime jog.

Alone in sweet solitude, away from the hounding press corps and congratulatory well-wishers, he finally had some time to put it all in perspective. "I took stock of my life," he remembers, "and I said to myself, 'You are blessed.'"

Round 4, August 7, 1972

HOLE	1	2	3	4	5	6	7	8	9	OUT	10	11	12	13	14	15	16	17	18	IN	TOTAL
Par	4	5	3	4	4	4	4	4	3	35	4	4	5	3	4	4	4	3	4	35	70
Gary Player	5	4	4	5	4	4	4	4	3	37	4	3	5	3	5	5	③	3	4	35	72

1972 PGA Championship,
Final Leader Board

1.	Gary Player	71–71–67–72	281	$45,000
2.	Tommy Aaron	71–71–70–71	283	$20,850
	Jim Jamieson	69–72–72–70	283	
4.	Billy Casper	73–70–67–74	284	$9,275
	Sam Snead	70–74–71–69	284	
	Ray Floyd	69–71–74–70	284	
7.	Gay Brewer	71–70–70–74	285	$6,384
	Jerry Heard	69–70–72–74	285	
	Phil Rodgers	71–72–68–74	285	
	Doug Sanders	72–72–68–73	285	
11.	Hale Irwin	71–69–75–71	286	$4,950
	Lee Trevino	73–71–71–71	286	
13.	Jack Nicklaus	72–75–68–72	287	$4,162

POSTSCRIPT

After the victory at Oakland Hills, Player went on to win seven more times on the PGA Tour, including both the Masters and the British Open in 1974, and the Masters again four years later. With the bulk of his 24 PGA Tour victories, including nine majors, coming in the '60s and '70s, Player was grouped with Jack Nicklaus and Arnold Palmer in a triumvirate that came to be known as "the Big Three." In what was perhaps a tribute to his dedication to physical fitness, the Black Knight went on to enjoy wild success after turning 50. He racked up 19 wins on the Champions Tour, including six majors, and 13 other senior victories, including three Senior British Opens.

All of his accomplishments on the golf course, however, pale in comparison to what Player contributed to the world off the course. In 1983, at the age of 48, he established the Gary Player Foundation to combat what he perceived as a growing educational crisis in South Africa's rural schools. The first project undertaken was at Blair Atholl Farm outside of Johannesburg, in which a primary school, community resource/media center, and upgraded nursery school were built to help feed, clothe, and educate 500 South African grade-schoolers. The foundation grew from there and now supports various causes that work to better the lives of underprivileged children all around the world.

Regardless of the amount of money he donated, or the resulting benefits, the purity of his actions would be forever tainted without a change in his perceived views toward segregation and a public statement of his ultimate stance.

In his book, *Gary Player, World Golfer*, written with Floyd Thatcher in 1974, Player unquestionably amends his views on equality. Without actually mentioning, or even alluding to the pro-apartheid statement from his book in 1966, he clearly states a new position. In the preface he wrote:

> *An authentically successful person—golfer or businessman or housewife—is one who has learned to respect and love other people.... Certainly I can't condone any form of social injustice. People of every race or creed must have equal opportunity and I will continue to work for them in my own way. But the universal principle remains the same: every one of us needs the acceptance and love of other people—to receive we must give.... In saying all of this, however, I certainly don't set myself up as a paragon of virtue nor do I mean to imply in any way that I've arrived at any lofty place or am a candidate for sainthood. Quite the opposite is true. I make my share of mistakes—more than I like—but I'll never give up and I intend to keep trying.*

Player seemed to be a man looking back at himself, introspective and fair, silently judging who he was, and determined to be somebody else in the future.

Taking his feelings a step further, Player went on record in a 1986 interview with Don Wade, the associate editor of *Golf Magazine*, saying, "Apartheid is a tragedy and we shall have a lot to answer to when our grandchildren ask how in the world we could have allowed such a system to prevail. Can you imagine the mind of the man who invented apartheid? We must be honest and admit we've made a terrible mistake and set about to solve this crisis fairly for everyone. We have no more second chances on this."

Player backed up his words with his actions over the remainder of his career. He made a point of playing practice rounds with some of the tour's first black golfers, like Lee Elder, and consistently hiring black caddies whom he treated well and generously. An African American man named Alfred Dyer was on Player's bag at the 1962 New Orleans Open. "He finished fifth in the tournament, and gave me $500," Dyer recalls. "I'd never seen that much money at once!"

Dyer reconnected with Player 10 years later at that fateful event at Oakland Hills and inquired about working for him again. Player promised Dyer he could caddie for him at the following week's World Series of Golf if Player gained entrance to the tournament with a win at the PGA Championship. A month later, just four days after pulling off that incredible 9 iron over the trees, the pair set out on the 1st hole of the World Series. Player went on to win the tournament, and the relationship between the two went on for the next 18 years. Together, they racked up more than 30 PGA titles.

In 1974 Lee Elder became the first black PGA pro to play in a tournament in South Africa. In that same event, Dyer became the first black foreign caddie. "Some people really didn't want that to happen, but Gary Player did," Dyer remembers. "He helped pave the way for that to happen. Gary Player was a sportsman, and he figured that everybody should play sports together. So Gary used his position to help promote desegregation in South Africa...he was a pioneer."

The July 2000 issue of *Golf Digest* ran a lengthy piece titled, "The 50 Greatest Golfers of All Time: And What They Taught Us." The interesting aspect to the series of vignettes was that somebody other than a traditional golf writer wrote the feature on each player. Player came in at number eight on the list, and his story was composed by the most widely known and well-respected figure in the fight to abolish apartheid, Nelson Mandela.

In part, it read:

> *Few men in our country's history did as much to enact political changes for the better that eventually improved the lives of millions of his countrymen. Through his tremendous influence as a great athlete, Mr. Player accomplished what many politicians could not. And he did it with courage, perseverance, patience, pride, understanding, and dignity that would have been extraordinary even for a world leader.*
>
> *There were people who thought he was partly to blame for apartheid in South Africa, when in truth he was no more responsible for that policy than Jack Nicklaus or Arnold Palmer were for racial conflict in the United States....*
>
> *Upon my release from prison, I met with Mr. Player and told him, "You have not received the recognition you deserve." I was very sincere in saying that.*
>
> *Mr. Player was voted the top athlete in the history of South Africa.... That is impressive, but it is important to note that Mr. Player also was voted one of the top five influential people in our nation's history. His accomplishments as a humanitarian and statesman are equal to, and may even surpass, his accomplishments as an athlete. That is a legacy that will last forever.*

Tom Watson watches his ball go in the hole after hitting out of the rough to sink a birdie on the 17th hole at Pebble Beach at the U.S. Open on June 21, 1982.

CHAPTER FIVE

1982:
Chip by the Cliffs

PRELUDE

Pacific Ocean waves crash relentlessly on a heavenly stretch of rocky beach 45 miles south of San Francisco. Mother Nature patiently and ploddingly takes her rightful share, regularly claiming tiny bits of the coast, but the land sitting high above, atop stately cliffs, has remained virtually unchanged for the better part of a century. On grassy green perches overlooking sparkling blue seas, many a golfer has stood transfixed, temporarily delaying play to breathe in the majestic beauty and soul-searing brilliance of Carmel Bay. There, among the Monterey pines and endangered California sea otters, lies a golf course so stunning, so magnificent, it feels sacrilegious to so much as take a divot.

Pebble Beach Golf Links does not brandish the history of St. Andrews, nor does it, or will it ever, wield the prestige of Augusta National. It does, however, undoubtedly own a unique and sacred spot in the golfing universe. Pebble Beach is greatness among greatness—the brightest shining light in an ultraluminous galaxy. It is Michael Jordan in a room rife with all-stars, Grace Kelly in a park packed with prom queens. It is a furious and unrelenting fighter in the boundless bout for superlatives, the undisputed heavyweight champion of splendor.

The fact of the matter, though, is when this resplendent real estate is played as a golf course, the beauty becomes a beast. It is Joan Collins in *Dynasty*, Sharon Stone in *Basic Instinct*—a heartless, devious, unscrupulous bitch, beckoning with her bare beauty and then breaking you with her veiled venom. It is the kind of place that will distract you with its scenery and then steal your wallet. Or your dignity. Or, on a windy day, both. The nearby waves aren't crashing, they're laughing at you. The greens have claws and the fairways have fangs. Yet what a treat it is to play.

Prior to its development, the land on which the course now sits was a small part of a stunning piece of the Del Monte Forest—coastline property with unique, breathtaking views and inimitable, timeless allure. In 1880 a foursome of California railroad tycoons formed the Pacific Improvement Company and bought several miles of the real estate for $35,000. They held the land for the next 35 years, minimally developing it before commissioning a sharp young man from Massachusetts to liquidate the property.

Samuel F.B. Morse, an entrepreneurial Yale graduate with a knack for business and the grand-nephew of the man acknowledged to be the inventor of the telegraph and Morse code, headed west. Morse had seen the Monterey coast seven years earlier and had been touched by the beauty inherent to the land. Taking a tour of his new employer's property, Morse found a buyer immediately: himself. In 1915, with visions of building a seaside golf course, he formed a company called Del Monte Properties and obtained funding to pay $1.3 million for 18,000 acres.

Originally, the plan called for homes along the shoreline, but in his heart of hearts, Morse knew that was the wrong way to go. Having experienced firsthand the appeal and inherent beauty of Pinehurst, an East Coast course designed along the ocean, Morse decided to build his own Pinehurst where the setting sun, not the rising sun, would be a superstar. He reconfigured his mind's-eye view of the layout, retraced his steps, and began to buy back the lots he had already sold.

Next he found his architects, taking what at the time was a radical step of choosing two men who were not course designers but players. Jack Neville, the California amateur champion in 1912 and 1913, and Douglas Grant, who had just beaten Neville at the Del Monte Mid-Winter Championships, agreed to take on the project. Both men were familiar with the Monterey area and quickly grasped and shared Morse's vision.

Whether or not they fully understood its eventual historical impact, the trio was dedicated to the concept of a course built along the ocean. It was a choice that assured for all time Pebble Beach's status among the world's elite golf courses. They broke all previously established rules of seaside golf-course design with their insistence upon sacrificing the large potential revenue of ocean-front home sales. Residences would eventually be built along the course, but the prime real estate was dedicated wholly to the course itself. What they agreed to forego in immediate profit was infinitesimal compared to what they gained in the purity of the project, designing what would ultimately become one of the most distinctive sporting venues on the planet.

Three years later, in 1918, Pebble Beach Golf Links was opened for play in a course-christening tournament. The players hated it.

Fairways were bumpy, the grass was uneven, and greens were patchy. Borrowing a trick used by courses in Scotland, Neville had, a few months earlier, brought in hundreds of sheep to graze on the grounds to keep them trimmed. What he didn't consider, though, is that the grass on the courses in Scotland had been there for decades. The grass at Pebble Beach had just been planted and had not had proper time to take root. The sheep tore it up, and despite the setback, Neville good-naturedly cracked, "They didn't replace a single divot!"

The designers, though, were not all that concerned, insisting the course, still in its infancy, simply needed one thing money could not buy: time. And they were right. The grass took root, the greens smoothed out, and the course opened to the public in February of 1919 to rave reviews.

In the late 1960s, not long before his death, an 80-year-old Samuel Morse relayed the story of Pebble's early development to Robert Trent Jones Jr., still in his twenties. Recalling a fateful day from a half-century earlier, Morse told the now-celebrated architect about a purposeful stroll through the grounds with his two course designers. "We simply walked the path from what was then a log-cabin lodge and drove wooden stakes for the tees and greens of the 1st and 2nd holes," he said. "Then we had to make a decision whether to turn toward the sea and the lovely vista in that direction or continue more or less along the inland route of Seventeen Mile Drive [the historic street that surrounds Pebble Beach]."

It is a perfect illustration of how taking poet Robert Frost's "road less traveled" can indeed make all the difference. The preeminence of the course lies in the intersection of style and substance. Despite the fact that each hole is a well-designed, thoughtfully laid-out piece of the overall puzzle, like any piece of real estate, location, location, location is a huge selling point.

"In many ways, if some of the individual holes were removed from the scenic surroundings—like paintings from their frames—they would lack specific greatness," the architect Jones once remarked. But the combination of the course design and the inherent beauty of the land makes the whole even greater than the already substantial sum of its parts.

The course has hosted a PGA Championship, several men's and women's U.S. Amateur tournaments, and four U.S. Opens, with a fifth scheduled for 2010. It is home to the AT&T National Pro Am, a yearly block party of a tournament formerly hosted by Bing Crosby and known as the "Crosby Clambake."

THE TOURNAMENT

U.S. OPEN, PEBBLE BEACH GOLF LINKS, PEBBLE BEACH, CALIFORNIA
JUNE 17–20, 1982

With its unique challenges and even more unique setting, Pebble Beach rolled out the seaside welcome mat for the world's best golfers in the summer of 1982. The U.S. Open, with all its prestige and history, was a perfect showcase for the course, which was hosting the event for the second time. One hundred fifty-three players made up the field, but according to Jack Nicklaus, "Maybe only 15 or 20 have a chance to win."

Look up "credibility" in the dictionary, and you might find Jack Nicklaus speaking about major championship golf at Pebble Beach as one of the definitions. Nicklaus won the U.S. Amateur title in 1961, walked away with three Crosby events in 1967, 1972, and 1973, and marched to the 1972 Open championship—all at the very course that was hosting the event beginning the next day. And Jack was dialed in. "This is a course where I have had a great deal of success and have played very well," he said. "So I think I can find my way around. The U.S. Open is the most important tournament in the world as far as I'm concerned, and it's probably the most difficult to win." Then, as if he needed to clarify, he added matter-of-factly, "And, yes, I consider myself one of those that can win it."

Nicklaus was one of four golfers to have claimed the national championship four times and was determined to be the first ever to win a fifth. To do so, he'd have to make his way through a field that sported several others with incentive beyond the $60,000 first prize.

Tom Watson, unquestionably one of the top five best golfers in the world after taking PGA Player of the Year honors in four consecutive seasons from 1977 to 1980, wanted desperately to cross the U.S. Open off of his personal "Important Tournaments I Have Never Won" list. Though just 32 years old, he had already won three British Opens, two Masters, and 25 other PGA events.

While Watson, with his recent honors and body of work, may have staked claim to the unofficial title of "world's best," Raymond Floyd hit town as the world's hottest. Floyd had won the last two PGA events in which he played and lost the one prior in a playoff. "I have never played as well in my life as I have the last three tournaments," he offered confidently in his first media interview upon his arrival. Having already won the Masters and the PGA Championship, a win at Pebble Beach would take Floyd a step closer, that is, just a single step away from a career Grand Slam.

Gary Player, who had long ago solidified a Grand Slam of his own, was in search of a second. With a win, he'd not only have multiple victories in each of the four majors, but would also finish off the feat in front of his son, an amateur who, that week, became half of the first-ever father-son duo to play in a U.S. Open. Twenty-year-old Wayne Player started the tournament with a nervous anticipation and an unquenchable love for the game. He'd finish it a bit differently.

Defending champion David Graham was also hungry for a victory. A win in 1982 would make him the first back-to-back Open winner since Ben Hogan in 1951. Well-versed in golf history, Graham fully understood the prestige of being mentioned in the same breath as the great Hogan, regardless of context. He arrived at Pebble Beach focused and determined.

Craig Stadler was also getting a share of the pretournament attention as he looked to keep a good thing going, coming off his Masters victory two months earlier. A career Grand Slam is one thing. Sweeping the majors in a single season is entirely another. For Stadler, a victory at Pebble would get him halfway to golf immortality.

ROUND I

With all the focus on the big names, it was a group of lesser-knowns doing most of the damage on opening day. A player named Danny Edwards, who also dabbled in auto racing, burned some major rubber on the opening lap of the tournament with a sizzling front nine of 31. Edwards was 6 under par through 13 holes, but skidded to a pair of double bogeys, which he called "blowouts" on the way in, to finish in a five-way tie for second with a 71.

At the top, sharing a first-round score of 2-under-par 70, sat the pair of 1981 PGA Player of the Year Bill Rogers and 44-year-old Bruce Devlin, a player who had spent more of the past few years in the broadcast booth than on the course. "If someone had told me before I teed off that I'd be sharing the lead today," Devlin gushed afterward, "I'd have told them they were mad. I had no reason to expect this."

While the leaders came in playing to smallish galleries, the marquee players with thousands of eyes upon them didn't even manage to get in position to make a run at the top of the board. Despite good conditions and a relatively tame and very manageable breeze, only Tom Watson, with a workmanlike 72, managed to shoot par. The other stars of the day struggled: Nicklaus and Tom Weiskopf both finished 4 shots off the lead with 74s. Stadler put up a 76. Floyd struggled to a 78. Seve Ballesteros and Arnold Palmer joined 34 other players who failed to break 80, limping in with dual 81s.

A decade earlier, Nicklaus won the Open at Pebble Beach with a four-day total of 2-over-par 290. Players agreed, however, that with shorter rough and softer greens, the course was now a kinder, gentler version of its former malicious self. The day before the tournament started, both Nicklaus and Watson predicted a winning score of around 281 or 282; 6 or 7 under par. With one day down, three to go, and increasingly tough pin placements along with tougher conditions likely ahead, those prognostications appeared to be as accurate as a blindfolded drunk hitting a 1 iron to an island green into the teeth of a whipping wind.

ROUND 2

Unlike Messrs. Allin and Thirsk in the PGA Championship 10 years earlier, improbable U.S. Open first-round leaders Bruce Devlin and Bill Rogers followed up their respective stellar opening 18s with strong second rounds. Devlin—who was winless on tour for an entire decade before hitting the Monterey peninsula, was floundering at 195th on the year's money list, and had missed the cut in half of his eight 1982 appearances prior to the Open—was unflappable.

Using a new "metal wood" that he tried for the first time Wednesday evening, he was at his best at both the beginning and the end of his round. On a cold and calm Northern California afternoon, the wiry-thin Australian racked up birdies in three of the first four, and three of the last four holes of the day. He bettered his opening round by a stroke, coming in with a smooth 69, which was good for a 2-stroke lead on the field.

"My game before coming to Pebble Beach was the worst I ever played," he said, almost bewildered after his round. "I will admit, though, I'm starting to think about winning." His score would have been even better, but a deadly accurate sand wedge on the par-5 18th bounced in and out of the hole, forcing him to settle for a tap-in birdie instead of an eagle. Rogers didn't fare quite as well, shooting a scrambling 73, but he was still very much in contention. The reigning British Open champion hit the halfway mark with the number four rather prevalent in his standing. He was in a four-way tie for fourth place, 4 strokes off the pace.

Taking Rogers's spot near the top was a player whose recent credentials were even less impressive than Devlin's. Larry Rinker—who had entered 17 tournaments to date in 1982, failed to qualify for five, and missed the cut in nine others— ripped through the shores of the Pacific like an angry winter wind. Rinker rode a red-hot putter to a day's best 67, vaulting him all alone into second place, 2 strokes back.

A shot behind Rogers's group sat Jack Nicklaus, who shaved 4 strokes off his first-round score, finishing at 2-under-par 70. Nicklaus fired at pins all day, and then fired again at a press conference. "Six [actually seven] guys in front of me is not very many," he boldly claimed. "Nobody is in command of this golf tournament. Pebble Beach is my favorite golf course, and two good rounds would put me back in the thick of things. There is still a lot of golf to be played."

Nicklaus shared eighth place with four others, including Tom Kite, who jumped into contention with a 71, and Tom Watson, who recorded a second straight round of even-par 72.

The cut line was set at 7 over par, with 66 players making it through to the weekend. Arnold Palmer, Seve Ballesteros, and Lee Trevino were among those whose stay was short. Another golfer who missed the cut was young Wayne Player. After taking an 8 on the final hole, the 20-year-old son of one of the sport's true legends stormed off the green without waiting for his playing partners, saying, "That's it. I'm giving up this game."

Jack Nicklaus II, at Pebble Beach to caddie for his father, tried to console Wayne, but was told, "I just hate this game and I don't want to play it anymore. Over the two days, I played the front side in 75 strokes. I played the back in 87. I couldn't take this course for another two days!"

Chalk up another victim of Pebble Beach.

Round 2 Leader Board

Bruce Devlin	70–69	139
Larry Rinker	74–67	141
Scott Simpson	73–69	142
Lyn Lott	72–71	143
Andy North	72–71	143
Calvin Peete	71–72	143
Bill Rogers	70–73	143
George Burns	72–72	144
Bobby Clampett	71–73	144
Tom Kite	73–71	144
Jack Nicklaus	74–70	144
Tom Watson	72–72	144

Round 3

Like an aging, once-dominant boxer with slowing reflexes, or a power pitcher with a sore arm, the heartless bully that is Pebble Beach was shown no mercy by its suddenly empowered intended prey on a wet and windless Saturday. Rendered essentially defenseless by the conditions, the course helplessly saw 13 of the 66 remaining players shoot rounds in the 60s. A steady drizzle softened the course, and with a barely detectable breeze whispering sweetly if at all, flagsticks became bull's-eyes and the golf-club-wielding marksmen of the PGA Tour took dead aim. In the first two days, even though the infamous

Pacific winds blew calmly, slick, dried-out greens led to a mere six of the 305 rounds played coming in under 70.

The name that had been a surprise at the top of the leader board the first day was back. Bill Rogers, who fell from a tie for first place on Thursday into a tie for fourth on Friday, birdied three of the first six holes and had at least a share of the lead for the rest of the day. He ended up with a 2-under-par 70, good for first place. But once again, he had company.

Thirty-two-year-old Tom Watson, who had been playing Pebble Beach for 15 years, had his best round of the week and joined Rogers at the top. Watson knocked down seven birdies on his way to a 4-under-par 68 for a three-day total of 2-over-par 212. As a freshman at Stanford in 1968, Watson would often wake up in the wee hours of the morning, drive from Palo Alto in the darkness, and be the first player on the course. He'd finish his round, drive back to school, and be on campus in time for his afternoon classes. Watson's day started as if he were still a college kid, with a bogey on the 379-yard, par-4 1st hole. He pulled it together immediately, though, stringing together four birdies in the next six. The highlight of his round came on the 204-yard, par-3 12th hole. "The 3 iron I hit there could be the key to my tournament," he said, recalling the blistering tee shot that cuddled up to within three feet of the pin. "I know one shot doesn't win over 72 holes, but just one shot, in the right place, can give you the confidence you need to win an Open. That one was that kind of a shot." He followed it by dropping the short birdie putt and took a share of the lead for the first time in the tournament.

"I hope the third time is the charm," Watson said after seven birdies and three bogeys left him with a 68. The comment was a clear reference to two previous close calls at the U.S. Open—when he led after three rounds at Winged Foot in 1974, and after two rounds at Medinah in 1975, before faltering each year. "I won't consider my career successful unless I win it," he added. "There's only room in the history books for one Sam Snead."

The statement spoke volumes about the immense meaning Watson put on the U.S. Open championship. It would be an honor for a golfer—any golfer, really—to be compared to the legendary Snead. The only major title that had eluded the old Virginian was the one Watson coveted most. Lost in the boldness of his declaration was the fact that, despite three British Open titles and two green jackets, Watson had not won the PGA Championship, either.

Watson was asked how he would spend the next morning awaiting his late tee time, and he said, "I'll watch *Sesame Street* with my two-year-old daughter, Meg. We'll count," he continued, "but not up to seven or eight."

Los Angeles Times sportswriter Shav Glick made an interesting point, noting that all week people had been describing Pebble Beach as an "English/Scottish type golf course." He opined that it should come as no surprise then that Rogers and Watson, the past two winners of the British Open, were tied for the lead with 18 holes to play.

Falling several spots was the man who just 24 hours earlier said he was "starting to think about winning." Bruce Devlin was one player who did not take advantage of the course conditions, following rounds of 70 and 69 with a Saturday 75. "There wasn't much joy out there for me today," he said. "I played awful. I struggled all day to keep from going under."

His round of 3 over par left him just 2 shots off the pace and still in relatively good position, but with his confidence level apparently rising and falling in the opposite direction of his scores, he seemed like a long shot.

On the other hand, confidence was sky high for Jack Nicklaus, who was headed to the final round in a seventh-place tie. Despite his own 71, made up of a bogey and just two birdies, Jack remarked, "It was a fairly easy day to play golf."

The Golden Bear had been golden indeed 10 and 20 years earlier, winning the U.S. Open in both 1962 and 1972, and as he looked toward the final round of 1982, said, "My position is not bad by any means. I'm putting all right, it's just that these greens are very, very difficult to read." And then the winner of the 1961 U.S. Amateur Championship, and several other events on this very course, took a jab at himself, adding, "I only have 21 years' experience on these greens. One of these years I'll learn how to putt them."

Round 3 Leader Board

Bill Rogers	70–73–69	212
Tom Watson	72–72–68	212
George Burns	72–72–70	214
Bruce Devlin	70–69–75	214
David Graham	73–72–69	214
Scott Simpson	73–69–72	214
Jack Nicklaus	74–70–71	215
Calvin Peete	71–72–72	215
Bobby Clampett	71–73–72	216
Dan Pohl	72–74–70	216
Larry Rinker	74–67–75	216
Craig Stadler	76–70–70	216
Lanny Wadkins	73–76–67	216

ROUND 4

Thirteen players started the final round within 4 strokes of the lead on a cool and clear Northern California June Sunday. The golfing Gods took it easy on the field with the winds fluctuating between mild and mildly bothersome. The dawn of the next morning would bring the first day of summer, and for one of the 13, the calendar's sweetest season would start in style.

Most eyes, of course, were on the final group of the day: coleaders Bill Rogers and Tom Watson. Watson took a brief lead with a birdie on the 2nd hole, but gave the shot right back with a bogey on 3. Rogers held the lead by himself briefly, but it was the roar of a bear from three groups up that got the attention of not only the entire gallery but every other player on the course as well.

Jack Nicklaus hadn't scored particularly well the first three rounds—at least not by his standards—but maintained a sense of calm that had to be somewhat disconcerting to any other contender paying attention. The fact was, Jack's game from tee to green was just fine. It was trouble with his putter that had prevented him from making the charge everybody had come to expect. According to *The New York Times*, Nicklaus had converted just four of 16 potential birdie opportunities through the first 54 holes. Once the putts started dropping—and "they will," predicted Nicklaus—his already giant presence would seem even larger.

Turns out, the days leading up to the final round were just the calm before the storm as Nicklaus went on an early rampage. After a bogey on 1 and a par on 2, those birdies that had been missing since the tournament began, came home to roost. Jack's best streak in his long and storied history at the U.S.

Open started with a 15-footer for birdie on the 3rd hole and picked up steam with a 23-footer on number 4. He racked up tweeters again on 5, 6, and 7, shaving 5 strokes from par in a span of five holes.

He went out in 33, cruising all the while in the leader board's northbound express lane, bypassing the bunched-up traffic near the top.

For about a minute, Bruce Devlin had the lead. Playing behind Nicklaus, Devlin birdied the 6th hole to move to 5 under par. However, as Jack was shaving strokes, Devlin was adding them, playing 7 through 9 in 3 over. Bye-bye, Bruce.

As Nicklaus teed it up for the back nine, holding a share of the lead at 6 under par, three holes back, Watson moved into position to take the top spot all for his own. One of the best putters in the history of the game, and certainly the best putter of his time, Tom had hit a gorgeous approach to within two feet on the par-4 7th hole.

Shockingly, he missed it. Barely even caught the lip of the cup, in fact. Shaking his head in frustration, he tapped in for par and walked off the green. It was as if he'd been logging hours at a slot machine and stood up only to watch the next guy hit the jackpot on the first pull. He had done all the work on the sometimes-stingy 7th but missed the payoff. Opportunities like two-foot birdie putts don't come often in the final round of the U.S. Open, and when they do, a player better take advantage.

Watson finished the front nine with another pair of pars, and momentarily took a 1-shot lead over Nicklaus and Rogers when Jack 3-putted for bogey on the 11th and Bill did the same on the ninth. As the final group made the turn, it was looking more and more like a three-horse race with the leader board stacked like this:

Player	Score	Through
Watson	-4	9
Rogers	-3	9
Nicklaus	-3	12
Devlin	-1	11
Graham	-1	11

It has long been said that major championship golf tournaments do not begin until the back nine on Sunday. If that's true, then Bill Rogers got off to a horrible start.

On the 10th, Rogers was in the green-side bunker, and Watson left his approach in the rough on a down slope off the green. But while Watson hacked out of the thick fescue and saved par with a 25-footer, Rogers needed 3 shots to get down for his second consecutive bogey. And then it got worse.

Rogers bogeyed the next hole as well, making it three straight. Meantime, Watson smoothly stroked a 22-footer for birdie, widening the gap to a suddenly substantial 4 over Rogers and 2 over Nicklaus, who, up ahead, had parred 13 and 14.

Jack heard the roar behind him and, by the time he reached the 15th tee, knew the reason for it. He saw Watson's birdie on 11 go up on the scoreboard and knew he was running out of holes. Two strokes can be a lot of ground to make up. Then again…

Watson played the par-3 12th while Nicklaus stepped up to the par-4 15th. Tom's tee shot was short and landed in the bunker in front of the green. He wedged his way out and needed 2 putts for bogey. Within a minute, Jack was standing over a 13-footer, unaware that a make would move him into a tie. Make it he did, and the sudden 2-shot swing put the two most popular and accomplished golfers of the day in a deadlock at 4 under par with precious few holes to play.

All around them, players dropped out of contention. Like a pro-wrestling battle royal, guys were figuratively getting thrown over the top rope left and right. Rogers, Devlin, Graham, Burns, Simpson—all of 'em—gone. The inherent pressure of Sunday at the Open, along with the subtle and not-so-subtle difficulties of Pebble Beach, knocked 'em out one by one until only the two most worthy contenders remained. Survival of the fittest with a Titleist.

Watson and Nicklaus were going head to head again. It's a battle that over the years became like a drug for golf fans—the more they got, the more they wanted. Most memorably, five years earlier in the British Open at Turnberry, the pair had fought it out in a duel for the ages, putting up identical 68–70–65 scores in the first three rounds. Paired together on Championship Sunday, Jack finished with a fantastic final round of 66 but was beaten by a single stroke when Tom dropped a monster 60-foot birdie putt on 16 and closed it out with a 65.

"My dreams were to be the best player in the world," Watson said in 2007, "and the only way you can do that is to beat the best, and that was Jack Nicklaus."

•••

Nicklaus's tournament-tying birdie sent him on a confident stroll to the 16th tee. He no longer needed to make up ground, but instead, he looked to apply pressure with steady play. Most world-class golfers in a stretch battle would rather be last to finish, but as he approached the final three holes, Nicklaus convinced himself that playing ahead of Watson could be used to his advantage.

Professional athletes are at their best when their minds are free of all thoughts other than the task at hand. It was the legendary basketball coach John Wooden who defined poise simply as the ability to be oneself. It is, in all walks of life, harder to simply be oneself when the brain is consciously or unconsciously consumed with situational details, outside forces, and perceived pressure. A birdie anywhere along the line by Nicklaus, and Watson would be hard-pressed to step up to his own ball without thinking about Jack's score and what was needed to beat it.

Watson's thinking, relayed in a 2007 interview was, "It really doesn't matter who teed off first. The one thing you do have to know in the last round is how you stand against the field. You have to look at the scoreboard and understand what you need to do. I knew that Jack was lighting it up. He made five straight birdies and it was, game on! It's daunting when you play against the best that ever played. You know you can't make very many mistakes, if any."

Watson played 13 the book: drive into the fairway, approach to the green, 2 putts. Tom was in for par while Jack unleashed a bomb off the tee on the par-4 16th. Nicklaus stayed clear of trouble and hit the green in regulation. His birdie putt, though, was a few inches off line, forcing him to settle for par. It was suddenly a game of match play despite the fact that the two leaders were three groups apart. In that vein, there was no blood. Still even.

The 14th hole is a 565-yard par-5 that had given Watson fits for years. Under the intense Sunday pressure, though, he put together two flawless shots, putting him inside 120 yards. He approached with a sand wedge that was directly on line but a bit too strong. The ball flew over the pin and came to a stop on the second cut at the back of the green nearly 40 feet from the hole.

With the green sloping severely, not only from back to front but significantly from left to right as well, the shot had potential trouble written all over it. Watson looked it over and conferred with his trusted caddie, Bruce Edwards. He took his stance over the ball and tapped it softly just to get it going, as if gently nudging a willing child from the top of a slide. From there, gravity took over. About halfway to the hole, the ball seemed to pick up speed. It bent on a perfect arc from about five feet outside the cup, tracking all the way. It ran toward the hole as if on rails and sped into the cup like a kid running off a diving board into a pool. *Splash*.

The green-side gallery roared its approval as Watson shot a smile at Edwards. "That was the best read I've ever given him," the caddie would say later. And Tom agreed.

"Humans 3-putt from there," remarked Rogers, blown away by Watson's uncanny ability to continually find the mark from long range.

Watson went to card a routine par at the 15th, while Nicklaus, now a stroke down, jabbed his tee into the earth at 17. Anybody watching, with any sense of golf history, had to be reminded of a shot that had become legend. A decade earlier, from that very tee box in this very tournament, Jack whistled a deadly accurate pin-seeking 1 iron that smacked the flagstick and died near the cup. He converted his birdie, propelling him to a 3-shot victory and the third of his four U.S. Open titles.

His shot this time was not as good, but good, nonetheless. He stuck it about 12 feet from the hole and needed another flash of the magic that emanated from his putter earlier in the round. But it wasn't there. He tapped in for another par and moved to 18 looking for his seventh birdie of a great final round that just might not be good enough.

Back to Watson. The man who had built his reputation with a deadly short game had been scorching it off the tee all day long. His accuracy had kept him out of the rough, and his length had allowed him to approach with short irons. On the par-4 16, though, his driver failed him. Watson pushed his tee shot badly to the right and wound up in the nastiest spot of a fairway bunker that was deeper than a Stephen Hawking dissertation.

Stepping into the trap and seeing the ominous wall of sand in front of him, he knew that trying to advance the ball forward was dangerous, at best. Leading by a stroke, he played his second shot sideways into the fairway, forcing him to hit his approach from a downhill lie. The ball came out with little backspin and scooted about 55 feet past the pin, which was cut in the front of the green. He made a great run at a big bending par putt, but had to settle for a tap-in bogey, once again dropping him into a tie for the lead.

Moments later, Nicklaus missed yet another birdie putt on 18, making it three straight holes in which he could have gained a stroke. Each of his 3 birdie putts was less than 20 feet in length, but Jack couldn't will a single one of them into the cup. He walked off the final green and signed his scorecard, knowing his round of 69 could have been better. His scores of 74–70–71–69 gave him a 4-under-par total of 284, which was a half-dozen strokes better than his winning score 10 years earlier. He walked to the clubhouse and arrived at a television monitor as Watson was teeing up his ball on 17.

THE SHOT

The last of the four par-3s at Pebble Beach, the 17th hole is a picturesque puzzle of sensory overload. The scenic sightlines from the tee are like no other hole in golf, with the hourglass-shaped green more than two football fields away, protected by thick, lettuce-like fescue grass all around. To the left of the green are jagged rocks atop daunting cliffs leading down to the Pacific. Over the trees beyond the green, on the June day that would see the Open decided, was a blue-gray sky that seemed to go on forever. The cloudless airborne landscape skewed the depth perception of the view toward the heavens, while the constant rumble of the surrounding water seemed both deafening and silent at the same time. The scent of the sea was everywhere while a late afternoon breeze blew right to left and a bit into Watson's face. He gripped his 2 iron and set his gaze on the hole, 209 yards in front of him, planning to draw the ball with the wind onto the green.

He made a good swing with his usual smooth tempo and sent the ball rocketing skyward. Dirt flew forward while the tee recoiled backward. At the apex of its flight, the ball seemed to be moving on a perfect arc toward the center of the green. As it descended, though, it began to work to the left—floating, wandering aimlessly like a wayward soap bubble. He knew he hooked it a touch more than he had intended and could only watch helplessly as the little white pellet meandered toward trouble like a stray dog crossing a busy highway. It reunited with the earth, grabbing a piece of the second cut on the left of the green, and then it was gone. The ball scooted into the thick, gnarly grass, which was deep enough to hide a cantaloupe. As it settled into the rough between a large bunker and the green, the crowd let out a collective groan. Watson clenched his teeth while Nicklaus watched with the stoic poker face of a seasoned cardsharp, thinking he had just won his fifth U.S. Open.

Watson was going over the possibilities of the shot that lay ahead as he and his caddie started toward the green.

Walking off the tee, Tom said, "That's dead."

Edwards answered back, "No, it isn't. Let's go get it up and down."

For years, Watson had made a habit of re-creating the game's most demanding shots: working the ball in the wind;

putting on superfast greens; playing out of tough spots; and, alas, chipping out of thick rough. "I've practiced that shot for hours, days, months, and years," he would later say. "It's a shot you have to be able to execute if you are going to survive in a U.S. Open where there's always high grass around the greens."

Arriving at his ball, Watson saw not disaster but, incredibly, opportunity. As if placed gently on the fescue, the ball was sitting up, practically begging to be struck cleanly; it far more resembled sunny-side-up than over-easy.

Still, it was a dreadfully difficult shot. The ornery grass was certain to grab the club as it came through, and the proximity of the ball to the green was such that strict precision in loft, speed, direction, and distance were all crucial. Watson and Edwards looked it over, figuring they were 16 feet away, roughly seven feet from the edge of the green and another nine feet to the stick. Making matters worse was a relatively severe left-to-right break in the green and two other slopes, both working against Watson.

He remembered, in a 2000 *Golf Digest* article, "The problem was, it was on a down-slope, and the ball was well below my feet—probably the most difficult position to chip from…that was compounded by the fact that the pin was also on a down-slope."

"Get it close," said the caddie, thinking ahead toward 18. "We gotta make 3 here."

"Get it close, hell! I'm gonna hole it," came Tom's response, seemingly as absurd as it was bold.

Watson took his stance—feet slightly open, knees bent, weight shifted toward his left side because of the slope. He lowered his left shoulder "to help get the club up more vertically." He settled into a comfortable position, dramatically opened the blade of his sand wedge, and drew the club back up in a smooth, outside arc about waist-high before pulling firmly downward. Executing a swing with a delicate balance of the solid pass needed to get through the rough and the soft touch needed to control the distance, he made the perfect stroke. He blasted through the top of the thick foliage like a chef chopping a thin slice from a head of lettuce. The ball popped almost straight up as if punched softly from below and floated gently forward, drifting tenderly like the feather in the opening scene of *Forrest Gump*.

The ball came down quietly on the fringe, as the minimal amount of backspin allowed it to check up just a touch before it began its forward roll onto the green and toward the flag. It picked up speed because of the slope, and as it headed downward, it also began to catch the break in the green and move to the right. Tom had estimated it would move a full foot side to side, and as he watched it roll toward the cup he feared it would not break quickly enough to drop. He began moving quickly to his left as if his own changing vantage point would help the ball slide harder. As he moved, he saw ball, hole, and pin come together in a joyous and memorable ménage-à-trois of golf history. The ball puckered up, sweetly kissed the pin dead-center, and dropped into the cup. Watson went wild. Or, at least he did the PGA version of going wild: raising his arms triumphantly as he broke into an all-out jog around the perimeter of the green. He waved his putter, pointed toward Edwards, and excitedly said, "I told you so!" His caddie merely smiled.

"It was an impossible shot," Rogers said afterward. "You could take 100 balls and toss them by hand from where he was and not make a single one of them."

Told of that analysis, Nicklaus chirped, "Make it 1,000 balls. In fact, you could have walked to the edge of the green and dropped a ball, and you would not be able to stop it at the hole. How are you going to do it with a wedge?!"

Actually, there was no way to stop the ball at the hole. A good part of the shot's greatness is the fact that the only way to stop it was to knock it *in* the hole. Watson estimated later that if the ball had not dropped it would have gone five feet past the cup. Rogers said 15 feet. Nicklaus went with 20.

•••

Watson moved to the par-5 18th, the 72nd and final hole of the tournament he had coveted since he was 10 years old, needing just a par to win it. He played it as if he were back in college, competing with only the morning dew and the rising sun. No pressure, no mistakes. He hit a good drive, was on the green in regulation, and closed it in style, rolling in a silky smooth 20-foot birdie putt to win by 2 strokes.

As he walked off the green, Watson looked up to see Nicklaus waiting for him. "You little son of a bitch, you're something else," Jack said with a smile.

As a boy, Watson would talk about the U.S. Open with his father, reciting the names of long-since-retired players and the years in which they won. The victory meant more to him than just another trophy. "This augments my other accomplishments," he said to the gathered media. "And to have it come down to Jack Nicklaus, the greatest player to ever play the game, and Tom Watson at Pebble Beach, which I consider one of the great golf courses in the world, is a scenario I'll never forget."

Later in the evening, the champion returned to the interview tent and was asked what he did in the hours before the final round started. "I watched *Sesame Street* with Meg," he said with a sly smile and then paused a beat for effect. "They only counted up to two."

U.S. Open
Round 4, Sunday, June 20, 1982

HOLE	1	2	3	4	5	6	7	8	9	OUT	10	11	12	13	14	15	16	17	18	IN	TOTAL
PAR	4	5	4	4	3	5	3	4	4	36	4	4	3	4	5	4	4	3	5	36	72
Nicklaus	5	5	3	3	2	4	2	5	4	33	4	5	3	4	5	3	4	3	5	36	69
Watson	4	4	5	4	3	5	3	4	4	36	4	3	4	4	4	4	5	(2)	4	34	70

Tournament Results

Tom Watson	72–72–68–70	282
Jack Nicklaus	74–70–71–69	284
Bob Clampett	71–73–72–70	286
Dan Pohl	72–74–70–70	286
Bill Rogers	70–73–69–74	286
David Graham	73–72–69–73	287
Jay Haas	75–74–70–68	287
Gary Koch	78–73–69–67	287
Lanny Wadkins	73–76–67–71	287

POSTSCRIPT

After receiving the trophy and, a bit less important to him, the $60,000 winner's check, Watson reflected on the amazing chip. With certainty and simplicity, he said, "That was the best shot of my life."

Certainly the 1982 U.S. Open will always be remembered for the unlikely tie-breaking birdie on the 71st hole—16 feet of unforgettable glory amidst nearly 7,000 yards of unequalled beauty—but no tournament is ever won with a single shot.

Watson actually hadn't played very well the first two days, but salvaged back-to-back rounds of par with birdies on three of the final four holes on Thursday, and on three of the last five on Friday. Although he might have seen his game as inconsistent throughout the event, he was the only player in the field of 153 to shoot par or better in all four rounds.

The win gave Watson his sixth major championship and, amazingly, the fourth in which Nicklaus finished second. Tom would go on to capture the British Open at Royal Troon that summer and recapture the British at Royal Birkdale a year later. In all, he won 39 PGA tournaments, including five British Opens, two Masters, and his all-time favorite, the 1982 U.S. Open. He would later say about his chip on 17, "That shot had more meaning to me than any other in my career."

Watson became eligible for the Senior Tour in 1999 and won at least one Senior or Champions event in each of the first seven years in which he played. Notably, he started 2007 with a victory at the two-man Wendy's Champions Skins Game, where he and his teammate took home first-place prize money of $320,000. His partner for the event? An old rival and friend named Jack Nicklaus.

As much as Nicklaus seemed to be victimized by Watson's heroics at Pebble Beach, an analysis of his own play reveals a four-day series of uncharacteristic missed opportunities by the Golden Bear.

On Sunday, with the tournament on the line, Nicklaus had potential birdie putts of 17 feet or less on each of the final three greens, and missed all of them. "I could have putted better," he'd admit afterward. "But at the U.S. Open, you could always say you could have putted better."

The final stretch of the final round, though, was merely a continuation of a tournament-long trend that ultimately delivered the crown to Watson. Breaking down each player's four-day perform-ance, it's easy to see it was the last three holes on the course where, with a 7-stroke swing, Tom got the better of Jack.

Tournament Totals, Final 3 Holes:

Hole	Watson	Nicklaus
Par-4 16th	-1	+1
Par-3 17th	-3	E
Par-5 18th	-2	E
Total	-6	+1

Although there is a lot of validity to Gary Player's views about finishing second, being the runner-up of a golf tourna-ment in which 153 players started has to be considered a great showing by anybody's standards.

For Nicklaus, second place was a pretty common spot; he now had four U.S. Open runner-ups to go with his four U.S. Open championships. By the end of his career, he would finish second in an incredible total of 19 majors. What might have eaten at him is not being second-best on a particular weekend, but the way he seemed to be cursed at the 17th hole.

In 1977 Watson had beaten him down the stretch at the Masters when he birdied 17. Later that year, in the British Open at Turnberry, when Watson shot that final-round 65 to Nicklaus's 66, it was a birdie on 17 that had made the difference.

Five years earlier, Jack played the British already having won the 1972 Masters and U.S. Open.

Because he closed out 1971 with a victory at the PGA Championship, a win at Muirfield would give him all four major titles simultaneously. Late in the final round, he was tied with Lee Trevino but, once again, came up a stroke short. It was

Trevino's birdie on, of course, the 17th hole that won it, stifling Nicklaus's bid for the Grand Slam.

And he sat in the pressroom at Pebble Beach, again facing the media after another 17th-hole miracle—again off of somebody else's club. The reporters made no mention of Jack's seemingly unlucky number. Maybe they didn't know about it. Maybe, less than an hour removed from Tom Watson's chip, one of the greatest shots ever, they didn't care. They did, though, respectfully yet relentlessly fire questions at Nicklaus about his inability to win the tournament.

He was asked whether there was a shot in the final round he would have played differently if he had had the chance. Always the good sport, and able to keep his sense of humor on a day that did not end well, he answered, "Yeah. Watson's chip at 17!"

Jack Nicklaus watches his putt drop for a birdie on the 17th hole at Augusta National on April 13, 1986.

CHAPTER SIX

1986:
The Olden Bear

PRELUDE

There is a sporting phenomenon unique to boxing in which a particularly brutal battle will cost one or both of the fighters involved a part of themselves they can never recover. The level of effort they put forth and the brutal punishment they endure renders them less skillful on their way out of the ring than they had been on the way in. They might walk out as the same person, but not as the same athlete.

Thankfully, that is not true about golf. Jack Nicklaus and Tom Watson were, physically, the same players they were the Monday after the 1982 Open that they were on that final and fateful Sunday. For Nicklaus, though, a transformation was taking place. He had reached the age at which the already traveled path in the rearview mirror was unquestionably a lot brighter than the road in front of him. He was, through no fault of his own, reaching an unofficial demarcation line in the game of golf.

History said, at the age of 42, Nicklaus's window of opportunity for winning major championships, although not completely shut, was closing quickly. Despite the fact that golfers are generally seen as a less-athletic brand of athlete than those in more traditionally physical sports, the early forties generally mark the same kind of slide in performance for golfers as they do for the others. Sure, there are once-in-a-generation guys like Rickey Henderson, Nolan Ryan, and Chris Chelios, who were productive well past their 42nd birthdays, and there are once-in-a-lifetime guys like George Foreman, Gordie Howe, and George Blanda, who continued to shine even as they approached 50. But in almost all cases, even those of megastars like Willie Mays, Kareem Abdul-Jabbar, and Jerry Rice, athletes in all sports see a dramatic decline in their skills just as they approach 42.

From where Nicklaus stood in 1982, the record books had not been kind to men his age. At the time, since 1920, only three men over the age of 42 (Julius Boros, 1963 U.S. Open, age 43, and 1968 PGA Championship, age 48; Roberto DeVincenzo, 1967 British Open, age 44; and Jerry Barber, 1961 PGA, age 45) had won major championships. Jack's greatness could not be denied, and his showing at Pebble Beach was proof that he still had the game to win, but that didn't change the fact that he simply had not been winning lately. Nicklaus did not register a single victory in 1981, and won only once in '82. Golfers of his stature measured themselves, and each other, not only by victories but especially by victories in major championships. In that category, Jack might have been starting to wonder, given his age and the competition around him, if his career total would end where it stood as he left California, at 17. There is that number again.

•••

In the next few years, Father Time, it seemed, began to tarnish the gold on the Golden Bear as his on-course performance fell off dramatically. The man who finished in the top 10 in an astounding 35 of the 40 majors played in the 1970s was suddenly almost a nonfactor. Following are Jack's results from the 14 majors between the 1982 U.S. Open and the 1986 Masters. The numbers told an unmistakable tale of his fall from golf's elite.

	1982	1983	1984	1985
Masters	15th	WD	18	6
U.S. Open	2nd	43	21	Cut
British Open	10th	29	31	Cut
PGA	16th	2	25	16

All finishes were ties other than 1983 PGA.

WD = Withdrew. Cut = Did not make it past second round.

Cranking it up for his 25th professional season in 1986, Nicklaus had won just twice in the previous five years, and the downward trend showed no signs of turning around. He missed three cuts in his first seven events of the new year (after never before missing more than two in any one season), and did not finish higher than 39th place. His earnings of $4,404 put him 160th on that year's money list.

On the Sunday before the 50th edition of the Masters, a tournament preview article titled "This Year Should Be a Wide Open Shootout," written by staff writer Tom McCallister, appeared in the *Atlanta Journal-Constitution*. In it, the author clearly and rather bluntly gave his assessment of the five-time champion's chances.

"Nicklaus is gone, done," McCallister wrote. "He just doesn't have the game anymore. It's rusted from lack of use. He's 46, and nobody that old wins the Masters."

And certainly nobody that old ever had. Gary Player's championship came in 1978 when he was 42, and Sam Snead won it in 1954 at the age of 41. But 46 is another story.

A few days later, another article appeared in the same newspaper quoting 1964 U.S. Open champion and current television analyst Ken Venturi. Referring to Nicklaus's having missed several recent cuts, Venturi said, "I haven't seen him play, because he hasn't been around to be on the air. Jack's got to start thinking about when it is time [to retire]. He's already said that he's got more things on his mind than golf. Even though he's preparing for the Masters and the other majors, it's not a switch you can turn on and off. He'd like to win again for everybody who said he was down and out, but, well, everybody would. The whole world is looking for Babe Ruth to hit another home run and Ben Hogan to shoot a 66."

Even other players were questioning Jack's ability—and young players at that. "I think the players now respect him more for what he has done and what he has meant to golf than they respect him for his game," commented Corey Pavin, a 26-year-old hotshot out of UCLA. "If I was going head to head with him, I wouldn't be afraid of him or fear anything, you know, supernatural," Pavin said. "I think when he was playing 10 years ago he was a man to fear."

What McCallister, Venturi, Pavin, and the rest of the golf world didn't know is that a few weeks prior to the start of the tournament, Nicklaus called on the counsel of swing coach Jack Grout. The pair got together and identified a pretty serious flaw—Jack was getting way too "handsy" in his swing.

That realization along with Nicklaus's reading of McCallister's article combined to make Nicklaus a better prepared, more determined competitor as he headed to Augusta National, the site of some of his greatest victories. "I still want to win and I think I can," Jack was quoted in the local papers. "If nothing else, I'm gonna do it just to show you guys I can still win."

THE TOURNAMENT

The Masters, Augusta National Golf Club Augusta, Georgia, April 10–13, 1986

The annual event in Augusta had come a long way since Gene Sarazen's double eagle in the second tournament in 1935. Other than 1943–1945, when it was canceled because of World War II, The Masters had been played every year since, making the 1986 version it's 50th edition—the unofficial golden anniversary.

Augusta National welcomed the field of 88 as a less-than-gracious host. Whipping winds and table-top slick greens made a difficult course even more so. Only 16 players managed to break par as a not-so-dynamic duo surged to the lead. Bill Kratzert, a former University of Georgia All-American in his 10th year on tour, survived not only the wind but the chill of his early-morning tee time as well. Kratzert's 4 under par was good for a share of the lead with one of the true characters of the game, Ken Green.

Green won six tournaments in the '80s but was known more for his antics on and off the course. He was fined by the PGA more than 20 times for stunts ranging from sneaking friends into Augusta National in the trunk of his car to swearing on the course, signing autographs during rounds, and drinking beer while playing in the 1997 Masters with Arnold Palmer. On this Thursday, though, it was Green's putter that grabbed the spotlight as he drained putts of 35, 40, 50, and 70 feet en route to his scorching opening-round 68.

In a star-powered group at 2-over-par 74 sat a trio of former champions: Jack Nicklaus, Raymond Floyd, and defending champ Bernhard Langer, who said afterward, "The greens were so fast, you couldn't stop the ball. It just kept going and going and going."

Nicklaus played very well tee to green but, just like in that U.S. Open at Pebble Beach four years earlier, couldn't drop a putt. Well, he did drop one putt—one of the 11 he tried from inside 15 feet.

Also having trouble with the flat stick was self-proclaimed pretournament favorite Seve Ballesteros, who said afterward, "It's near impossible to stop the ball near the hole." The fiery Spaniard, who had the backing of the odds-makers, as well, had registered four top-three Masters finishes in the past six years and shot a 71 as he opened his quest for a third green jacket.

ROUND 1 LEADER BOARD

Ken Green	-4
Bob Kratzert	-4
T.C. Chen	-3
Gary Koch	-3
Dave Barr	-2
Tom Kite	-2
Tommy Nakajima	-2
Greg Norman	-2
Bob Tway	-2
Tom Watson	-2
Seve Ballesteros	-1
Ben Crenshaw	-1
Dan Edwards	-1
Hubert Green	-1
Roger Maltbie	-1
Corey Pavin	-1

Round 2

It was another bright and windy day in east-central Georgia as players filed in at the crack of dawn to start round two. Quickly falling off the leader board, Ken Green effectively nullified all of his great work in the opening, giving back all 4 of his strokes under par and then some. By the time Green made the turn, he was already 1 over, and by the end of the day, his 78 had him off of the leader board.

Kratzert, on the other hand, backed up his strong first round with an even-par 72. Two of his three birdies of the day came on the final six holes, and he headed toward the weekend just a shot off the lead.

The man he was chasing was Seve Ballesteros, who had actually been banned from playing in most of the PGA Tour events in 1986 because he did not appear in the required minimum of 15 tour events in 1985.

Ballesteros birdied the 2nd hole, bringing back memories of three years earlier when he tore up the early holes as if his clubs were backhoes. In the final round of his victorious 1983 Masters, Seve began his day going birdie, eagle, par, birdie, in a dazzling dash from the 1st tee in which he needed merely a dozen shots to get through the first four holes.

On this day, though, it wasn't a strong start that propelled him into the lead but a steady round with a game plan pulled off to hear perfection. His approach was all about the approach. The greens once again were mowed tremendously short—like a fresh crew cut on a marine—and Ballesteros made sure to come in below the pin, avoiding downhill putts at all costs. According to plan, he hit the low part of the slope on 16 of the 18 greens. Ironically, one of the approach shots that missed the mark came on the final hole when he left himself a Carl Lewis–fast 20-footer, which he delicately rolled home to close the show with a day's best 68. He finished with an eagle, four birdies, and two bogies for a two-day total of 5 under par, sending him to the weekend leading the pack.

"When I came in here this week I was very confident and strong mentally," Ballesteros said. "Determination has always been a part of me."

Seven players finished within 3 shots of Seve, including Greg Norman, who had a brief share of the lead after birdies on the 6th and 8th holes. However, an Augusta special—a 4-putt on the 10th—took a big bite out of the Shark, sending him in with a round of 72 for a 2-under-par total.

Defending champ Bernhard Langer played the front side in even par but brought his round home in style with four back-side birdies, including a chip-in at 12. Langer's 68 left him tied with Norman and three others, 3 off the pace.

Jack Nicklaus followed up a pretty good opening round with an even better second round, shooting a 1-under-par 71. Given his recent results, Nicklaus would not have hesitated if offered a two-day total of 145, but it could easily have been in the low 140s. "On Thursday, I had 11 putts inside of 15 feet and made one," he said. "In the second round, I had 12 putts inside 15 feet and I made only four. Those are what I call makeable putts, inside 15 feet. If I could just putt, I might just scare some-body. Maybe me!"

Jack's old buddy and nemesis, Tom Watson, saw a poten-tially great round slip away at the par-3 12th, where he hit his first shot into the water and his third shot into a bunker. He ended up taking a triple-bogey 6 on the hole and finished for the second consecutive day at even-par 72.

Eighty-eight had started; 40 got the axe. The cut line was established at 5-over-par 149 and sent several former champions packing. Gary Player was gone, as were Arnold Palmer, Ray Floyd, and Craig Stadler.

A flurry of activity in the fading daylight just an hour before, Augusta National was suddenly dark and quiet. The course, nestled into a quiet corner of the Deep South, was alive with a decidedly international flair remaining in the day's afterglow. Five of the top eight players on the leader board were foreign-born, outplaying and outnumbering America's best golfers in an all-out assault of the country's most exclusive golfing grounds.

Round 2 Leader Board

Ballesteros (Spain)	68	139
Kratzert (U.S.A.)	72	140
Nakajima (Japan)	71	141
Chen (Taiwan)	73	142
Crenshaw (U.S.A.)	71	142
Edwards (U.S.A.)	71	142
Langer (West Germany)	68	142
Norman (Australia)	72	142

A quartet of Americans, including Mark McCumber, who blistered the course with a great second round of 67, were stacked together 4 shots back. He, Corey Pavin, Bob Tway, and Gary Koch all stood at 143 in the tournament headed to the weekend.

ROUND 3

What was shaping up to be a veritable League of Nations tournament welcomed in yet another well-traveled member on Saturday, when a man who was born in South Africa, grew up in Rhodesia (now Zimbabwe), carried a British passport, and would apply soon for U.S. citizenship, dominated the field and the course itself. There had never been a round, in the long and storied history of the Masters, like the round Nick Price put together on the third day of the tournament in 1986. Never.

After a bogey on the 1st hole, Price settled down and dialed in. He waltzed through the old course on a day so calm the limbs on the trees appeared to be frozen in a snapshot. Price racked up 10 birdies and seven pars over the final 17 holes to come in with a record-setting 63. It would have been 62, but his 30-footer for birdie on 18 lipped the cup and stayed out. It was the only bit of bad luck he had all day. Price moved around Augusta National like a machine, hitting long and straight drives and deadly accurate approach shots, and finishing holes with a precision he called the "best round of putting in my career."

He was an equal-opportunity scorer, punishing all areas of the course. Price started hot on the 10th hole and kept the sizzle going through a famous stretch known as Amen Corner. Holes 11–13 have been the demise of many a promising round over the years, but not on this day, not for Price. He played the first four holes of the back nine to practical perfection, taking just 12 strokes as he breezed through them like a free spirit out for a Sunday drive on a Saturday afternoon. He played the two par-4s in 3, the par-3 12th in 2, and the par-5 13th in 4, stringing together a dazzling run of four straight birdies they're still talking about at Augusta nearly a quarter-century later.

Price's third round was almost as startling when viewed by itself as it was in the context of the way he had started the tournament. Just 29 years old, Price hadn't yet fulfilled the promise he showed when he won the World Series of Golf in his first season on tour three years earlier, and the 1986 Masters appeared as if it were going to be just another missed cut. But after an opening-round 79, he bounced back with a sure-handed 69 on the second day to make the cut by a single stroke. "I just went out Saturday hoping to break 70 again," he said. And he did. By a lot. His all-time course best of 63—a mind-boggling total—put him in a tie for second place in a foursome that included Ballesteros, Langer, and Donnie Hammond.

In conditions far better than the previous two days, Augusta National played like what Tom Watson described as "an under-par golf course." However, with easier pin placements, slower greens, and no wind to speak of, Ballesteros failed to capitalize. The overnight leader was still a shot up on the field after a birdie on 15, but stumbled from there. He 3-putted the 17th green and hit a spectator with his tee shot on 18 to come in bogey-bogey for an even-par 72, a stroke off the pace. "I'm not happy with the way I finished," said Ballesteros. "But I'm happy where I am."

Never one to miss an opportunity to get in another player's head, Tom Watson said to the press afterward, "You'd have thought that on an easy day Seve could have distanced himself from the field. It looks as if he hasn't taken advantage of it. It's still a horse race."

And the horse out in front was a thoroughbred from Australia.

Greg Norman's jockey apparently went to the whip down the stretch as Norman birdied five of the final 11 holes to finish with a 68. His three-day total of 210 was 1 stroke better than Price and the other three at 211.

Norman finished fourth in his first Masters appearance in 1981, but not better than 25th in the four years since. Taking the lead to the final round, he acknowledged, "Sometimes I have a hard time controlling my ego here. I try to play the golf course too aggressively, and you can't really do that because of pin positions and the speed of the greens. I've changed my line of thinking. I'll now opt for laying it up or playing for the center of the green."

Watson and Tom Kite equaled Norman's 68 and stood 2 strokes behind in a group that included Tommy Nakajima, a pleasant, solid pro who exorcised a haunting demon on his way to a round of 4 under par.

Nakajima's eagle 3 on the 13th hole was a full 10 shots better than his score there eight years before. Ten shots. In one of the most miserable and memorable holes in major championship history, Nakajima registered a 13 on 13 in 1978. He drove into a ditch, took a penalty stroke with his drop, hit an iron to the fairway, then a wedge into the creek in front of the green. Playing from the creek, he hit another wedge that popped up in the air and came down on his foot for a 2-stroke penalty. Then, handing the club to his caddie to get it cleaned, Nakajima grounded the blade in the hazard for another 2-stroke penalty. He then hit a wedge over the green, chipped on, and, naturally, missed his putt. Thirteen.

On this day, though, it all seemed so simple. He hit a driver to the fairway, 5 wood to the green, and then drained a 25-footer for a ghost-busting eagle. "This hole is my friend now," Nakajima said afterward with a smile. "I feel I have more than redeemed myself for that bad day."

Also of note, Jack Nicklaus came in with a 69 to finish the third round 4 shots behind Norman. As if to stay under the radar (to the extent that a five-time champion can), he commented afterward that it was "the first time I've broken 70 since I can't remember when."

With 18 holes to play, Nicklaus was certainly within striking distance. A player can make up 4 strokes in the first four holes at Augusta, so the five-time Masters champ could certainly do it in 18. The problem was the logjam in front of him and the company to his sides. He left the course on Saturday in a group of seven at 214 with eight more players lower than that.

ROUND 3 LEADER BOARD

Norman	68	210
Price	63	211
Ballesteros	72	211
Langer	69	211
Hammond	67	211
Kite	68	212
Nakajima	71	212
Watson	68	212
Nicklaus and 6 others		214

Preparing his column for the following day, legendary *New York Times* writer Dave Anderson posed an interesting question. He asked the five former multiyear champions playing in the tournament which shot on the back nine is the most difficult with the Masters on the line. Interestingly, Ballesteros, Watson, and Player agreed that it was the tee shot to the shallow green on the 155-yard 12th hole over Rae's Creek. Palmer said it was the approach shot on the 500-yard, par-5 15th with the pin cut near the front and the downslope toward the pond in the back. In vintage Nicklaus fashion, Jack refused to answer. Always positively thinking about always thinking positive, he explained, "I don't want to be standing over a shot and remembering that I've said this was the toughest shot. On the back nine at Augusta, every hole is tough."

Round 4

Nicklaus woke up Sunday morning with that beautiful old dizzying feeling, a once-familiar friend that had somehow become a stranger. All of the great athletes know it. Most love it; some live for it. It is a perfectly balanced recipe of equal parts anticipation and excitement topped with a teaspoon of nervousness and encrusted in a thin layer of anxiety. It all comes together in the pit of the stomach and is tossed gently like a salad by those butterflies you always hear people on the brink of greatness talk about. The combination of ingredients is common to many, but the exact measurement of each is intimately known to precious few.

Before leaving for the golf course, Jack got a phone call from his 23-year-old son, Steve, wishing him good luck. "What's it gonna take, Dad?" he asked.

"I think it'll take 66 to tie," answered Jack, "and 65 to win."

"That's the number I had in mind, too," replied Steve. "Go shoot it."

Nicklaus in his prime was known not only for identifying a final-round total that would win a tournament, but also for being able to go out and shoot it. As he hung up, he had to know 65 was within a shot or two of the right number, but actually going out and shooting it was a different story. Even the best version of Nicklaus, which at this point was a decade-old memory, would be hard-pressed to go that low on Sunday at the Masters. Hell, the now two-day-old course record was only 2 shots better, and people had been playing the course for half a century.

Another magnificent morning broke in Augusta on a day that will be remembered for as long as golf is played. Describing the conditions, Bob Verdi of the *Chicago Tribune* wrote, "It was a day so choice it shouldn't have had to end."

Blue and green never went together so perfectly as the Georgia sky and the prestigious jacket did on this special Sunday.

The front nine on the final day of a major is like the early rounds of the NCAA basketball tournament. Players can either stay alive or get knocked out of contention, but nobody is securing a tournament victory there regardless of how well they play. Nicklaus had a round of even par going before closing out the front with a birdie on 9 for 35. The leaders, playing behind Jack, were jockeying for position, with the more-seasoned players keeping the big picture in mind. Veterans of the game understand the relative importance of birdies and bogeys in the early stages of Sunday golf, where conservatism is the better part of valor.

Nicklaus got a little something going with birdies on the 10th and 11th to make it three straight, but he gave back one of those shots with a bogey on 12. Rare is the time that a bogey spurs a player on to victory—especially when that bogey leaves the player 4 shots off the lead with six holes to play. Jack's 4, however, on the par-3 12th, turned out to be significant. As he walked to the 13th, he says he was angered by his play on the previous hole. Shooting at the fat part of the green, he had pulled a 7 iron to the back fringe. From there, he chipped but got a bad kick to the left, leaving him six feet for par. A spike mark pulled his putt offline, and he settled for the bogey that would change his approach the rest of the round.

As he stood over his tee shot on the par-4 13th, he later recounted, "I figured if I was to have any chance at all, I've got to kick myself in the rear, get aggressive, and just go."

Nicklaus's older son, Jackie, who was caddying for Jack that day, recounted in a 2006 *Golf Digest* article written by Guy Yocom, "If a ball catches one of the branches on the left at 13, it's going in the water. It almost always does. He used a 3 wood and pulled it a little. It missed one branch by a foot. I told him, 'Dad, that's not good on a 24-year-old's heart.'"

According to playing partner Sandy Lyle, Jack's reply was, "What about me? I'm 46!"

Nicklaus went on to birdie the hole to move to 5 under par, and with late afternoon shadows growing long, the leader board was stacked like this:

Ballesteros	-7	(12)
Kite	-6	(12)
Haas	-5	(18)
Stewart	-5	(16)
Nicklaus	-5	(13)
Norman	-5	(10)

Within minutes, Nicklaus's suddenly manageable 2-stroke deficit disappeared in a flash. While Jack chipped his 3rd shot to tap-in range for par on the 14th, Ballesteros whipped up a little magic two holes back with his second eagle of the day—a 3 on the par-5 13th. At this point, even as well as the Golden Bear was playing, he trailed by 4 strokes, and there simply were not enough holes left to catch Ballesteros without a bit of help from Seve himself. There was also the matter of Tom Kite, who was a stroke ahead of Nicklaus, and Payne Stewart, who headed to 17 tied with Jack at 5 under par.

Two holes back, overnight leader Greg Norman tried to swing his way out of a daylong malaise. At 1 over par through 10 holes, the Shark was about to ditch his stated conservative strategy and play golf the way he was born to play it: aggressively.

The 15th hole, a sometimes certifiably insane par-5 monster fronted by water that has swallowed up so many golf balls and hopes over the years, was on this day rather reasonable. With almost nonexistent winds and a deep pin placement, players were taking dead aim on the shot that Palmer identified the day before as the hardest on the back nine. In fact, when Nicklaus stepped to the tee, three of the previous four golfers to play the hole—Corey Pavin, Mark McCumber, and Gary Koch—had eagled it. On the very hole that Gene Sarazen rode to glory 51 years earlier, Jack ripped his drive right down the middle. As the Nicklaus duo arrived at the ball in the fairway, Jack said to Jackie, "How far do you think a 3 will go here? And I don't mean the club."

Jackie knew his father wasn't referring to a club because, first, they were 204 yards from the hole, which was a certain 4 iron, and, second, because they were both thinking the same thing—eagle.

"I think it will go a long way, Pops," came the reply.

Jack took his stance and put that old sweet swing on the ball, spanking an arrow-straight missile. He rocked back slightly on his follow-through, then started walking forward confidently as the ball traveled toward the green. He brought his right hand to his forehead to shade his eyes from the sun, almost as if he was saluting the shot. With their backs to the sun, the greenside gallery tracked the ball on its way in, and began to cheer as the ball was still in flight. The noise level grew as it came down on a nearly perfect line, landed about a foot short of the cup, bounced about six feet forward, checked up, and rolled another seven feet, stopping within a couple paces of the back edge of the green, about 12 feet from the cup.

With about 500 yards behind him, the four yards that remained were all that stood between Nicklaus and his eagle. As playing partner Sandy Lyle putted out, Jack and Jackie surveyed the green, looking at the putt from every angle. Jack stepped up to it, just to back off when the sound of distant applause broke his concentration. And then again. Finally, as he stood over the ball for the third time, he set it in motion. Both the line and pace were perfect, and as it tracked toward the hole, the result was not in doubt. To the cheers of the gathered spectators, the ball dropped. Jackie couldn't contain his excitement. The roar of the crowd seemed to lift him off the ground. He jumped about a foot and a half in the air, while Jack pumped both his fists about head high and retrieved his ball from the cup.

As he walked off the green within 2 strokes of the lead, he flashed a smile that seemed at once both shy and sly. The pair moved on to the 16th tee as the old man said to the kid, "If you jumped like that all the time, you could've played basketball at North Carolina."

The junior Nicklaus chuckled to himself. He had felt the same kind of excitement four years earlier caddying for dad in that great U.S. Open at Pebble Beach. In 2006 he was quoted by *Golf Digest*, saying, "In the final round [at Pebble] he birdied 3, 4, 5, 6, and 7 to share the lead. I was beside myself, and on the 8th hole, I said, 'Dad, this is great! Keep it going!' He promptly bogeyed the hole.

"I didn't want a repeat of that. [So, at the Masters] I was very careful not to distract him. I'd say matter-of-factly, 'Nice birdie. Let's make another one.' By then I knew enough to try to help him to stay in the moment."

When Jack's putt fell on 15, looking on were four spectators who hadn't bought tickets. Watching from the fairway waiting to approach was the twosome of Tom Watson and Tommy Nakajima. Back on the tee waiting to hit were Ballesteros and Kite. There is no way to know to what extent the eagle and subsequent roar of the crowd had an effect on them, but in that all-important space between a golfer's ears, the moment certainly resonated, and perhaps hung around a while.

On to the par-3, 170-yard 16th. When Nicklaus got to the tee box, the leader board suddenly had only one player ahead of him.

Ballesteros	-9	(14)
Nicklaus	-7	(15)
Kite	-7	(14)
Watson	-6	(15)
Norman	-5	(13)

Jack stood over his teed-up ball and focused for a second before stepping back. He replanted his right foot as if to check the firmness of the earth below and decided he didn't like it. He picked up the tee and ball and checked several other spots before finding one to his liking.

Taking his 5 iron back in that classic familiar arc, his head stayed fixed over the ball. He brought the club through, and the instant he made contact, the crowd collectively began to quietly rumble. As the ball traveled, Nicklaus took his eyes off of it, stepped forward, and bent down to pick up his tee. Jackie demanded, "Be the right club." Jack casually shot back, "It is."

He straightened up as the ball sped beyond the water to the front-left of the green and toward the waiting short blades of grass. "I knew it was going to be close," he later said. But how close?

The ball landed about five feet short of the pin and a bit to the right. The bounce on the green, which had been firmed significantly from the hours of sunshine, took it three to five feet beyond the cup. Instead of rolling forward, though, that sucker bit like a junkyard dog and spun back and took the slope down to the left, heading close enough to the pin to set the gallery into a frenzy. The ball missed the cup by about three inches, and continued on until it settled and stopped within four feet of the hole. Ho-hum, just your basic pressure-filled pin-seeking dart from a 46-year-old, five-time past champion.

Nicklaus watched as Lyle converted a birdie putt before stepping up to drain the three-and-a-half-footer that he insisted was "no gimme" for another bird of his own. He smiled again as he took in another round of wild applause, handing the putter to his son with his right hand while acknowledging the crowd with his left. He had played holes 9 through 16 in 6 under par to move to 8 under for the tournament, 1 shot off of Ballesteros's lead. Speaking of Ballesteros...

Seve hit a 302-yard cannon shot from the 15th tee and undoubtedly heard the roar of the pro-Nicklaus gallery up ahead as he slowly chased it up the fairway. The talented Spaniard reached his ball, sitting 198 yards from the pin, dead center of the fairway, and chose his weapon for an approach that could go a long way toward a green jacket. He and Kite had to wait several minutes for Watson and Nakajima to putt out, and when the green finally cleared, Kite hit first. Tom hit a beautiful approach of more than 200 yards and stuck it to within 20 feet of the cup, looking at birdie at the worst.

Whether it was the pressure of holding a shrinking lead, the long wait to hit, or a combination of those and other factors, Ballesteros then hit what might have been the worst shot of his professional career. Like a weekend duffer playing the local muni, the eventual winner of 49 European tour titles, nine PGA tournaments, two Masters, and three other British Opens, badly snap-hooked a 4 iron that had disaster written all over it. The ball was working hard left from the start, traveled only about 170 yards and, like a hungry gannet spying a fish in the ocean below, made a beeline for the water.

As the ball disappeared, there was actually cheering from the gallery. The usually staid, always-polite Augusta crowd had seen Nicklaus's score go up on the leader board, realized Jack actually had a chance, and simply reacted with their hearts when Seve's ball went Greg Louganis.

Nicklaus heard the reaction and had spent enough time on golf courses to understand it. "It was a loud roar with a deep groan underneath. Not a nice sound," he said. "I've never wished anyone bad, but I knew exactly what had happened. People were yelling, 'It's in the water! It's in the water,' and I'm thinking, 'I know that.'"

Former player and modern-day announcer Ken Venturi was quoted by *Golf Digest*, saying, "There have been three great types of roars at Augusta. Arnold Palmer got wild, whooping roars. Ben Hogan got a roar that really was very loud, sustained applause. Jack that year had a roar unlike any other, and Seve got a full dose of it. It got into his head. If it had been any other player who had made the eagle at 15, Seve wouldn't have given a damn; he would have been over the water, easy.

"Hogan always said there were three ways to beat somebody: you outwork them, you outthink them, and you intimidate them. Jack intimidated Seve, there's no way around it."

Nick Price added, "Seve heard those cheers, and it crushed him."

•••

Nicklaus, Nicklaus, and Lyle, along with Sandy's caddie, Dave Musgrove, headed toward the 71st hole of the Masters in a surreal scene of sound and sunshine. The old golf-clap had been sent to pasture hours before, and its replacement, thunderous applause, suddenly had friends. The traveling twosome of Whoop and Holler arrived at Augusta, and made themselves rather comfortable, as if they owned the place, which, at this point, they kind of did.

Perhaps caught up in the chaos, Nicklaus pulled his tee shot on 17. The ball drifted far left, off the fairway, well beyond the ropes, and into some thick grass between two pine trees about 125 yards from the center of the green. A few yards longer or a few yards shorter, and the trees would have interfered with either the ball path or his stance, but this day being what it was, Jack had a clear look at the green.

Back on 15, Ballesteros took his drop, chipped up, and missed his par putt. A few minutes earlier he had been lying in the middle of the fairway looking at possible eagle. He walked away, seething with bogey. Kite, meantime, took 2 putts for birdie, and suddenly a trio came together in what had to be the most exciting threesome until the movie *Wild Things* was released 14 years later.

Ballesteros	-8	(15)
Kite	-8	(15)
Nicklaus	-8	(16)
Watson	-6	(15)
Norman	-6	(14)

Now in a tie for the lead, Nicklaus stood over his ball between the trees. He hit a wedge high in the air but short and left of the flag, which was in the back-middle. Had the ball come out with normal backspin, it would have been trouble. Since he hit out of the rough, though, the ball bounced forward and rolled nearly to the back of the green, stopping about six feet short of the fringe. It was an outstanding approach, but there was still a lot of work to do.

THE SHOT

At about 20 feet, the length of the potential birdie putt was challenging but wasn't the bulk of the problem. The hole sat on a crest that ran through the green, making for a tricky read and an almost-indiscernible proper line. "It's hard to appreciate on TV how hard that putt was," Jackie recalled. "I took a look and told Dad I thought the ball would break a little to the right."

Jack acknowledged that it would break right but added, "I think it's going to come back left at the hole because Rae's Creek is going to have an influence at the end of the putt."

Wearing white shoes, old-school plaid pants, and a yellow polo-style shirt with a small golden bear logo over the heart, Nicklaus slowly approached his ball and settled into the silence. He was bent slightly at the waist, his back at a 45-degree angle with his head hanging parallel to the green, eyes over the ball. He looked up at the cup and then back down at the ball. He repeated the motion over and over, checking his line four times. He was in his stance for a full 18 seconds before drawing back his MacGregor Response ZT putter.

"He missed a couple of putts on the front nine," remembered Jackie in that *Golf Digest* 20-year-anniversary article. "Dad's tendency in putting was to peek, to lift his head. Early in the week he told me to remind him to keep his head still. I did that on every single putt. A few times he peeked anyway, and when he did, I told him. Needless to say, there was no peeking on the back nine."

With his head down and still, Nicklaus sent the ball rolling smoothly forward and on a line a few inches to the left of the hole. About a quarter of the way to the cup, the murmur in the gallery started to rise and, with every revolution of the ball, got louder. Halfway there, it started its slight break to the right. Four feet from the hole, as Jack predicted it would, the ball began to move back to the left. It wasn't really breaking as much as it was seemingly fighting the green to hold the line to the hole. Jack was still in his stance, but now narrowing his eyes to focus in on the ball as it approached its intended target. As it got within about two feet of the cup, Nicklaus had the club in his left hand and started to dip his torso and move the putter forward. He jabbed the club in the direction of the hole as if to give emphasis to a final telepathic push, and with a thrust, straightened his body upward quickly while raising the putter in an arc skyward. The ball dropped perfectly into the cup, and the crowd erupted in a joyous booming convergence of celebration and relief before it even hit the bottom. Nicklaus reacted with a double fist-pump, starting shoulder high and punching upward above his head.

Like a runner taking a festive victory lap after a race, he walked toward the hole to get his ball with the throngs cheering wildly. He walked off the green with a slight smile, let out a quick exhale, and rolled his eyes upward. The CBS cameras, of course, were tight on Nicklaus's face and later showed a freeze frame of the gesture—the old champion exiting a grand stage, gazing toward the heavens, unmistakably saying a silent "thank you" for the blessing of an unforgettable moment.

"He knew he had to make it, and it was such a hard putt," Lyle remembered. "Not only could it break either way, it would have been easy to hit it six feet past. And he just lasered it in there."

Smooth and understated television announcer Verne Lundquist, who called the putt with a simple, "Yes, sir!" says he will never forget the crowd reaction to the beautiful birdie.

"It had the quality of a roar you hear in an enclosed arena, where the noise has nowhere to go. It was like the sound bounced off the sky and came back at us. It made my tower tremble."

Strangely, decades later, Nicklaus says, "I've putted that putt a thousand times since, and it's never broken left again."

After three days of golf, and 98 percent of a fourth, Jack Nicklaus had taken his first lead of the 1986 Masters. The birdie on 17 allowed him the luxury of approaching the final hole without needing to make up strokes. He left the driver in the bag and hit a 3 wood safely into the fairway.

It seemed as if the entire gallery had been sucked in by Jack's march, like wayward debris to a black hole. Still, there was significant action playing out behind him. Ballesteros and Kite each parred the 16th, and Norman was headed toward a potential eagle putt on 15. As Nicklaus made his way toward his ball, fans lining the 18th fairway reacted as if they were witnessing the reincarnation of Elvis. This wasn't Augusta, it was a rock concert. Jack still had work to do, but he soaked in the applause that many felt he would only hear again as he rode off into his career sunset in the rocking chair of a once-great champion, not on the white horse of a resurrected hero. As the gallery settled down and Jack gripped a 5 iron, the leader board stood like this:

Nicklaus	-9	(17)
Ballesteros	-8	(16)
Kite	-8	(16)
Norman	-6	(14)
Watson	-6	(17)

Nicklaus had left himself 175 yards to the two-tiered 18th green. The Sunday pin placement was deep, about midway between the steep upward slope that ran through the middle of the green and the back fringe. Seemingly unaffected by the pressure, he put his old, classic swing on the ball, sending it flying on course toward the flag. He said later that he hit the ball exactly as he wanted to, but as soon as it left the club, he felt a breeze kick up. The wind was strong enough to win a battle with the ball, which landed on the slope and rolled back to the lower plateau. It stopped about 40 feet from the cup, leaving him a dangerous long putt over the ridge.

There is a crucial aspect to golf known as "local knowledge." It usually refers to a player's familiarity with a course he plays often. A tidbit of information known by one player and unknown to another can be the difference in a tournament. As Nicklaus surveyed the potentially precarious putt, he relied on a nugget of a more intimate bit of local knowledge that made him quite comfortable with the shot.

Over the years, some of the greens at Augusta had become too severely sloped, and it was Nicklaus's course construction company that was commissioned to level them out. The 18th happened to be one of them, so naturally Jack putted extensively on the green earlier in the week. He knew exactly what the ball would do when it came over the ridge, and he gauged both the line and the speed nearly perfectly. The ball was directly on target, but stopped about four inches short of the hole. Jackie later said the putt was the best shot his father hit all day.

Nicklaus marked the ball to let Lyle putt out and had a laugh with his son. When Sandy finished, Jack tapped in to close out one of the most memorable rounds in major championship history.

Jack fished his ball out of the cup, bared the pearly whites in a broad smile, and raised his arms in triumph. He shook hands with Lyle and Musgrove, and then embraced Jackie in a Golden Bear hug. To thunderous applause, father and son exited the green with their arms around each other's shoulders, as if walking off screen in the final scene of a cinematic tear-jerker.

A man who just four days earlier was widely considered over the hill, tore up one of the most challenging courses in the world under extreme pressure to take the final-round lead into the clubhouse. He would say afterward, "I played today like the guy I once knew."

He had blistered the back nine with five birdies and a bogey, coming in with a 6-under-par 30 for a Sunday total of 65—the exact number he said he would need to win.

But he hadn't won yet.

Two holes back, Norman registered his second straight birdie to move to 8 under par, 1 stroke behind Nicklaus. On 17, Kite held steady at 8 under with a par, and Ballesteros fell to 7 under with a 3-putt bogey.

Nicklaus made his way into Jones Cabin, worrying only about the fit of his sixth green jacket. "Walking off, I thought I had it won," he said in an interview before the 20th anniversary of the '86 tournament. "I knew Ballesteros had self-destructed, and I didn't realize Norman was going to make a whole bunch of birdies. I hadn't even thought about Kite."

Suddenly, though, as he followed the action on television, he must have felt like a holed-up fugitive watching news reports of authorities closing in on him.

The first to fall was Seve, who had been in command of the tournament just an hour before. He needed a miraculous eagle on the final hole to force a playoff, but could not find the magic. Next up was Kite, who needed a birdie to tie. His approach on 18 was far better than Jack's had been, as he deftly rifled a sugary 6 iron over the ridge and onto the upper shelf, leaving himself about 10 feet short and to the right of the pin. Just 10 feet.

With a playoff a distinct possibility, "I probably should have gone to the practice tee," acknowledged Nicklaus in a 2006 interview with CBS's Jim Nantz, "but if I had done that, I wouldn't have had near as much fun!"

Kite, who had finished in the top 10 in nine of the previous 11 Masters, was very much alive for his first major victory. He stepped up to hit the most meaningful putt of his life and made a beautiful stroke. The ball was heading for the center of the cup as it neared the hole but broke slightly left in the last couple of feet and barely slid by on the low side, coming to a stop about two inches from the cup, as if to mock its maker. Kite collapsed into a catcher's crouch, laying the shaft of the putter on his head. The club fell to the grass, tumbling like Kite's bid at the green jacket. Exasperated, he would later say that he had putted on that exact line seven or eight times in the practice rounds, and the ball never once broke left.

Still sitting on the couch watching the events unfold on television, Nicklaus turned his attention to the only man remaining who could turn this glorious day into a lifetime of what-ifs.

Norman was a solid player, appealing in most every way. He had more than his share of supporters at PGA Tour stops around the United States, just not at the moment. Having never won a major, and entering the year with only two PGA wins, Norman went to the 72nd hole with an enormous opportunity. A par would force a playoff; a birdie would win it.

He hit an easy 3 wood off the tee, leaving himself in the middle of the fairway, 200 yards from the front edge of the green. Norman's caddie handed him the 4 iron and said simply, "It's the perfect club."

The man called "the Great White Shark" would ultimately suffer an unbelievable amount of heartbreak in major championships, but more often than not, he was the victim of an opponent's greatness. On this day, on this hole, on this shot, he was victimized by his own mistake. He left his clubface open as he came through the ball, sending it flying far to the right toward the mass of humanity standing off the side of the green.

Longtime golf analyst Ken Venturi said he was shocked by how poor of a shot Norman hit, opining that from where the ball was in the fairway, Greg would make 10 birdies to every bogey.

However, bogey appeared likely, and certainly all thoughts of a tournament-winning birdie died an instant death. In a matter of a few seconds, Norman went from a playoff-at-worst scenario to a playoff-at-best. His first inclination was to putt the ball, despite the fact he was still about 15 feet from the green. However, once the spectators were cleared out, he noticed there were indentations from portable seats all over the grass. Forced to chip, he left himself about 12 feet for par. The usual short murmur that follows a crucial shot became a sustained buzz, which accompanied the Shark to his ball like a taunting serenade.

As Norman moved into putting position, Augusta National, grew silent. Thumping hearts pounded in spectators chests all over the grounds while every eye in the place turned toward a single shot that may or may not decide a championship. He stroked the putt firmly. No sense in leaving it short.

The ball approached the hole at a good pace, but was inches offline. It ran about four feet by, but the wheels on the most unlikely of victory celebrations were set in motion before it came to a stop. Norman made the come-backer for a disastrous bogey and a tie with Kite for second place. But the Masters has never been about second place.

The TV cameras were turned toward Jones Cabin, from which moments later, Nicklaus emerged. He smiled that smile again—half in triumph, half in disbelief. Uniformed police officers, some of whom were failing miserably in any attempt to hide their own joy, escorted him. They were half armed escort and half Golden Bear fan club. One of the cops can be seen clearly on television raising both arms in victory while grinning from ear to ear. Jack, meantime, looks almost incredulous at having survived the course, the competition, and the declaration of his demise.

Nicklaus zigzagged through the crowd, heading to Butler Cabin, taking a beating from well-wishers slapping him on the back with congratulations along the way. He stepped inside the cabin, where a few minutes later, in front of a national television audience, 1985 champion Bernhard Langer, seemingly a bit in awe, spoke softly as he slipped the coat on the Bear. The fit was perfect.

POSTSCRIPT

CBS Announcer Jim Nantz, who has become synonymous with the Masters, tells the story of an incident that took place in the Augusta darkness following the events of that fateful Sunday. As Nantz was walking toward the parking lot, Venturi came up behind him in a golf cart and offered him a ride.

Venturi, who was 55 years old and a lifelong golfer, asked the young broadcaster how old he was.

"Twenty-six," Nantz answered.

Venturi, who finished second in the 1960 Masters, smiled at the sheer youth in the answer. "Let me tell you something," he said. "I don't know how many of these tournaments you will announce, but I can assure you, you will never see a greater day here than the one you saw today."

Sandy Lyle's caddie, Dave Musgrove, who worked bags in professional golf for 35 years, had the best seat in the house for Nicklaus's win. As Jack's playing partner, Lyle finished in 11th place, but Musgrove remembers that gorgeous April Sunday because of what the "other guy" did. In 2006, after a lifetime in the game, which included four major championships for his own player, Musgrove said that the final round of the 1986 Masters was, "Quite simply, the most wonderful day I ever enjoyed on a golf course."

Later that summer, Jack finished tied for eighth in the U.S. Open, his last top 10 at a major not played in Augusta, Georgia. At the Masters, though, he seemed to always find a bit of magic somewhere along the way to either make the cut or make a run. The following year, as defending champion, he finished in a tie for seventh place. In 1990, at the age of 50, he came in sixth. And, perhaps most impressive, at age 58, four years away from current-day eligibility to collect social security, Nicklaus finished a mere 4 strokes off the lead, in a tie for sixth. One of the many players he beat that year was the defending champion— a young superstar in the making named Tiger Woods.

Nicklaus played in his 44th and final Masters in 2005. Missing the cut, his appearance was limited to 36 holes. As he finished, he shared a private moment with his caddie, Jackie, and, a year later, revealed through tears what he said.

In 1969, Jack explained, his father was sick with cancer and was being wheeled into surgery. The senior Nicklaus picked up his head and lightheartedly said to his family, "Don't think it ain't been charming!"

Thirty-six years later, walking off his final green at the Masters, Jack repeated those exact words to Jackie.

Nicklaus says to this day people approach him to tell him where they were and what they were doing the day he made time stand still. Grown men—men in their seventies and eighties—might not be able to remember birthdays or anniversaries but they remember, in detail, the final round of the 1986 Masters. Why was that slice of golf history so meaningful to so many?

Legendary *L.A. Times* columnist Jim Murray wrote of the event:

> *Well, we're all 20 years younger today. [Nicklaus's winning] brings a sense of order, stability to our world. The rest of it may be in change, ferment, chaos, but you think, "Well, it can't be too bad. Jack just won The Masters." It's 1963 again, and there's no Kadafi, inflation, Central America.*
>
> *What does the old song say? "I'd Give You a Million Tomorrows for Just One Yesterday"? Well, Jack gave us one more yesterday. Tomorrow can wait. He is not going gently into that good night. He's going to eagle it.*

There may have been more talented players, and perhaps there have been more dutiful ambassadors for the sport, but nobody has ever meant more to the game of golf than Jack Nicklaus. He was portrayed as the villain in his early years—a cocky fat kid with sights set on taking down the King. He was painted as a hero in his later years. As long as Jack was playing golf, all of our dreams were alive and youth was our companion. In between, he was a rock-solid omnipresent tour de force—an awesome combination of physical tools and mental toughness. He not only played on another level, but he thought on another level too. If he was entered in a tournament, he was the odds-on favorite to win. If he wasn't entered, it was not an important tournament.

He racked up win after win, year after year, decade after decade. All the while, he played the game with a grace and dignity befitting royalty. There were no public spats, no run-ins with the law, and no vulgar behavior. He played the game the way it was meant to be played—always a sportsman, always a gentleman, and with an unwavering code of honor. The extent to which he values the ethics that are at the very heart of the game is evident in a long-ago incident that, according to *Sports Illustrated*, still bothers him to this day.

The year was 1974. Nicklaus was one of three golfers trying to make up ground on leader Gary Player in the final round of the British Open. Caught in a large pot bunker less than 100 yards from the green, Nicklaus took a mighty swing, but the ball hit the front wall of the trap and rebounded back toward him. There were chunks of sand and little rocks flying everywhere. Jack ducked to avoid the ball but clearly felt something hit him on the back of the shoulder.

Joe Dey, a powerful figure in the golf world for the past half-century, was a rules official that afternoon, standing within a few yards of the bunker. Nicklaus asked Dey if the ball had actually hit him. Dey said that the ball had gone entirely over Nicklaus and it must have been a piece of debris that Jack felt on his shoulder.

Jack continued play, finished the round, walked into the scorer's tent, and sat down to go over his scorecard. One more time he asked Dey whether he was sure it was not the ball that hit him. Dey assured Nicklaus he was, and Jack signed the card for a 71.

The total was good for a third-place finish, 5 behind Player and 1 behind Peter Oosterhuis. The problem, as Nicklaus saw it, was that he finished a stroke ahead of Hubert Green, but if that ball did in fact hit him, the 2-stroke penalty would have left him with a 73, a shot behind Green.

The difference in the prize money would have been £500, mere pennies over the course of a lucrative golfing lifetime, but the principle of the matter is what was at issue.

Amazingly, 32 years later, he says, "It still bothers me."

That, as much as all the talent and all the titles, is Jack Nicklaus.

Greg Norman, shown here with the British Open trophy he won at Turnberry Scotland in 1986, was at the height of his career in the mid-'80s and was in an epic battle for the 1987 Masters.

CHAPTER SEVEN

1987:
A Native Son

PRELUDE

Dealing with his loss in the 1986 Masters could be considered a mere training ground for the sporting heartbreak that lay ahead for Gregory John Norman. Born in Queensland, Australia, in 1955, Norman won his first professional tournament at age 21 and later burst onto the American scene as a veritable freak show of good looks, athleticism, and a quiet charisma that attracted a Sunday morning gallery like free Bloody Marys. He was tall, handsome, and eminently likable. He was as cool as Fonzie with a Popsicle in the dead of the Alaskan winter, the all-time tour leader in cool. He even talked cool. His features were so distinct and chiseled, sportswriter Jim Murray remarked, "You could chop wood with his face."

After 20 worldwide victories, Norman broke through on the PGA Tour in 1984, winning both the Kemper and Canadian Opens. That year he finished second at the U.S. Open and tied for sixth at the British.

Following his disappointment at Augusta in '86, he suffered another one at the next major. As he did in the Masters, he led the U.S. Open after three rounds but didn't win that tournament, either. In a classic meltdown, Norman shot a final-day 75, 9 strokes worse than winner Raymond Floyd.

At the British Open, he once again led after three rounds, and despite many golf insiders whispering about another inevitable fourth-round collapse, he played a solid and steady round of 69 to win his first major, dominating the field by a full 5 strokes.

Heading into the 1986 PGA Championship at the Inverness Club in Toledo, Ohio, the Australian was the clear-cut favorite. He gave nobody any reason to believe he didn't deserve the pre-tournament hype as he took the lead on the first day and bulked up his edge to a full 6 strokes during the third round. One man, however, did apply a bit of pressure. Bob Tway, whose only three PGA tournament wins to date had come earlier that year, stormed in with a course-record 64 to cut Norman's lead to 4 shots.

Greg was growing quite familiar with the 54-hole lead; he left the course that night as the only man in history to hold the top spot in every one of a season's four majors through three rounds. Considering he led the previous three by a single stroke, he was particularly comfortable with the 4-stroke bulge in Toledo.

If he could hold on the following day, he would join the great Walter Hagen, who did it in 1924, as the only player to win the British Open and the PGA Championship in the same year. Norman had not only flexed his golfing muscle to become widely accepted as the best golfer in the world, but he was drawing comparisons to the best ever.

"He's playing at a level comparable with Jack Nicklaus in his prime," said Peter Jacobsen, whose view of Norman was from behind—far behind—as he went into the final round in a distant third place, a half-dozen strokes back.

An unrelenting rain on Championship Sunday forced a postponement of a round in which the leaders were only able to complete one hole before play was halted. Both Norman and Tway parred the first, leaving 17 holes to play on what became Championship Monday.

It didn't take long for things to get interesting as Norman bogeyed the 3rd hole and Tway birdied it. In an instant, a comfortable 4-stroke lead had been cut in half.

On the 9th, the roles were reversed. Norman rolled in an 18-footer for birdie while Tway missed a short par putt and walked away with bogey. Nine holes down and nine to go, the lead was back to 4, exactly where it had been after three rounds.

Heading to the 10th tee, Norman said to his caddie, "There's still a long way to go. Let's put in a real solid nine holes." After the round he commented, "I had 4 shots with nine to play, and you should feel pretty secure with that."

Two holes later, half of that security was gone. It was more bad luck than bad golf that led to a double bogey for the Australian who hit a strong tee shot into the fairway only to see the ball roll into a divot. He then picked the ball clean with a 2 iron that drifted into a green-side bunker and another bad lie. He blasted out into some wiry rough from which he chipped out, took 2 putts, and walked away with a double bogey. Tway, meanwhile, had a far-less adventurous experience, taking a run-of-the-mill par to get back to within 2 shots.

One of the best drivers on tour, Norman could always rely on his prodigious length off the tee but sometimes went through stretches in which he lost his accuracy. Unfortunately for him, one of those stretches started on the 12th hole as he hit the first of four consecutive tee shots that missed the fairway. There was no blood on number 12; Tway pulled to within 1 with a birdie on 13, and pulled even with a par on 14 while Norman scrambled for a bogey.

In what suddenly felt like match play, the men stayed tied with pars on 15 and 16. Norman seemed headed for a 1-shot edge on 17, but Tway executed a cotton-soft sand wedge that rolled perfectly on the sloping green to within three feet. He got his par, and they remained tied.

The final twosome on the course moved on to the 17th hole of the day, the 18th of the round, and 72nd of the tournament: two men, one hole, one prize.

Off the tee of the 354-yard par-4, both players' tee shots came down flirting with the edge of the fairway. While Norman's ball took a mostly forward bounce into the light rough, Tway's 1 iron kicked to the right, disappearing into the next cut, which was made up of far heavier rough. Advantage Norman.

Relieved to see his ball wasn't buried, Tway approached with a 9 iron, but found more trouble, landing in the front-right bunker. Norman's shot, a wedge from 123 yards, landed on the green but spun back off the putting surface, nestling in some green-side rough.

Working in Tway's favor was the fact that his ball was resting on the upslope of the bunker. Working against him was the way the green sloped away from him toward the hole. He stepped into the sand, dug his heels in as if doing the Twist, and told himself, "Get it close."

He opened the blade of his sand wedge and struck a smooth blow, popping the ball out softly in a perfect arc. It came down on the green beyond the fringe and began rolling toward the flagstick, picking up speed as it went. It took the slope, broke a bit to the left, hit the pin with a thud, and disappeared into the cup. Tway, craning his neck, saw the ball drop and started jumping around with his arms in the air as if he had just holed a shot from the sand on the 72nd hole to win a major championship.

"I wasn't trying to make it. I'm not that good," Tway said later. "I was just trying to get the ball close. It's just like a putt that you lag. Sometimes they go in." And sometimes they miss the cup and roll 20 feet past, as Norman said later it would have had it not hit the stick.

Greg, of course, after the final-hole debacle at the Masters and the final-round disaster at the U.S. Open, could only watch and shake his head. He still had a shot to tie, but given his lie and the slope of the green, his chip was a tougher shot than Tway's. Not wanting to leave the ball short, he put down his sand wedge in favor of a pitching wedge and took dead aim.

All of the day's 18th-hole miracles, though, had been used, and Norman's run at a tie rolled 10 feet past the cup. He 2-putted on the way back for a final-round total of 76, including a 4-over-par 40 on the back nine. He hit just six greens in regulation during the final round and blew a 4-stroke lead with eight holes to play. His 76 was the worst score of any player to finish in the top 10, and when viewed in comparison to his first three rounds of 65, 68, and 69, had to be considered, despite his British Open title, another piece of evidence of the ever-growing case against Norman as a player who did not perform well under pressure.

According to a *Chicago Tribune* article the following day, Pete Bender, Norman's caddie, was first to greet the Shark in the locker room after the postmatch press conference. "Jack Nicklaus dropped by a minute ago to say he's sorry," said Bender. "Sorry about your tough day."

Norman smiled warmly at the sentiment and then coldly at the irony of from whose lips it had come.

He had just made his way through a crowd of about a hundred fans outside the locker room asking for an autograph. "I'll be down to sign in a few minutes," said a still-shocked Norman, "but first, I'm going to grab me a beer."

THE TOURNAMENT

THE MASTERS, AUGUSTA NATIONAL GOLF CLUB AUGUSTA, GEORGIA, APRIL 9–12, 1987

The early-April sports week started with the epic, long-awaited fight between Sugar Ray Leonard and Marvin Hagler. Leonard came out of retirement to take the bout for which he had to fight as a middleweight for the first time in his career. He walked into Caesars Palace in Las Vegas as a heavy underdog and walked out as the WBC middleweight champion, winning in a split decision. *Ring* magazine later named the fight boxing's "upset of the decade."

The next morning, across the country, players began arriving in Augusta for the 1987 Masters. Like Hagler, Greg Norman was an odds-on favorite, but he had company. Seve Ballesteros, who had suffered through his own bad shots and the gallery's bad manners on the final nine a year earlier, returned, and was a strong second choice.

Seve, who had won six tournaments worldwide in 1986, appeared poised to forget his Masters collapse, but an entire year later, he refused to forgive the gallery for its cheering as his hopes disappeared in the water on the 15th hole. Largely ignoring the paying customers through practice rounds, Ballesteros did not even acknowledge fans around one of the greens as they serenaded him with a chorus of "Happy Birthday" on the day he celebrated his 30th. Asked about his obvious indifference, he answered simply, "Some things you don't forget."

Norman checked into town with a quiet confidence and sky-high hopes for the season ahead. His 1986 "Saturday Slam" might have been maddening as he went through it, but in retrospect had to be viewed as clear-cut proof of his potential to be not just the best player, but a dominant player on the PGA Tour.

Norman, now 32 and the winner of 42 tournaments worldwide, ranked first on the circuit's money list with more than $650,000 in earnings the previous year and was both walking and talking like a man on a mission.

"What I did in 1986 helped create a plateau for me," he said before the 1987 Masters. "It has allowed me to project myself into the future. Last year was all a positive, and an incentive, as well. The positive and the incentive come from having been on the doorstep to the Grand Slam. Now, I'm more determined to go out and bust the door off its hinges."

The implication was, of course, that Norman had sights set not only on winning the Masters, but also on winning every major. A reporter pointed out that nobody in history had won the Grand Slam in a single season. Norman did not miss a beat in replying, "It only takes one guy to do something special. Somebody ran a four-minute mile, and pretty soon everybody was. Al Geiberger shot a 59, and everybody said that if he could do it, so could they."

Regarding his devastating loss a year earlier, he said, "As of 6:00 that Sunday, I've been determined to come back, play well, and try to win the tournament. Jack performed something that was great to see for golf and him. But I've been keen to get back here ever since. That's just a part of my inner makings, what pushes me and makes me so determined."

While handicapping the tournament, how could anybody overlook Jack Nicklaus? Hadn't the entire golf world made that mistake a year earlier? There were several players whose Las Vegas odds were shorter than Jack's, but a year removed from his electrifying 30 on the back nine, and despite shooting par or better in just half of his 14 competitive rounds in the new season, he had to at least be part of the conversation.

"I'm not as good as I once was," Nicklaus said before the tournament. "I know that and it's obvious the guys who play against me know it, too. But I'm still going to have my moments where I can play good golf. I happened to find a pretty good moment here last year, and I might find another one or two this year at the majors, as well."

And lastly, Bob Tway, who had, after all, won the previous major, even if it did take a miracle out of the sand to do it. Tway finished tied for eighth in the Masters in '86, just his second time playing the event. Practice rounds in '87, though, were hellish for him as he fought through a runny nose and watery eyes just to finish. An unusual amount of pollen in the Augusta air was bothering Tway's allergies, leading him to say, "Maybe I'll try using light sunglasses between shots."

Round 1

There is no way to ever know for certain exactly what the Augusta National Committee's intentions are. Suffice to say, the international espionage community has what can be considered "loose lips" compared to the ultraexclusive, megasecretive group that assembles clandestinely on a regular basis regarding the state of their tournament. It was pretty clear, though: they had issues with the greens seeming to get progressively softer and more puttable over the years. The Augusta National greens were switched from Bermuda grass to the faster bent grass in 1981 but had been kept moist since—until this year.

Players began to get a feel for the changes to the putting surfaces early Thursday morning, and frustrations on the greens continued all day. In the new math of the Augusta greens, a six-foot putt called for three feet's worth of power from a putter. Surfaces were cut so short and left so dry that an even slightly downhill putt had little chance of stopping at the hole.

Norman and Ballesteros both opened with respectable 73s, while Tway sneezed his way around with a 78. Greg said afterward, "I had a putt on 16, where the only way I could hit it soft enough was to whiff it and let the air get the ball rolling. They're going to have to water the greens or they'll lose a couple of them. At numbers 11 and 13, the grass is blue because it's so dry."

Payne Stewart shot a 71, leaving him 2 strokes off the lead, and commented, "I'm sure they didn't intend for the greens to get like this. Go out and look at 18—for about 15 feet around the hole, it's starting to turn purple. The grass [has started] dying!"

Blue, purple, whatever the color, the greens were the main topic of conversation after an opening day on which only eight players broke par. Leading the way was John Cook, a 29-year-old Floridian who, ironically, had been putting horribly since the beginning of the season.

In his first Masters in three years, Cook, who, like Nicklaus, was a star at Ohio State, had the benefit of playing the morning before the constant, dry, swirling wind hardened the greens even more. He took just 24 putts en route to a day's best 3-under-par 69. "I played Muirfield one year when they said they had the fastest greens of all time, and these are comparable to those," Cook said afterward. "I can't imagine them any faster, but they are so good, so smooth, it's a matter of pace. If you miss it, you just go hit it again."

Cook, ranked 82nd on the tour's putting list, was the serendipitous beneficiary of a luggage problem while traveling. "An airline lost my clubs," he said, forcing him to call home to have an old set, which included the brass Bullseye putter he used in college to win the 1978 U.S. Amateur, sent to him.

The putt that made Cook's round was a slippery big bender on 16. "That was one of the scariest putts of my life," he said. "It started breaking and broke into the hole, but I guarantee you if it hadn't hit any part of the hole it was off the green. It was probably the only 12-footer I've ever had that I didn't want to putt."

Cook's playing partner also had a great round. Augusta native Larry Mize took just 25 putts to gingerly play his way through round one. Birdies on the final two holes left him a stroke behind Cook, all alone in second place.

One man not complaining about the greens was Jack Nicklaus. "I like the golf course the way it is, hard and fast," he said after opening with a 2-over-par 74. He did, though, have a tough time getting started as he snap-hooked his drive off the opening tee through the trees and into the 9th fairway. "I opened defense of my title with the worst tee shot of my life," he half-joked. Perhaps Jack was satisfied with his number because it was exactly what he shot in the opening round a year before. And we know how that one ended.

Round 1 Leader Board

John Cook	35–34	69
Larry Mize	36–34	70
Curtis Strange	33–38	71
Calvin Peete	34–37	71
Tom Watson	37–34	71
Bernhard Langer	34–37	71
Corey Pavin	37–34	71
Payne Stewart	35–36	71
Five others		72

Round 2

Greens were still fast but far less firm as a gentle Friday breeze replaced the swirling Thursday winds on a gorgeous 78-degree Georgia spring day. John Cook nearly parlayed his first-round lead into a halfway-home disaster with bogeys on each of the final four holes on the front nine, but pulled it together and finished strong. Birdies on both 17 and 18 left Cook with a second-round 73, good enough for second place. "It was one of those days, and I'm glad it's over," he said. "When you make four bogeys in a row, you start to wonder a little bit."

The only player able to creep ahead of Cook was Curtis Strange, a 10-year tour veteran with nine PGA wins to his credit. He led the tour money list two years earlier and would lead it again in 1987, but had yet to win a major.

It was a Strange day, indeed, as Curtis surged to the lead by registering five birdies, five bogeys, seven pars, and an eagle. His round of 2 under par came on the heels of an opening-round 71, and put him a shot ahead of the field with a 3-under-par total of 141.

For a while, it looked like everybody would be chasing Corey Pavin, who rolled through the front nine in 4 under par. Pavin, though, lost his touch on the back and came in at 39 for a total of 71. He joined Cook in second place, as did Larry Mize and Roger Maltbie.

Known best for a careless loss following a dramatic win a dozen years earlier, Maltbie shaved a full 10 strokes off his opening round 76, smoking Augusta National with seven birdies against a single bogey en route to a day's best 66.

In 1975, after winning the Pleasant Valley Classic in Boston, Maltbie went out to celebrate at a tavern called T.O. Flynn's. Somewhere between finishing off one drink and ordering the next, Maltbie's $40,000 first-place tournament check disappeared. "I had a lot to drink," he recalled. "I remember showing the check to some people, but I have no idea what happened after that."

When he discovered the check was missing, he called the tavern in vain to see if anybody had found it. He then called the tournament sponsors and was relieved to find out they were happy to issue a new one. Later that day, the tavern owner tracked down Maltbie, saying a janitor had found the check.

Maltbie told him it had been canceled, so for years, the winner's check to the 1975 Pleasant Valley Classic hung framed on the wall of a fine drinking establishment in suburban Boston.

It was a good day for Jack Nicklaus, who shot an even-par 72, including nine straight pars to finish his round. Jack hit the weekend 5 shots off the lead, a stroke better than he stood the previous year through 36 holes. He said afterward he simply needed to shoot a round in the 60s on Saturday. "You'd be surprised what that will do for you. I'm playing well enough. If I just get some putts to fall…you never know." Then, in case anybody had forgotten, he added, "I've been known to shoot 65 out here."

Ballesteros and Norman made it through to the weekend, as well. Seve earned a 71 for a two-day total of even-par 144 and a tie for ninth place, three strokes back. Greg got off to a great start that included an eagle on number 2, but he could manage no better than a 74 for an aggregate of 147 and a six-way tie for 24th place. Norman claimed to take no joy in the fact that Bob Tway missed the cut.

Also missing the cut was Scott Verplank, who registered a 10 on the par-5 15th hole, while Jumbo Ozaki did him 1 worse with an 11. That pair was in good company, though, as stars such as Arnold Palmer, Ray Floyd, and Lee Trevino also played higher than the cut line of 151. Trevino fired a parting shot on his way out of town, telling the media, "I'd rather go milk cows than look at one more of those four-foot side-hillers."

Round 2 Leader Board

Curtis Strange	71–70	141
John Cook	69–73	142
Larry Mize	70–72	142
Roger Maltbie	76–66	142
Corey Pavin	71–71	142
Tom Watson	71–72	143
T.C. Chen	74–69	143
Bernhard Langer	71–72	143
Seve Ballesteros	73–71	144
Joey Sindelar	74–70	144
Andy Bean	75–69	144
Jay Haas	72–72	144
Lanny Wadkins	73–72	145
Ben Crenshaw	75–70	145
Mark Calcavecchia	73–72	145
David Frost	75–70	145
Bobby Wadkins	76–69	145
Howard Clark	74–71	145
Jack Nicklaus	74–72	146
Payne Stewart	71–75	146
Mark McCumber	75–71	146
Jodie Mudd	74–72	146
Nick Price	73–73	146
Norman and 7 others		147

Round 3

One of the great personalities in golf history, Sam Snead used to work a vintage gag on a new young playing partner at Augusta.

Snead would point to the towering pine trees that provide a barricade for the dogleg along the 13th fairway and say, "Son, when I was your age, I'd mash my tee shot clear over them trees and cut this sucker down to a par-4."

The kid, whoever it might have been, already in awe of the legend, would invariably crane his neck, lifting his eyes to the impressive treetops, likely wondering if the tale was true. He'd look back to Snead, who would put his hand chin-high and say with a smile, "'Course, when I was your age, those trees were about yea high."

In a practice round before the 51st Masters, Jack Nicklaus retold that story to Greg Norman, offering a challenge to the Australian who was known as a prodigious hitter. Norman accepted, and swung mightily, barely clearing the trees, which had grown to nearly 100 feet tall.

In round three, Norman made his move, quickly climbing the leader board. As he came to the 13th, he thought back to his round with Nicklaus and looked again toward the treetops. "I asked my caddie about going over the trees," he said after the round. "But I didn't have enough you-know-what today. Maybe tomorrow. If I'm desperate enough."

Hard to imagine his being desperate after a sizzling Saturday 66 pulled him to within a shot of the lead. Without a single bogey, Norman shot the low score of the day and the best of his 27 rounds in Masters competition. He sounded afterward very much like a man who had forgotten about the disappointment from a year earlier.

"Maybe my first two rounds [73 and 74] were a blessing in disguise," he opined. "Maybe I had been trying too hard, and fading back a bit made me relax. I was 6 or 7 shots out and I decided to go out and enjoy the course. I love this course. I love this tournament. I love this place."

Greg was a shot behind a twosome of Roger Maltbie, who fired a third-round 70, and 1984 champion Ben Crenshaw, who dramatically lowered his score for the second straight day. Crenshaw, who insisted he had been playing the best golf of his life recently, followed his opening round 75 with a 70 on Friday and a 67 on Saturday.

Gentle Ben shot even par on the front, then went on the tear that took him into the lead. He made four straight birdies beginning on the 12th hole, missed makeable birdie putts on 16 and 17, and closed it in style with a 12-footer for birdie for a "pack your bags, we're on the move" back-nine of 5-under-par 31.

Even though two others were ahead of Norman, many of the players challenging for the lead had their focus directly on the Shark. Nineteen eighty-five champ Bernhard Langer, who, like Norman, finished the third round a shot off the pace, was to be paired with the Australian favorite for the final round. "I've played with Greg many times," Langer said, looking forward to Sunday. "I'll just have to play my own game and let him play his. If he drives it 300 yards, and I hit mine 260 or 270, I'll just have to find mine and hit it again."

Echoing the big-hitter sentiment, Crenshaw added, "The ground shakes when Greg tees off. It can be intimidating just to watch."

Even Nicklaus, the defending champ and an obvious candidate for "best of all time," pointed to Norman's round-three leader-board ascent as an example of the ground a player could make up in 18 holes. Jack, for the third straight day, did not manage to break par, and his 73 left him with a total of 219, 7 strokes behind. "But look what Norman did today and look where he is," Nicklaus pointed out. "He was 3 over par when he started and now he's up there. I'm at 3 over and I'll let you take a guess at what a 65 might do for me."

Well in front of Nicklaus and slightly behind the leaders was a capable foursome, tied for third, 2 shots back. The group included Ballesteros, who was looking for his third green jacket and shot a 70 for his best round of the tournament; Larry Mize, who fired a second consecutive 72; Curtis Strange, the man who carded a miserable 80 in the opening round of the 1985 Masters but rallied to lead by 3 strokes before collapsing on the final nine; and T.C. Chen, best remembered for his double-hit of a chip shot in the 1985 U.S. Open.

Fifty-four holes down, 18 to play, and the overnight star-studded standings were stacked with five major-championship winners among the top 10 on the board:

Ben Crenshaw	75–70–67	212
Roger Maltbie	76–66–70	212
Bernhard Langer	71–72–70	213
Greg Norman	73–74–66	213
Seve Ballesteros	73–71–70	214
T.C. Chen	74–69–71	214
Larry Mize	70–72–72	214
Curtis Strange	71–70–73	214
Lanny Wadkins	73–72–70	215
Mark McCumber	75–71–69	215

Round 4

The April warmth and just enough of a breeze made for pleasant conditions on a Sunday that far surpassed any possible expectation of drama in Augusta. The lead changed hands like the mustard bottle at a hot dog stand with a different player seeming to take over on each hole. At times there were five-way ties at the top, and rare was the moment that saw the lead belong to a single player.

As is often the case in a major championship, the final nine holes saw players fall away one by one, orchestrating their own tournament demise with the deadly weapons of conservatism, bad decisions, poor execution, or ill-timed bravado.

Nicklaus made some noise early, going out in 34, and really got the place going with a 3 wood/3 iron/15-foot-putt eagle on the 13th, but missed makeable birdie putts on each of the final three holes to come in with a 36. His Sunday 70 was the defending champ's best round of the tournament, but he finished 4 strokes off the lead.

As the groups finished and the scores went up, the list of players who could win dwindled. It was subtraction by attrition.

Larry Mize fell out of a briefly held lead with bogeys on 14 and 15. But on the final hole, he came up big in the clutch, hitting an almost perfect 9-iron approach to set up a five-foot birdie putt for a final-round 71. As he walked to the clubhouse, he did so with a tenuous 1-stroke edge on the field, but still on the course were a half-dozen guys who were looking to steal a jacket like a thief working a coat-check closet. The players who had a shot to knock off Mize made up the final three groups of Ballesteros/Chen, Norman/Langer, and finishing last, Crenshaw/Maltbie.

Strange, playing with Mize, started the day 2 back and pulled to within a single stroke of the lead with an even-par 36 on the front. The back, however, was a different story as he started: bogey, double bogey, and bogey, on his way to a 40 to check out of contention.

Ballesteros/Chen: Arriving at 17, Seve was in a dead heat with Mize. On the par-4 17th, the tournament-tested Spaniard hit a gorgeous approach to within six feet. He converted the birdie putt and headed to the 72nd hole leading by 1. That lead, however, vanished moments later with Mize's clutch birdie on 18, leaving Seve needing a par to tie and a birdie to take back the lead.

Ballesteros, who had insisted all week long that he had entirely forgotten his debacle from the previous year, smoked a perfect drive down the middle of the fairway on 18. He pulled out an 8 iron and, perhaps with the memory of his snap-hook from '86 not entirely forgotten, left the shot out to the right. It caught the edge of the trap and rolled in, effectively killing his chances for a win in regulation.

Remember, though, as a *Sports Illustrated* article pointed out later that week, "Seve in the sand is like Brer Rabbit in the Brier Patch. Long before he ever played a real golf course, Ballesteros was hitting sand shots on the beach of Pedrena...that is still his home."

He channeled all that experience and dropped it into one perfect swing, sending the ball spinning softly out of the bunker and onto the green, where it rolled to within six feet. He calmly rolled his putt into the heart of the cup and walked off tied with Mize, his chances for a third green jacket still alive.

Just like Curtis Strange, Seve's playing partner, T.C. Chen saw his own chances disappear with a double bogey on the 11th hole and a back-nine 40. Chen shot one of the day's worst rounds, falling from a tie for fifth into a tie for 12th with a 76.

Langer/Norman: Bernhard Langer, the eventual winner of 69 tournaments worldwide, including two Masters, saw his hopes all but disappear early on the back nine with bogeys on 10, 12, and 14. They did disappear on 15 when his second shot found the water. He limped to the finish with a 76, a tournament total of 1 over par, and a tie for seventh place.

Norman, who had used that incredible back-nine birdie run to get into contention on Sunday the previous year, shot 37 on the front and started the back with consecutive bogeys. Heading to the par-3 12th, he was even par for the tournament and in danger of falling out of contention completely when once again, he went on a tear. The big Aussie birdied three of the next four holes to get back to his day's starting score of 3 under. A bogey at 16 dropped him back to minus 2 and a tie with Mize, who, two groups ahead, moved to 18.

Word of Mize's birdie on the final hole reached Norman at 17, where Greg answered with a birdie of his own. Norman then went to the final hole in effectively the same situation he had been in 12 months earlier against Nicklaus—par to tie, birdie to win. As Seve finished with a par ahead of him, Norman stood, for the moment, in a three-way tie with Mize and Ballesteros.

Regardless of any athlete's mental toughness, and no matter how hard a person might try to forget a past failure, there is no way 1986 was not running through Norman's head as he stepped to the tee. He considered the layout of the final hole, and unlike the previous year when he opted for a 3 wood, he instead pulled out the big dog, his driver. He teed up his ball and crushed it with a mighty swing designed to carry the 285 yards over the back end of the two-part bunker on the left side of the fairway. Carry it, he did. The drive was well struck, flying as if it should have had a stewardess aboard. It took a big bounce to the left, then rolled through the gallery and into an open area, 314 yards from where it started.

As he walked up the fairway, he moved without pause past the spot from which he approached the year before. As he passed, he shook off thoughts of one of the worst shots of his career, which ultimately cost him the most prestigious title in golf. Now, 364 days later, he continued walking another 104 yards. Despite being so far left, he had a clear look at the green.

As he set up for his approach, he gripped not a 4 iron from 200 yards out, but a sand wedge from a mere 96.

Another good shot. The wedge landed with a thud, leaving him about 22 feet for a championship-winning birdie.

Success can sometimes be like an eraser to a chalkboard full of failure. Norman had a chance to wipe away the sting of the defeat from the year before, and stroked what he thought was the perfect putt. It was on target the entire way as Norman stood as still as a statue—not wanting to move, almost for fear of changing any single molecule of the current structure of the universe. The ball, though, started to break left about half a foot from the cup and slid softly by, missing the lip by mere millimeters. Norman watched incredulously and then fell to his knees. A minute later he tapped in for par, completing an erratic round in which he registered six birdies, six pars, and six bogeys.

"I honestly don't know how it stayed out of the hole," he insisted later. "I mean, a foot and a half from the hole, I said to myself, 'Don't move. Don't say a word. It's going in.' I was just waiting for the place to erupt."

It would erupt all right, but not for another hour or so.

Maltbie/Crenshaw: The final pairing of the day came to the par-4 17th tee in an interesting situation. With Ballesteros and Norman both playing ahead of them, Roger Maltbie and Ben Crenshaw were looking at Larry Mize's minus 3 as the score to shoot for, but uncertain if it ultimately would be. Crenshaw was at that very number, and Maltbie was 2 strokes back at minus 1.

Crenshaw gave himself a golden opportunity to take the lead as he put his drive safely in the fairway a mere 134 yards from the green. His caddie, Carl Jackson, suggested the pitching wedge, but Ben insisted on his 9 iron. "I've had him for a dozen years here," Crenshaw would say of Jackson after the round. "He's a fantastic caddie, and I don't overrule him often."

He did, though, in this case, and paid for it dearly. The 9 flew toward the back of the green, skipped, and rolled a few inches onto the fringe. His chip from about 20 feet ran uphill halfway to the cup, and downhill eight to 10 feet past it. He 2-putted for bogey, losing a crucial stroke to fall to minus 2.

Maltbie, on the other hand, birdied, gaining a stroke to minus 2.

By the time they reached the 18th fairway, they knew that minus 3 was indeed the leading score. Neither player, though, could manage a 72nd-hole birdie. Crenshaw missed a 20-foot putt, and Maltbie, a 35-footer, as they each settled for par and final totals of 2-under-par 286.

After the round, the men both reflected on what could have been, Crenshaw with seemingly more regret. "Seventeen will live with me for a while," said Ben. "If I had listened to my caddie, I might have been in the playoff."

Maltbie, known as a free spirit often seen with a cigarette in one hand and a beer in the other, looked at it a bit more casually. "At least I had a chance to tie for the Masters championship," Roger said. "I just didn't do it."

He did, though, win more than $30,000 for his tie for fourth, and the check did, in fact, make it into his bank account without incident.

THE PLAYOFF

After four days and 72 holes, three men stood above the rest, and you could not find a more diverse trio anywhere.

Getting together on the 10th tee to start the fourth three-way playoff in Masters history were Seve Ballesteros, the fiery Spaniard; Greg Norman, the charismatic Australian; and Larry Mize, the soft-spoken American who was born and raised in, of all places, Augusta, Georgia. Drawing numbers out of a straw hat, it was determined that Seve would hit first, followed by Norman and then Mize.

The 10th hole at Augusta can always be problematic, but on this day it was closer to diabolical than it was difficult. Half of the 54 men who had played it on Championship Sunday left with bogey or worse. The other half parred. There were no birdies. None.

The hole, as complex as it is beautiful, measures 485 yards. The key is to drive to the left side of the fairway, which runs downhill to a green that is a full 75 feet lower then the tee box. Leaving the ball out to the right is effectively creating a par-5 with a long approach from a side-hill lie, the playoff equivalent of suicide.

Ballesteros and Norman each hit their tee shots well, landing within five yards of each other in the center of the fairway. Mize, clearly the underdog in the threesome, stepped up huge, ripping his shot down the left side, traveling at least 30 yards past the two superstars.

Just like their drives, Seve's and Greg's approach shots from about 180 yards were very similar, both winding up on the back edge of the green—Norman's back left, Ballesteros's back right. They made their way up the fairway, stopping about 50 yards beyond Mize's ball, pausing only so Larry could hit, as if the American were merely a pesky hindrance to the business at hand. The two foreigners, perhaps feeling that this was their playoff, didn't even bother looking back. They stood focused on the green, moving forward again only after hearing the sound of Mize's club make contact with the ball.

What they saw from there may have made them change their thinking. Mize's shot from 145 yards was right on target. It landed in the middle of the green about a third of the way from front to back. As late as it was in the day, the greens were as hard as they had been for the opening round, and Mize's ball didn't bite a bit. Instead it just rolled forward, heading toward the pin, which was cut about 20 feet from the back edge. It came to a stop just eight feet from the cup.

Seve was away and putted first. It was a difficult putt—a slippery, downhill, left-to-right breaker that he missed a few inches to the right, rolling five feet by. Norman was next. He too missed, but rolled just three feet past.

Suddenly, Larry Mize was looking at an eight-footer to win the Masters. He understood the magnitude of the moment and put a good stroke on the ball, starting it at the right edge of the cup, or maybe a touch outside. Rolling slightly uphill, the ball took the break, but a couple of inches before arriving at its destination, it broke just to the left of the front lip and stopped about two inches to the left of the hole. Two inches: it was all that separated Larry Mize from a green jacket.

Ballesteros stepped up to take his par putt, but shockingly, he missed it. He rolled it by on the left without even grazing the edge of the cup. He picked up his head and stared straight forward as if he had seen a ghost. And just like that, he was one.

Norman converted his par, and as he and Mize moved from the 10th tee to the 11th green, every single spectator on the grounds moved right along with them. There were no other groups to follow. There was nothing else to watch.

Going against traffic was a heartbroken Severiano Ballesteros, the two-time former champion, making a livid and lonely walk back to the clubhouse. Scores of newspaper reports the next day say he was crying as he went.

"It was a shock for me to see Seve 3-putt," Norman would say later. "Of all the people in the world in head-to-head competition, he's the last one to do that because he doesn't give things away."

But in this case, he did. With only two men left to beat, Ballesteros apparently let the pressure get to him, and suffered his second straight soul-shaking Masters disappointment. The just-turned-30-years-old Spaniard should have been in the prime of his career with at least a decade of productive golf ahead. Turns out, although he did win the British Open the following year, his career peaked early. His best golf was played in his twenties, and he would never again come so close to a third green jacket. He returned to play Augusta every year through 2003, but in those 16 tries, he managed just two more top 10s and did not make a single cut after 1996. In 2007, after a three-year hiatus, he tried again, but again couldn't manage to make the weekend.

Suddenly it was tee for two under a setting Southern sun. Norman and Mize stood on the box ready to drive the 455-yard par-4 that plays downhill with a fairway slightly sloped from right to left. At the green, the fairway opens to the right, but the green curls to the left, leaving the front part of the putting surface guarded by a dangerous pond in front. To the right of the green is a large sand trap, and as an added bonus, just in case players aren't completely preoccupied with the other hazards, Rae's Creek awaits placidly behind the entire width of the green.

It is a green that is so well protected, with so much potential trouble, some feel it is best to leave an approach shot short and try to par by getting up and down with a pitch and a putt. In fact, it was the great Ben Hogan who said, "If you ever see me on that green in two, you'll know I mishit my second shot."

Only four players had birdied the hole in the final round, but it had been a friend to Mize the entire tournament; he birdied it in the opening round and parred it in the next three. Norman had sandwiched a pair of pars between a pair of bogeys.

THE SHOT

Both men shrugged off the pressure of the moment and laced good drives, leaving them manageable approaches. Norman hit first, an aggressive but safe shot that stayed clear of the water but still caught a piece of the green. He ended up on the right fringe, about 40 feet from the hole. It would be an extremely difficult birdie putt, but par was quite likely.

Mize, perhaps worried a bit too much about the water, left his 5 iron from 190 yards out way to the right. *Waaay* to the right. As soon as the ball left his club, he turned quickly in disgust. "Oh my gosh!" he muttered forcefully and disgustedly as he turned back to watch the ball land well off to the right of the green.

Huge advantage Norman.

Mize was a total of about 140 feet from the pin, but there was a lot to consider in that space and beyond. The ball was a good 80 to 90 feet off the front fringe, and then another 50 or 60 feet to the pin. There were several ways to play the shot, but with the green sloping to the left and downward toward the back, Mize went through a mental trial-and-error to decide on the right one. He thought a pitch landing on the green would probably not hold and a high wedge shot landing in the rye grass in front of the green might stop dead. He opted for a bump-and-run.

The strategy was to hit a low wedge that would bounce before the green, but have enough momentum to roll up softly toward the pin. The best information he had to work with was his knowledge of the slope and speed of the green. In a fortunate twist of fate, he had made a 20-foot par putt from virtually the identical line earlier in the day. Leaving a reasonable chance at par was the goal.

He settled into his stance, alternately looking up and down, checking the angle of his clubface to the ball and visually measuring the variables of the terrain between he and the flag-stick. He brought the club back about thigh high and came through crisply as Norman watched from a vantage point in between Mize and the hole, but off to the right. Norman's line was similar enough to Mize's shot that he could learn something by getting a good look at the roll of Larry's ball.

The ball came off Mize's wedge straight and true—hard enough to get through the grass surrounding the green but soft enough to stay on the putting surface. The ball bounced first about 10 feet short of the green, and then again about six inches short. It settled into a roll, moving at an interesting speed and falling off to the left as it went. With each foot, each revolution, the shot looked better and better. Twenty feet from the hole the gallery started to murmur. It was not one of those shots that is obviously right on target from the begin-ning, but as the ball began to slow down and follow an arc toward the hole, it was becoming clear that this was not going to be just a good shot, but a great shot. Ten feet from the hole, the crowd noise rose and got louder with each fraction of a second that went by. As if shot from a gun by an expert marksman, the ball smacked into the dead center of the pin and then disappeared like a quarter going into a parking meter. The crowd roared. Mize lifted his arms with clenched fists, punching at the Augusta air. He broke into a slow, jubi-lant jog alternately clapping his hands and pumping his fists. He put both hands over his face, picked up his head, and raised his arms with his hands open as if to thank the heavens for his good fortune. With the crowd still cheering, he made his way to the hole, retrieved his ball, and walked off, looking down. As he exited the green, he put both hands up, taking in the applause and asking for quiet at the same time. The tour-nament wasn't over.

Norman could only stand and watch as his caddie, Pete Bender, patted him on the back, whispering something—likely, some kind of optimistic nonsense about prolonging the playoff by dropping the 40-footer. For the snake-bitten Australian, it had to feel like some kind of twisted, Satan-inspired déjà vu. Same shit, different major.

Norman hit his putt harder than he usually would to make sure it got to the hole, but in truth, it never had a chance. Even with the extra pace, the ball broke too hard to the left and missed on the low side. Before it even got to the cup, Greg accepted his fate and turned to walk toward Mize. A man feeling the throbbing sting of another unimaginably hard-luck loss was the picture of class, offering a genuine nod, kind words, and a congratulatory handshake.

On his way off the course, Mize spoke with the on-course reporter from CBS. Asked how he felt, he could manage just a few jumbled words, saying, "It's kind of walking on air right now."

Norman later said, "I couldn't believe it. I saw the ball rolling along, rolling along, rolling along, and I said to myself, 'Well, if it misses, it'll probably be four or five feet by.' I was just watching it to get the speed of the green, and as it got closer and closer to the hole, the more it looked like it was going in, and I said, 'Awwwwwww.' I just couldn't believe what was happening.

"When he tried to bump it on, I was happy," Norman continued. "I was thinking he might chip it all the way into the water. I thought he might try to land it on with a high soft sand iron. That's what I would have done. If I was where he was, I'd have been happy to make 5."

Mize made three.

And he didn't see a choice of shots. Looking back in a *Sports Illustrated* article in 2007, he said:

The nice thing is that there was only one shot I could play. I had to use my sand wedge and land it short of the green. If I landed it on the green or used a less lofted club, the ball could have run too hot and landed in the water on the other side.

When it went in, I threw my club in the air and ran around like crazy...then I thought, Larry, don't be yelling here. I picked up the ball, tried to quiet the crowd, and told myself to calm down and get ready to go to the 12th tee because you always have to expect the worst. I'm glad we didn't have to go.

Larry Mize was born in Augusta in 1958, attended both elementary school and junior high school in the small town, and finished high school at Augusta Prep. Augusta National, though often in his thoughts, was not available to him as a junior golfer. Growing up, he would play Augusta Country Club, which is located next to Augusta National, and he admitted "always looking at this course through the fence."

Asked in the post-Masters news conference whether he ever hopped the fence or played the legendary course by hook or by crook, Mize chuckled. He said, "No. You don't sneak onto Augusta National. My father knew some members, and he played here a couple of times, but I didn't. I wanted to earn my way on it."

Suffice to say, he did. Forever.

The victory netted Mize $162,000 in prize money, making him the 75th player in PGA history to reach the $1 million mark in earnings.

As if anything could make winning the Masters any better, Mize was helped on with his green jacket by his personal hero. Once upon a time, as a 13-year-old boy, Mize worked the scoreboard at the 3rd hole of the Masters and savored the moments he could get a mere glimpse of Jack Nicklaus. Now, here they were, forever linked as Masters winners, with the current champ slipping into the jacket being held for him by the former champ.

Mize was wearing a shirt with thick horizontal stripes. The bottom stripes were a deep violet color. The middle stripes were purple, and the top two, light purple. On his way in to the course that day, somebody commented on his attire, and he answered, "Hey, anything goes with green around here."

In his acceptance speech at the awards ceremony, Mize said, "As a little kid, you always have the one big dream that you hope will come true. Mine finally came true, and it's unbelievable."

FINAL ROUND

	HOLE	1	2	3	4	5	6	7	8	9	OUT	10	11	12	13	14	15	16	17	18	IN	TOTAL
	PAR	4	5	4	3	4	3	4	5	4	36	4	4	3	5	4	5	3	4	4	36	72
Player (Start)	(-2) Ballesteros	4	5	4	3	4	4	4	5	3	36	4	5	3	5	4	4	3	3	4	35	71
	(-2) Mize	4	4	5	4	4	2	3	5	4	35	5	4	2	4	5	6	3	4	3	36	71
	(-3) Norman	3	5	5	3	3	4	5	5	4	37	5	5	2	4	4	4	4	3	4	35	72

1987 MASTERS, FINAL SCORES

Mize*	70–72–72–71	285
Norman	73–74–66–72	285
Ballesteros	73–71–70–71	285
Crenshaw	75–70–67–74	286
Maltbie	76–66–70–74	286
Mudd	74–72–71–69	286
Haas	72–72–72–73	289
Langer	71–72–70–76	289
Nicklaus	74–72–73–70	289
Watson	71–72–74–72	289
Weibring	72–75–71–71	289

* won on second hole of playoff

POSTSCRIPT

"I didn't think Larry could get down in 2 from where he was, and I was right."

Greg Norman's declaration got a good chuckle from the gathered media, who were uncharacteristically treading lightly. The man had an incredible knack for finding a way to rise to the top of the substantial pile of still-smoldering rubble left from his on-course disappointments.

Searching for a bright side, he said, "When Tway got me in the PGA, I didn't have any majors left. At least now, I've got three to go this year."

The questions kept coming, and he stood there answering all of them. He didn't have a trophy or a green jacket, but he was conducting himself far more like a champion in defeat than many others ever had in victory. "I can't tell you how tough that shot was," he said of Mize's chip. "I just cannot tell you."

He was then asked which shot was harder, the one Mize just made or the one Tway made to beat him at the PGA Championship.

"Larry's," he said quickly and with certainty. "Bob was coming out of the bunker. You can spin it, stop it, make it run, whatever. But Larry's looking at water, looking at the green running away from him, different grasses cut different ways. Larry's was 30 percent harder than Bob's."

Whether or not it had yet occurred to Norman, the miraculous chip cost him far more than a golf tournament. Greg had a $300,000 bonus clause for winning the Masters written into his endorsement contracts. "I think I'm more disappointed now than any golf tournament I've ever played," he said. "It's probably the toughest loss I've ever had. I've got to swallow the pill, as hard as the pill is to swallow. I have a hollow feeling because Larry's shot is the toughest shot to make in golf. I don't think he could speak when he did it. I know I couldn't."

Greg Norman's golfing legacy to the casual fan will always be that of a hard-luck loser. Much in the same way that Bill Buckner will be remembered for a misplay of a ground ball, Scott Norwood for a missed field-goal attempt, and Chris Webber for an untimely timeout request, Norman will be forever linked with heartbreaking losses. It is fair to point out, however, that unless a golfer is in contention on the final hole of a tournament, there is no way he can suffer a devastating loss or, even worse, be victimized by another player's singular moment of greatness.

Norman pulled off a miracle finish of his own in 1990, roaring back from a 7-shot Sunday deficit in the Doral-Ryder Open, blistering the famed Blue Monster with an all-time course record.

His final-round 62 was just good enough to get him into a four-way playoff with Paul Azinger, Mark Calcavecchia, and Tim Simpson. The red-hot Norman continued his rampage on the first hole of sudden death, quickly putting the others out of their inevitable misery with a perfectly executed 22-foot, tournament-winning chip for eagle.

His greatest disappointment came at the site of two previous well-known failures. In 1996, a full decade after falling to Nicklaus in Augusta, Norman suffered a colossal final-day Masters meltdown for the ages.

Holding a 6-stroke lead going into the fourth round, Norman holed a bunker shot on his final swing of warm-ups and then headed for the 1st tee. It was all downhill from there.

A deadly mix of bad shots and bad luck, an atypical conservative approach, and a rock-steady, hard-charging challenger in

Nick Faldo combined to obliterate Norman's seemingly comfortable lead by the 12th tee. The unflappable Faldo shot a final-round 67 to Norman's 78. It wasn't even close. A special Sunday that seemed to be about a coronation ended instead in a long, drawn-out, nationally televised disaster. Watching the back nine, fans couldn't bear to look. Nor could they look away.

Yet, once again, the proud Australian handled himself with a grace beyond most people's comprehension. Stuck for hours in a nightmare seen by millions, Norman never once displayed anything short of perfect sportsmanship and golf etiquette. He estimates he received 20,000 letters of support in the weeks following the tournament.

Again facing the media after a memorable loss, he was asked to compare the loss to Faldo with the loss to Mize.

"In '87, Larry made the shot," he said. "If it was one in 10,000 or one in a million, he played the shot and was trying to make it. Here, I had a 6-shot lead. I had control, and I screwed up. It was nobody else's fault. I had no one to blame but myself, and you move on with it. Destiny wasn't going to let me win that golf tournament."

Hard-luck loser? Not exactly. Norman won 20 times on the PGA Tour and is credited with 69 other victories worldwide. True, he never won the Masters, but after the 1987 event, he went on to rack up 19 more top 10s in majors, including his second British Open championship in 1993. He dominated the weekly world rankings for a full decade, coming in at number one 331 times. No player, other than Tiger Woods, has been at the top for even 100 weeks.

Norman was the first golfer to exceed $10 million in career earnings and went on to build a business empire that made that figure look like chump change. Great White Shark Enterprises is a global corporation with companies dedicated to golf-course design, field turf, event management, wines, restaurants, sportswear, e-commerce, and more.

The numbers on the scorecard were low. The numbers on the financial statements are high. All things considered, despite the heavy dose of career heartbreak, Greg Norman is one of the most successful athletes in the history of sports.

The 1999 U.S. Ryder Cup team erupts in a spontaneous and controversial celebration on the 17th green.

CHAPTER EIGHT

1999:
International Incident

PRELUDE

With new uniforms on their backs and sharpened cleats on their feet, a talented and dynamic group of baseball players came together for spring training in March of 1927, on its way to becoming the most exciting and entertaining team in America's sporting history.

At the time, all was well in the United States. A complete victory in World War I turned the evils of a global fight into a fading memory. The stock market crash, still more than two years away, was a wildly unlikely scenario—not even considered a possibility in this developing era of great prosperity.

The time was right and the nation was ripe for heroes from the world of sports, and the New York Yankees were in the dead center of the white-hot spotlight. Babe Ruth had just signed a new three-year contract for $210,000, making him the highest-paid athlete ever, and went on to eat up everything that ensued—from the unprecedented publicity to opposing pitchers to hot dogs by the dozen. Like Ruth's in general, the public's appetite for a living legend was insatiable. With every Yankee's victory and every mammoth home run slugged by the Babe, his fame and popularity grew. The world of sports was in strong and capable hands.

On April 5, 1927, as the Yankees broke camp in Florida to make their way to New York, the American selection committee for the inaugural Ryder Cup met in Chicago. The group put forth rules for the upcoming international competition, deciding most notably that only golfers born in the United States could be part of the team that would face the British squad later that year.

The origins of what became the Ryder Cup are the subject of debate among golf historians, but it is known that the countries faced each other in friendly, unofficial competition for the first time in Scotland in 1921. The British made easy work of the Americans, winning the match 9–3.

In 1926, with the best golfers from abroad in the United States for regional qualifying for the U.S. Open, another match was arranged. The British teamed up with players from Ireland and once again had no problem defeating the United States, taking them out 13½ to 1½. In attendance was Samuel Ryder, an English entrepreneur who kind of stumbled upon the game of golf at the relatively advanced age of 50.

Ryder had built a fortune starting a company that packaged and sold gardening seeds. He worked such long hours building the business that his health began to suffer. Advised by his doctor to stick to a daily regimen that included exercise and fresh air, he took up golf. He became so passionate about the sport that he hired British professional Abe Mitchell to be his personal teacher and was in attendance as Mitchell beat British Open champion Jim Barnes to secure the 1926 aggregate win over the American team.

After play concluded, Ryder met Mitchell and teammate George Duncan for tea, where two American players, Emmett French and Walter Hagen, joined them. Though they were not actually playing the game, the men became one of the most significant foursomes in golf history as they sketched out plans for the first Ryder Cup competition, which was to take place the following year.

At stake: a sparkling, 17-inch-high, nine-inch-wide, silver and gold chalice, paid for and donated by Ryder. On the top of the cup, at Ryder's insistence, is a figurine of a golfer, made in the image of Abe Mitchell. Also at stake: international pride and bragging rights.

On June 3, 1927, as the Yankees cruised along in first place with a 30–14 record, already having outscored opponents by more than 100 runs, the first shot off the first tee of the first Ryder Cup match was fired. The United States team, captained by Hagen, hosted Ted Ray and the British team at the Worcester Country Club in Massachusetts. The squads were made up of eight golfers who each played one singles match and one alternate-shot doubles match. All competition was played over 36 holes under the match-play format. Despite losses in the previous two international team competitions, the Americans impressively rolled through the British team in the inaugural Ryder Cup, winning 9½ to 2½.

Other than a hiatus from 1939 to 1945, forced by World War II, the event was held every odd year with the teams alternating as host. Through several tweaks to the format, including increasing the total number of matches, the United States dominated the series, winning 14 of the first 17 competitions. The 18th, held at Royal Birkdale in 1969, is still being talked about to this day.

In the closest Ryder Cup duel ever, 17 of the 32 matches were not decided until the final hole. Tied at eight wins apiece after the first day, the British won five of the eight morning singles matches to put themselves in a strong position, needing only to split the eight afternoon matches to win the cup.

The American team, captained by the great Sam Snead, came back to win four of the first six after lunch. The aggregate score stood dead even at 15–15. The penultimate pairing of Billy Casper against Brian Huggett was halved, leaving only one match to decide the winner.

As golfing nations looked on, two young, evolving stars battled for the Ryder Cup and all it symbolized. Twenty-nine-year-old Jack Nicklaus and 24-year-old Tony Jacklin went to the final hole of their match all-square. Nicklaus dropped a clutch four-footer for par, putting a world of pressure on Jacklin to make a testy two-footer to tie.

With the pressure of a continent pressing on Jacklin's shoulders, Nicklaus moved toward him, extending his hand in one of the all-time great gestures of sportsmanship. Nicklaus conceded the putt, allowing Jacklin to halve the hole and halve the match. The two men shook hands with their respective teammates looking on, and the great international competition ended in the first tie in Ryder Cup history. Minutes later, as Jacklin expressed his appreciation, Nicklaus said, "Tony, I don't think you would have missed that putt, but in these circumstances, I would never give you the opportunity."

Under Ryder Cup rules, in case of a tie, the side holding the cup prior to the competition would retain it. The Americans once again left England with the cup but, because of the move by Nicklaus, were champions in more ways than a trophy could represent.

The American dominance continued for the next decade, and finally, with the United States having taken 16 of the previous 17 events (other than the tie in '69), both sides realized something had to be done.

During the 1977 matches, it was Nicklaus who approached the PGA of Great Britain, urging them, in the name of competition, to consider expanding the current British/Irish team to the rest of Europe. With the approval of both Samuel Ryder's descendants and the PGA of America, the new Ryder Cup would pit an American team against a European team, and as expected, the event quickly became far more than an every-other-year flexing of American golfing muscle over an overmatched British team.

Though the U.S. did win the first three matches under the new format, the Europeans broke the streak with a convincing win in 1985, and two years later defended their title with a 15–13 win in Ohio. The captains for that 1987 match: Tony Jacklin and Jack Nicklaus.

As the Ryder Cup moved into a more competitive era, sports in general became a high-stakes business, and media coverage grew, the matches began to take on a bit of an edge. There were unpleasantries exchanged and accusations of cheating between Paul Azinger and Seve Ballesteros in 1989, with the bad blood spilling over to an intense doubles match in 1991. There, Ballesteros and partner Jose Maria Olazabal beat Azinger and Chip Beck 2 and 1 in what is still accepted as the best pairs match in history. Despite the Europeans' angry victory, the Americans took back the Cup, winning 14½ to 13½.

Tempers cooled, as they will with a two-year wait between tournaments, but the tone of the matches seems to have forever changed. The events of 1989 and 1991 can be considered the unspoken beginning of a not-so-kind, far-less-gentle approach to the Ryder Cup, but the duel eight years later is one that will live forever as the obliteration of any pretense of goodwill.

What happened in the final international golf fight of the 20th century will never be mistaken for the intended spirit of the Ryder Cup. In fact, quite the contrary. It was a case of gamesmanship winding up and slugging sportsmanship right in the face with one hand while sliding a whoopee cushion under its all-too-polite-and-proper ass with the other. A new-age attack on an old-school approach. Anybody who saw the events of the 1999 tournament unfold, though, has to acknowledge that, even with a sense of civility and decorum missing, it certainly made for some damn good theater.

THE TOURNAMENT

Traveling in style, Jose Maria Olazabal set a world record within a world record. As the European team made its way to the United States aboard the Concorde, Olazabal cleared the aisle and walked to the front of the airplane. There, he set his sights on a makeshift hole near the back of the plane and stroked a ball with a putter borrowed from British Airways captain David Studd. Down the carpet it rolled, straight and true for the entire length of the 150-foot aisle, directly into the cup. With the Concorde traveling at nearly 1,300 miles per hour, and the putt taking 26 seconds to complete its journey, the ball was actually in motion for 9.2 miles, a world record. The flight from London to Boston took just 186 minutes, also a world record. A week later, Olazabal would figure prominently in the sinking of another long putt.

With the dawn of a new millennium just three months away, the teams got ready to compete in what had become a nearly dead-even matchup. After the early years of American domination, no more than two points had decided any of the past six Ryder Cups. The European team won three, the U.S. team won two, and there was one tie. In the new 28-match format, 15–13 had been the largest margin of victory, with three of the six ending in 14½ to 13½ scores.

Seventy-two years after the first official Ryder Cup event was played, the Yankees were back in first place, on their way to another World Series championship, and the great international golf tournament was back in Massachusetts with another team of Yanks coming in as heavy favorites.

At the same club at which an unknown 20-year-old amateur named Francis Ouimet shocked the golf world by winning the 1913 U.S. Open, Ryder Cup captains Ben Crenshaw and Mark James gave their teams a final Friday-morning pep talk before the start of play. The opening-day format called for only doubles competition—four alternate-shot matches in the morning and a quartet of four-ball matches in the afternoon.

The American team got off to an unexpectedly slow start, losing two matches, winning one, and tying one against a European squad that trotted out four of its seven Ryder Cup rookies. It wasn't so much Europe's 2½ to 1½ edge that was disappointing, but the particular matches the U.S. team lost.

The two most powerful American pairs came up short, with Tiger Woods and Tom Lehman losing to Sergio Garcia and Jesper Parnevik 2 and 1 (2 holes up with 1 to play), and Phil Mickelson and David Duval falling to Colin Montgomerie and Paul Lawrie 3 and 2.

Woods and Lehman took an early lead, going 2 up through 5 holes, but their success ended right there. The pair didn't win a single hole after the 5th, with Woods failing to capitalize on a perceived advantage off the tee as his prodigious length was canceled out by an uncharacteristic lack of accuracy. Lehman left birdie putts short on 13, 15, and 16, and slid one by on 17, where the Europeans closed them out.

In the other match, David Duval caught a glimpse of his own frustrating future, driving erratically while managing to hit just two fairways. For his part, Mickelson missed three putts inside eight feet, and the duo never led after the 6th hole. Credit, too, to Montgomerie and Lawrie who played the entire round without a bogey and needed just 16 holes to chalk up a point for Europe.

If the morning results were a disappointment for the Americans, the afternoon four-ball session was a downright disaster. Even Woods and Duval, the top two ranked players in the world, couldn't get a win playing together.

All-square with Darren Clarke and Lee Westwood through 16 holes, Woods and Duval went down 1 when Clarke birdied 17. On 18, looking to halve the match, Duval sliced his ball badly off the tee, missing the fairway by a good 70 yards, and Woods drove into the rough. Their second shots were not much better, and despite halving the hole, they walked away with another U.S. loss, 1 down.

Mickelson, teamed with Jim Furyk, missed two short birdie putts in the final three holes to lose to Garcia and Parnevik. And a pair of old veterans, Jeff Maggert and Hal Sutton, dropped their match to Jose Maria Olazabal and Miguel Angel Jimenez.

The only bright spot for the Americans was actually only bright in comparison to the others. Davis Love III dropped a 30-foot birdie putt on the final hole to lift himself and partner Justin Leonard to a tie with Colin Montgomerie and Paul Lawrie.

All the hopes and expectations the home team had as the sun came up that frenzied Friday lay in ruins when darkness fell. The afternoon's 3½ to ½ score gave the Europeans a 6–2 advantage overall. A competition that had been won by razor-thin margins over the past 10 years had all the makings of a dominant runaway in what had become the visitor's own suburban Boston "Tee" Party.

"Good day for us—only one out of three, though," said European captain Mark James, who, in his typical understated way, clearly didn't want to further upset the American team.

U.S. captain Ben Crenshaw was a bit more blunt about the situation, saying, "I can't believe we are looking at a 4-point differential."

Friday Results
Foursomes: Morning

Duval/Mickelson lost to Montgomerie/Lawrie (3 and 2)
Lehman/Woods lost to Parnevik/Garcia (2 and 1)
Love/Stewart halved with Jimenez/Harrington
Sutton/Maggert beat Clarke/Westwood (3 and 2)

Four-balls: Afternoon

Love/Leonard halved with Montgomerie/Lawrie
Mickelson/Furyk lost to Parnevik/Garcia (1 down)
Sutton/Maggert lost to Jimenez/Olazabal (2 and 1)
Duval/Woods lost to Clarke/Westwood (1 down)

Day 2

It was a far more serious American team that emerged Saturday morning with another round of alternate-shot doubles the first order of business. With 20 matches still to play, the U.S. team certainly was not out of it but felt it was imperative to take at least a chunk out of the 4-point deficit.

American pairs were far more competitive on the second day, but after the futility of the first day, it was hard not to be. The teams split the four morning matches with each of the American victories coming by the score of 1 up, and both European wins ending after just 16 holes by the score of 3 and 2.

In the afternoon, each side won one four-ball match, and halved the two others. With both teams taking 4 total points, the day was effectively a wash. The Europeans, however, were one day closer to victory, still leading by that 4-point margin.

Seemingly unshaken, outwardly at least, U.S. Captain Ben Crenshaw wrapped up his Saturday evening press conference by saying, "I'm going to leave you all with one thought…I'm a big believer in fate. I have a good feeling about this."

SATURDAY RESULTS
Foursomes: Morning

Sutton/Maggert beat Montgomerie/Lawrie (1 up)
Furyk/O'Meara lost to Clarke/Westwood (3 and 2)
Pate/Woods beat Jimenez/Harrington (1 up)
Stewart/Leonard lost to Parnevik/Garcia (3 and 2)

Four-balls: Afternoon

Mickelson/Lehman beat Clarke/Westwood (2 and 1)
Love/Duval halved with Parnevik/Garcia
Leonard/Sutton halved with Jimenez/Olazabal
Pate/Woods lost to Montgomerie/Lawrie (2 and 1)

SCORE THROUGH TWO DAYS

	United States	European Union
Friday morning	1½	2½
Friday afternoon	½	3½
Saturday morning	2	2
Saturday afternoon	2	2
Total	6	10

Day 3

Sunday, September 26, 1999, dawned with a soft splash of sunshine flowing over a quiet morning in Massachusetts.

Players woke up with remembrances of the previous night when, despite the significant deficit weighing on their collective mind, the American team had gotten together at a joyful Saturday night dinner. The event, attended by the golfers, their wives and girlfriends, and team officials, made for an enjoyable and uplifting evening.

A video put together by team captain Crenshaw and his wife, Julie, showed highlights from each player's career and included wishes of good luck from celebrities and other professional athletes. Clips from movies ranging from *Caddyshack* to *Patton* were spliced in for added humor and inspiration. Crenshaw's longtime friend, George W. Bush, at the time the governor of Texas, appeared in person to read a letter written by Col. William Travis in 1836, saying he would give up his life to defend the Alamo. The message was clear: never surrender.

With wives and girlfriends participating, everybody gathered in a large circle and spoke, one by one about the experiences of the week that was. Players later admitted that, along with the laughs, a lot of tears flowed throughout the two-hour bonding experience.

Not a negative word was uttered. Each player, in his own way, expressed his belief in himself and the team. Afterward, they all said good night, perhaps with a different outlook on the big picture.

The stillness of the next day was broken by the thud of early edition newspapers hitting doorsteps all over the state. The whipping the American team had been taking on the golf course continued in sports sections throughout the country.

Many columnists echoed the sentiments of fans who had tuned in to see the beating administered by the Europeans, saying the result is truly not that surprising given the respective approaches of the two teams. The Euros were looked at as a cohesive group that traveled together, lodged together, ate together, and practiced together. The Americans, on the other hand, were a group of individuals—highly paid prima donnas. Rich, spoiled brats used to courtesy cars, five-star hotel rooms, and rock-star treatment from fans, tournament organizers, and sponsors.

It had been pointed out that the visiting team's hats had only their team logo on them, while the home-team players each had their own names stitched on the back. True, an innocuous, possibly meaningless detail, but as one little piece of a bigger developing theme, it somehow seemed to matter. It was becoming clear that fans were witnessing a team of 12 against 12 individuals in what was undoubtedly a team competition.

A *Chicago Tribune* story written by Skip Bayless was headlined, "Fittingly, Singles Last Hope of U.S. Ryder Cuppers."

In it, Bayless declared:

> *It's all but over now. The inconceivable has become the inevitable. Now the only hope for the United States Ryder Cup team is if its stars flaunt what has helped doom them. Now they get to be me-first individuals. Countries unto themselves. One-man conglomerates....*
>
> *Now eight of America's 12 must win singles matches and one must tie. Anything less and Team Europe pops its corks and sings its silly songs on the 18th green as Sunday's sun sets. Could eight of our stars win? On talent, no doubt. On unified passion, doubtful....*

To paraphrase a late president from this neighbor-
hood, too many of our players came asking not what
they could do for their country, but what The Country
Club could do for them.... Time to fly solo. Time, per-
haps, to find that one also can be the loneliest number.

When seen in the dim light shed by doubting columnists, Crenshaw's parting statement the previous night was an almost desperate expression of support. Of dying hope, really. Crenshaw, always the optimist, may or may not have actually felt the sentiment he expressed, but what else could he say?

The words didn't seem to mean much the next morning as the teams emerged to start play with the Europeans needing wins in just four of the 12 singles matches to retain the cup. Both captains knew that in the 10 competitions since the international side was extended to include all of Europe, no team had ever come back from anything larger than a 2-point deficit on the final day to win.

On the other hand, a month earlier, when all 12 players on both teams competed as individuals in the NEC Invitational in Ohio, the U.S. aggregate score over the four rounds was a full 80 strokes better than the Europeans.

The first pairing was on the tee at 10:38 AM, with each of the 11 subsequent groups going off in 12-minute increments. In one of the crucial elements of the captain's duties, Crenshaw and James took a different approach to stacking their Sunday line-ups. Needing to make up ground to at least have a shot by the end of the day, the American team sent out not necessarily its most talented, but certainly four of its most experienced and unflappable players first. Tom Lehman, Davis Love, Phil Mickelson, and Hal Sutton, with an average age of 36 and a collective nine previous Ryder Cup teams among them, were the first four off the tee. The Europeans countered with Lee Westwood, Jean Van de Velde, Jarmo Sandelin, and Darren Clarke—average age of 30 with a total of a mere two years of Ryder Cup experience.

By 12:50 PM, as the final pairing of Payne Stewart and Colin Montgomerie arrived on the 1st tee, the action in front of them had a decidedly red, white, and blue tint. After seeing the events of the first two days unfold, Stewart, perhaps the most passionate Ryder Cupper among the Americans, was likely regretting a comment he made about the European team a few months earlier, saying, "On paper, they should be caddying for us." Now, on the final day, Payne was hooked up with the man who was (and still is) considered the best European Ryder Cup player of all time. American galleries perceive Montgomerie, an outspoken perfectionist born in Scotland and raised in England, as a gruff elitist. His on-course demeanor and repu-tation, the situation at hand, and the very nature of Boston-area sports fans made for a volatile mixture that got ugly on Ryder Cup Sunday.

Fans who had been mildly heckling Monty early in the tour-nament turned up the heat as the points became more critical. Shouts of, "Hey, Mrs. Doubtfire!"—a reference to Montgomerie's resemblance to the Robin Williams movie character—followed him all over the course. As golf analyst David Feherty wrote, "The worst of the abuse was directed at Monty, who, bless his soft heart and thin skin, attracts morons the way Arnold Palmer attracted pretty girls." The heckling got so bad that Colin's father left the course.

The U.S. team, wearing what would eight years later be voted in an AOL poll as the third-worst jerseys in sports history (behind only No. 1, the Vancouver Canucks' bright V-shaped stripes of the early '80s, and No. 2, the Tampa Bay Bucs' glowing orange of the late '70s) stormed out to big leads in each of the first five matches.

By about 2:00, matches were ending seemingly every couple of minutes and with every result that was posted, U.S. designs on a record comeback became more and more realistic.

The Americans were not only winning, but winning easily. Lehman closed out Westwood in 16 holes. Love barely broke a sweat beating Van de Velde 6 and 5. Mickelson made quick work of Sandelin, winning 4 and 3, while future team captain Hal Sutton beat Darren Clarke 4 and 2. David Duval, who struggled all weekend and had been unable to win any of his three doubles matches despite being paired with Woods, Mickelson, and Love, cruised to victory, as well.

On the 3rd green, Duval's opponent, Jesper Parnevik, was four to five feet above the hole while Duval was about a foot closer and below the hole. "Good, good?" Jesper asked. "Nah, let's putt 'em," David responded. Duval made it; Parnevik missed it, giving the American the hole. Duval also went on to birdie the 4th, and win 6, 7, and 8 en route to a 5 and 4 thrashing in just 14 holes.

Like Sandelin and Van de Velde, Scotland's Andrew Coltart was a rookie who did not get his first taste of Ryder Cup competition until Sunday's singles matches. After sitting out the first two days, Coltart was the sacrificial lamb pulled from the blind draw to battle with Tiger Woods. To his credit, Coltart held his own early, matching Woods shot for shot for the first six holes. From there, though, Tiger went on a three-hole run, carding a par and two birdies to close out the front nine by winning the 7th, 8th, and 9th on his way to a comfortable 3 and 2 victory.

It was becoming a massacre. Everything that had gone right for the Europeans the first two days was suddenly going wrong. The fickle winds of fate blew through The Country Club, rippling the flags and crippling the stumbling team from abroad.

After Woods came in with his win, Steve Pate finished off Miguel Angel Jiminez to make it seven straight match victories for the Americans. With five groups still out on the course, the U.S. team had turned the event completely around. The score stood at 13–10 in favor of the Americans, with the pressure shifted entirely onto the European team, which needed to win four of the remaining five matches to tie the aggregate score and retain the cup.

Remaining Matches

Mark O'Meara vs. Padraig Harrington
Jim Furyk vs. Sergio Garcia
Jeff Maggert vs. Paul Lawrie
Justin Leonard vs. Jose Maria Olazabal
Payne Stewart vs. Colin Montgomerie

O'Meara was one of only two American players who did not see action on Friday and lost in his only appearance on Saturday. The man who had won two PGA events each year since 1995, climbed to the top of the golf world with wins in both the Masters and the British Open in 1998, but the season leading up to the Ryder Cup was a far different story as O'Meara failed to win a single tournament. A 31st-place finish was all he could muster in defense of his Masters crown, and his return to the British ended prematurely when he missed the cut. But as the afternoon shadows grew long, he suddenly had a chance to taste victory again.

All-square with Irishman Padraig Harrington, O'Meara rolled in a clutch eight-foot par putt on the 17th green. As the ball dropped in the cup—in a foreshadowing of a moment that will live in golf infamy—Tom Lehman charged onto the green to hug O'Meara. In part because Lehman ran near Harrington's line, and in part because it was inside two feet, O'Meara conceded his opponent's putt to halve the hole.

As he walked off the green, O'Meara pieced together the big picture and got a grasp on exactly what the final hole—the par-4 18th—actually meant. Two of the matches being played behind him had ended in the previous few minutes. Jim Furyk had systematically whacked the charismatic pulse of the European team, Sergio Garcia, taking him out 4 and 3, while Scotsman Paul Lawrie wiped out Jeff Maggert by the same count. The respective wins added another point to each team's total, making the aggregate score 14–11, putting the United States just a half-point from victory.

Despite having two teammates still on the course, O'Meara came to the realization that American success or failure would likely depend on him. The on-course scoreboards told a bleak story with Justin Leonard trailing Jose Maria Olazabal by 2 as they played the 14th hole, and in a colossal battle of wills between a pair of steely veterans, Payne Stewart was also down 2 as he slugged it out with Colin Montgomerie on 13.

Needing just to halve the final hole to halve the match and win the cup, a bad day with the driver got even worse for O'Meara. With both the stakes and the pressure at the high point of the weekend, he hit his tee shot into the fairway bunker. He then hit a 6 iron from 180 yards into the green-side bunker.

In the meantime, Harrington seemed oblivious to the immediacy of the moment. Swinging as smoothly as if he were playing a $2 Nassau, he put his ball on in regulation, a mere 12 feet from the cup. An up-and-down by O'Meara would force Harrington to hit a midrange putt under immense pressure, but the 42-year-old North Carolina native chunked his bunker shot and landed in the rough between the sand and the green. He failed to hole out his next shot, and when Harrington lagged his putt to within inches, the European team took the match and the crucial point to cut the American lead to 14–12.

As O'Meara walked off in painful defeat, four holes back, teammate Justin Leonard dutifully marched on like a marathoner trying to make up significant ground in the final few miles. It had been a tough day from the beginning for the 27-year-old former NCAA national champion from the University of Texas.

His opponent, Jose Maria Olazabal, took the lead on the 1st hole, setting the tone for what had become a long day for Leonard. Justin tied it on the 2nd, but again went 1 down on the 4th and had trailed ever since. Olazabal won the 6th, 9th, and 10th to take a commanding 4-up lead with just 8 holes to play.

The prospects for a comeback seemed bleak. Any golfer good enough to go 4 up through 10 holes is probably good enough to avoid losing 4 of the final 8 holes. And Olazabal wasn't just any golfer. Playing in his sixth Ryder Cup, the 33-year-old Spaniard was unlikely to be affected by the pressure. Having won his second Masters five months earlier, he was tournament-tested and obviously knew how to close.

Following a double bogey on the 9th and a bogey on the 10th, Justin was waiting to hit on the 11th tee, when he was greeted by Lanny Wadkins, Ray Floyd, and Hal Sutton, who all gave him a pat on the back and an encouraging word. It didn't seem to help much, though, as Justin bogeyed yet again. He was saved from going 5 down only when Olazabal missed a par putt from inside 10 feet. Yes, he had dodged a bullet, but at this point, every hole that went by was a step closer to defeat unless Leonard cut the gap.

As he walked dejectedly to the 10th tee, Leonard recalls being approached by Davis Love, who said, "You know, he's going to give you 2 holes. So you just have to win 2 others."

Sure enough, Olazabal started giving. On 12, he hooked his drive in a big way, sending the ball beyond the ropes down the left side, while Leonard stroked his tee shot into the middle of the fairway. Justin capitalized with a five-foot par putt, cutting the deficit to 3 with 6 holes left to play.

The 13th hole worked out, as well. Again Olazabal drove far to the left and landed behind a tree, forcing him to punch out laterally to the fairway. Leonard again was smooth and steady, getting on the green in regulation. He missed a 12-footer for birdie, tapped in for par, and won the hole when Jose Maria bogeyed. The American was now 2 down with 5 to play, and the gallery cheering for Leonard was growing by the minute—as Justin's confidence.

As if working in a package deal, as Leonard's tee-to-green game came together, the putter began heating up as well. On 14, he dropped a 10-footer for a hole-winning birdie—just his second of the day—to pull to within 1. Moving on to the next tee box, Leonard was in a new frame of mind. He looked around and noticed many of his teammates had started to gather: Woods, Mickelson, Duval... They were all there, watching him.

On the par-4 15th, both players hit the green in regulation. Leonard was 25 feet from the cup closer than Olazabal, who putted first. Justin went to school on Jose's attempt, which came up about three feet short. Knowing the green was playing on the slow side, Leonard gave his putt a touch of extra power and, to the roar of the gallery, dropped a delicious second consecutive birdie to pull even in the match. "That was as excited as I'd ever been on a golf course," he'd say later.

Incredibly, after winning just 1 of the first 11 holes, Leonard had reeled off 4 straight to pull even in a battle that seemed all but lost just an hour earlier.

"We talked about it the night before," said Leonard after the round. "Let's not think about the result, but play each shot one at a time. You win a couple holes in a row, the momentum shifts."

The match was now dead even, but with the aggregate score 14–12 in favor of the Uinted States, the advantage lay with Leonard. Needing only a half point to secure the cup, the Americans would gladly take a draw. They moved another step closer when both Olazabal and Leonard hit the green then 2-putted the par-3 16th, leaving just 2 holes for the Spaniard to pull out a match he had led most of the day.

To 17.

THE SHOT

By the time the players reached the very hole that saw history made 86 years earlier, the tournament was taking on the feel of an English soccer match.

Ouimet's U.S. Open win in 1913 came largely on the strength of birdies on the 17th hole in both the final round and the playoff. In 1999 the gallery at the hole had swelled to huge proportions, but unlike a regular tournament where many in attendance cheer for all of the players, the crowd at this event was divided very clearly by rooting interests.

Leonard hit first off the tee and drilled what he later said was probably "the best drive I hit all week." It went his two favorite ways—straight and far.

Olazabal followed with a shot not nearly as straight and not quite as far. Jose Maria pulled his ball into the left rough about

120 yards from the stick. The green was relatively deep but narrow, with the pin in the back-middle. Olazabal's approach shot was on line but short, leaving about 25 feet for birdie. Immediately after seeing the ball land, Jose turned and pointed into the gallery behind him and began chewing out a spectator who had apparently tried to rattle him by making noise in his backswing.

Leonard was next. He put a great swing on a wedge from about 100 yards out and sent it flying about 10 feet past Olazabal's ball. Two hops brought the ball to within about eight feet of the hole, but it put on the brakes and slammed into reverse like a getaway driver spotting a police car blocking the road ahead. The ball rolled a few inches to the side of the other ball and quickly past, then down a ridge, not stopping until a good 50 feet from the cup. Boy, sometimes backspin is a bitch.

As the players walked up to putt, they were greeted by an almost tangible wave of emotion emanating from a gallery stacked 20 deep around the entire green and down the fairway. Fans were waving American flags and chanting, "U.S.A.! U.S.A.!" The foreign contingent countered with a far-less-forceful show of support, singing the old European sporting venue chant, "O-ay, o-ay, o-ay, o-ayyy!" in hopes of urging on Olazabal.

The crowd began to settle down as Leonard studied his putt. NBC cameras zoomed in on Justin bent in a crouch—hat pulled low, grip of the putter near the side of his head, a worn strip of white tape wrapped around the middle knuckle of his right ring finger. A caddie casting a 15-foot sideways shadow tended the pin, which was bathed in sunlight. As several team members knelt close together by the side of the green, Leonard took his stance 45 to 50 feet away in the center of the green, covered completely by the generous shade of a huge, lazy green-side tree.

The gallery grew quiet, although a palpable nervous energy practically screamed through the late-afternoon silence. Leonard put a firm stroke on the ball, sending it rolling straight at its target and up a slight incline. Midway to the hole, the ball cleared the ridge and began moving to the right. Leonard's caddie, Bob Riefke, pulled the stick and quickly moved backward. Moving at enough pace to send it six to eight feet by, but cutting in a perfect line toward the center of the cup, the ball disappeared into the hole like a sugar cube into a cup of coffee.

"Pure pandemonium" is probably the best way to describe what followed. Leonard raised his arms victoriously, right hand clenched in a fist, left hand extending the putter straight to the heavens. The gathered masses erupted in cheer. Smiling broadly, Justin began moving to his left, picking up speed as he went. He was in nearly a full sprint as he approached the fringe and made an arc toward the front of the green. Still running, he was now being chased by most of the other American players, many of their wives, caddies, and team officials. They all came together in what looked like an on-field World Series celebration in baseball—jumping up and down and hugging. Chants of "U.S.A.! U.S.A.!" rang out again as the emotion of the magical moment seemed to invade and take over the bodies of the euphoric revelers.

There were, though, a couple of problems.

First, this was golf, not professional wrestling. Second, the victory they were celebrating was not yet actually theirs to celebrate.

Olazabal, who stood in stunned silence watching the impromptu ho-down play out before his very eyes, still had a 25-foot putt to halve the hole and potentially win the match on 18.

O'Meara, who had arrived minutes earlier after his own stinging defeat, was perhaps the first of the U.S. contingent to realize the behavior was inappropriate, insisting everybody clear the green. Leonard himself was also active in restoring order, holding up his hands head high, making a pushing motion and saying forcefully to the gathered group, "Off the green, off the green!"

As the crowd quieted, Julie Crenshaw sat down green-side and began to cry. "I'm sorry they got on the green," she whispered to Jarmo Sandelin. "That's just too much," he replied angrily.

Olazabal had a similar line to that of Leonard, but was putting from about half the distance, around 25 feet. All was now quiet, but certainly not normal, as Jose Maria stood over his ball, feeling the immense pressure to unring a raucous bell that had prematurely but, in all likelihood, signaled the end of this great competition. He set his feet, looked down at the ball, up at the cup, down at the ball, and then stepped away. Again he stepped up, went through his pre-putt routine, and set the ball in motion. To his credit, he made a nice run at it, but rolled it a couple of inches left of the cup and about two feet by. The miss made it official. The comeback was complete.

The American contingent once again rejoiced, but a bit less euphorically. The second gathering on the green felt like a group of partygoers trying to re-create a New Year's Eve celebration at 10 past midnight. It just lacked spontaneity and had lost a bit of its true, pure flavor.

By the time the players reached the media center, accusations of poor sportsmanship and inappropriate behavior were flying like balls off a jam-packed driving range.

"It's the most exciting day I've ever spent in sports," said Bob Denney, at the time the PGA of America's manager of media relations. "It had all the ramifications of a Super Bowl and national championship game all wrapped into one. I still get goose bumps from it. But once everyone got to the media tent, the controversy blew up. It was brought up immediately."

The European team, although acknowledging the great final-day play of the U.S. team, spoke almost solely of the celebration on the 17th green, while the American team tried in vain to steer the postmatch discussion toward their historic comeback. While the talk continued, many of the American players appeared on a third-story balcony of a building called the Locker House. There, in the late afternoon of a beautiful New England fall afternoon, with zero precipitation in the forecast, they made it rain. All of the players simultaneously opened bottles of champagne and sprayed the adoring minions below while they all sang the national anthem.

"It was kind of surreal," remembers Jeff Maggert. To stand up there and look out over the 18th fairway, to see the mobs of people waving flags."

Nearly a decade later, the impromptu scene at the Locker House is one of the enduring images of perhaps the greatest Ryder Cup of all time. As great as that was, though, it will never surpass Justin Leonard's magical moment on 17. It is a putt that has established permanent residence in the penthouse of golf lore. It just has a bothersome celebratory roommate it can never evict.

LEONARD VS. OLAZABAL

HOLE	1	2	3	4	5	6	7	8	9	OUT	10	11	12	13	14	15	16	17	18
PAR	4	3	4	4	4	4	3	4	5		4	4	4	4	5	4	③	4	4
Leonard	5	2	4	5	4	4	3	4	6		5	5	4	4	4	3	3	3	4
Olazabal	4	3	4	4	4	3	3	4	4		4	5	5	5	5	4	3	4	3

Sunday Singles, September 27, 1999

Lehman beat Westwood (3 and 2)

Sutton beat Clarke (4 and 2)

Mickelson beat Sandelin (4 and 3)

Love beat Van de Velde (6 and 5)

Woods beat Coltart (3 and 2)

Duval beat Parnevik (5 and 4)

O'Meara lost to Harrington (1 hole)

Pate beat Jimenez (2 and 1)

Leonard halved with Olazabal

Stewart lost to Montgomerie (1 hole)

Furyk beat Garcia (4 and 3)

Maggert lost to Lawrie (4 and 3)

(Results listed in order of tee time, not finish.)

POSTSCRIPT

It is a mostly forgotten fact that Olazabal holed a birdie putt on the 18th hole of his duel with Leonard, sending the match officially and indelibly into the record books as halved. And, it is a mostly unknown fact that Ryder Cup hero Justin Leonard never won a single one of his eight matches in the international competition.

Leonard followed his 0–2–2 performance at Valderrama in 1997 by going 0–1–3 in Massachusetts in 1999. That final half point, however, on that incredible putt against Olazabal is the one that put the U.S. team over the top.

In a *Golf Digest* interview a few months later, Leonard reflected on the cup-winning putt and the craziness that followed. "I can't blame myself for what I did. I think it was a moment, when we're all standing there and jumping up and down, and I'm being carried around, I wouldn't trade for anything in the world.... It would be nice if Ollie had already putted. But I don't think it had anything to do with his putt, because I don't think anybody ran through the line."

The question of whether the celebration carried into Olazabal's line became a major issue in the days that followed. Dealing with an opponent's celebration of a game-changing moment is simply part of the job description for a world-class athlete competing on an international level—especially if the competition is being played away from home. Regardless of what is accepted as "normal behavior" on a golf course, a mentally tough player, with so much at stake, should be able to at least temporarily disregard a spontaneous display such as the one that played out on the 17th green, as it seems Olazabal did with a good effort on his putt that followed. If, however, the player is put at a competitive disadvantage as a result of the display, that is something else entirely.

"There is one line you must not cross in golf—the line of your opponent's putt," wrote Frank Malley, the British Press Association chief sports correspondent. "It is written as indelibly in golfing etiquette as the fact that the club president gets his own parking space."

An article in London's *Evening Standard*, titled "Barbarians to a Tee," took it a step further.

> *Exuberance is one thing, but trampling across Jose Maria Olazabal's line before he'd taken his putt is simply cheating. Worse, there's something uniquely nauseating about American jubilance. It has nothing in common with Sergio Garcia's puppyish Spanish joy.*
>
> *Theirs is the kind of celebration that you learn in business school—vitriolic, bloodthirsty, and smug.*

> *They operate with a totally different ethos from us, one in which no achievement means anything unless it's at someone else's expense, and no victory is complete without a graceless pageant of supremacy.*

Another piece in the *Standard* was even more pointed. Columnist Matthew Norman wrote, "Let us be painfully honest about it. They are repulsive people, charmless, rude, cocky, mercenary, humorless, ugly, full of nauseatingly fake religiosity, and as odious in victory as they are unsporting in defeat."

Scathing reports poured in from newspapers throughout Europe. "Joy of Ugly Victory Brings Out the Ugly American," screamed Britain's *Guardian*. *The Daily Mirror* referred to the U.S. team as the "United Slobs of America," while periodicals in France, Italy, and Ireland ripped the U.S. players as well.

Even an American columnist, George Kimball of the *Boston Herald*, wrote:

> *Jeff Maggert may have set the stage for all of this earlier in the week when he proclaimed the U.S. Ryder Cup team 'the 12 best golfers in the world.' Whether they upheld that claim with Sunday's comeback performance may be open to some debate, but there is no disputing that the U.S. golfers showed themselves to be the world's 12 biggest assholes. The infantile celebration which accompanied Justin Leonard's improbable 45-footer that all but iced the Cup was a thoughtlessly appalling breach of sportsmanship.*
>
> *That Crenshaw might have done the gentlemanly thing and ordered Leonard to concede Olazabal's putt seems to have occurred to no one.*

European captain Mark James was predictably depressed

following the heartbreaking loss, but his criticism was more far-reaching than most, focusing on what he felt was a three-day pattern of unacceptable behavior by the American galleries. In addition to claiming his wife was spit on by an overzealous American backer, he cited examples of fans distracting his players in their backswings, cheering missed putts and wayward shots, heckling, and purposely pointing Andrew Coltart to the wrong area as he searched for his golf ball.

James, who resigned as captain after the match, placed a lot of the blame for the fans' actions on the drinks served at on-course concession stands, calling for the ban of alcohol at all future tournaments. "I'd hate if we lowered ourselves to that level. A lot of players will not be bothered competing in America again," James said. "Certainly that is the case with me. We don't need to be treated like this."

Asked about the day of domination, James conceded, "I think right from the start, the momentum was with the States. Putts and chips were just going in from all angles, and it seemed like we couldn't do anything to stop it. I could have rung in a bomb scare, I suppose."

James's American counterpart was caught in a strange predicament after the cup was clinched. While popping champagne corks with one hand, Ben Crenshaw was waving off criticism with the other. After initially apologizing for the events on the green, Crenshaw began to explain—if not justify—his team's actions. "This isn't the first emotional display at a Ryder Cup," he said. "In Europe, they've been excited before too. There was never any ill intent on anyone's part. I am sorry, but it was an incredible comeback and it was impossible not to get caught up in the moment."

Several players on the United States team spoke similarly; acknowledging the manner in which the celebration on the green took shape was not optimal. They did, though, reiterate Crenshaw's sentiments regarding the unexpected sight of that long putt disappearing into the cup and the sudden victory that came as a result.

Just as the team captains had differing viewpoints, several writers in the U.S. saw the events in a much different light than their colleagues from overseas. "Now we know why the English talk like they're sucking on lemons. Sour grapes, to be precise," wrote Steve Marantz, a colleague of Kimball's at the *Boston Herald*. "The mental collapse of the European team was one of the most astounding in golf history, and should be the cause of psychoanalysis rather than whining. Maybe next time the Europeans will use shrinks instead of caddies.

"The charge that American golfers were unfair to poor Jose Maria Olazabal in celebrating Justin Leonard's climactic putt proves that the Europeans are out of touch and irrelevant. What we are seeing is the Tigerization of golf, in which the game is being stamped with the passion, exuberance, and venality of American popular culture."

The truth is that while the European team had every right to express its distaste of the American team's behavior, no rules were actually broken. Longtime officer with the PGA of America, Ken Lindsay, who is currently a rules official on the Champions Tour, was the man in position to make a call.

Seated with announcers Dan Hicks and Johnny Miller in the broadcast tower at the 18th hole, Lindsay's job was to communicate with match referees and explain rulings on controversies to the television audience. In this instance, he was not even called on to appear.

"There was no question of a rules infraction at the time," recalls Lindsay, saying the Europeans did not call for a ruling or even bring it up as an issue until the match was over. And, alas, it would not have mattered if they had.

"We proved by means of videotape that there was no infraction," he insists. "Once Leonard made the putt he ran directly to his left, and that's when the others began to chase him and jump on him. They ran along the left side of the green and on the fringe. I saw a wide-angle view of the green during the incident and am 100 percent sure there was no infraction."

Match referee Jim Deaton, now an appointed member of the PGA rules committee and a pro in Greensboro, North Carolina, was standing next to Olazabal when Leonard's putt fell. He remembers, "I'm thinking, 'Now, wait a minute. This match isn't over,' and Jose looked at me and said, 'You need to do something.'"

"If you watch the videotape of the match," continues Deaton, "you can hear me yelling at people to get off the green. I got Ben's attention, and he kind of snapped back to reality and began helping me clear the green. It seemed like a long time, but I've put a stopwatch on the videotape. It's actually less than 20 seconds between the time everybody rushed out and the time the green was clear."

Deaton says that Sergio Garcia, who was walking with Colin Montgomerie in the group behind Olazabal's, sprinted up to the green and confronted Deaton. "He said, 'Excuse me, sir, how can you let this happen?' And then he starts cussing at me.

"I responded by telling him that I didn't let it happen, and I was the one who cleared the green," Deaton says. "But then his language got worse and he kept saying that f-word. I took about as much as I could take and told him if he said it again, he'd be outside the ropes."

Deaton laughs at the memory, adding, "I saw Sergio at Bay Hill three months later. I went up to him and told him I had a picture of he and I, and asked if he would sign it. Sergio said 'Sure,' not remembering me, and I took off to get the picture."

Deaton returned a few minutes later with a picture that appeared in a Boston newspaper the day after the Ryder Cup. In it, Garcia is clearly angry, arguing with Deaton, but Jim has his hands up as if to say, "Enough."

"Garcia took a look at the picture, looked up at me, looked back at the picture, looked at me, and said angrily, 'These people should not be on the green!'"

"I was kind of surprised," Deaton says, "but an instant later he smiled and we both had a good laugh. I still have the picture in my office. It says, 'To my friend Jim. All the Best, Sergio Garcia.'"

Deaton is certain there was no rules violation in 1999, saying, "Had there been any damage to the green, we either would have repaired it or allowed Jose to move his ball, but nobody even came near his line. Since then, though, as a direct result of what happened on 17, we have greatly restricted access at tournaments like that. At the time, players could get anybody they wanted inside the ropes, friends, relatives, whoever. Now players get a limited amount of passes."

The United States team party went on deep into the night with tequila shots replacing golf shots. Players and their wives, who had bonded over the course of the week in Brookline, laughed, cried, and drank their way through a final, precious few hours together.

"It was hard to go to sleep that night. Hard to wake up, get out of bed, and go home," recalled Jeff Maggert in a *Golf Digest* article the next year. "We're sitting at the airport and it was almost a depressing feeling, like, 'Gosh, it's over with.' It was a pretty amazing thing. You may not see something like that for another 100 years."

Lost amidst all the accusations of bad behavior and poor sportsmanship that fateful Sunday was a gesture of goodwill from an experienced and respected player. Payne Stewart, known in part for his passion for the Ryder Cup and its principles, may have enjoyed the final day of competition far less than anyone else on the American team.

Facing Colin Montgomerie in the tournament's last match, Stewart was witness to the onslaught of derisive taunts directed at his opponent. Others likely would have stood silently by. Stewart did not. Several times throughout the round, Payne approached Colin and offered to "take care of it."

"I was disgusted with some of the actions and some of the name-calling and the heckling. He doesn't deserve that. That is not what this event is about," Stewart said after the match. "All I can say now is that I'm sorry for some of our fans. It was not right that they behaved that way."

On the final hole, Stewart and Montgomerie were all-square. The fact their match had become inconsequential in regards to the Cup was meaningless; these were two of the world's best golfers in full-competition mode. Still, in the name of sportsmanship, Stewart conceded Montgomerie's 20-foot birdie putt for the match. The point went to Europe, 1 up.

That gesture was a final public display of the man Payne Stewart had become. A month later, at the tender age of 42, Stewart was traveling from Orlando to Dallas when the Learjet he was on gradually lost cabin pressure, effectively suffocating all six people aboard. The plane flew on autopilot across the country, ran out of fuel, and crashed into a field in South Dakota.

A week later, about three thousand people, including more than a hundred past and present PGA players, packed a church in Orlando for a memorial service. In attendance were Jack Nicklaus, Greg Norman, Tiger Woods, and three Ryder Cup captains: Ben Crenshaw, Tom Kite, and Lanny Wadkins.

Stewart was the winner of the 1989 PGA Championship and just months earlier had claimed his second U.S. Open title, but his on-course accomplishments barely received a mention in the two-hour service. People instead spoke of his dedication to his family, his religion, and his values.

The Ryder Cup tournament, completed less than a month earlier, somehow seemed a blur. The controversy over the events on the 17th green was put squarely in perspective. Golf, like life, is delicate. But in golf, there is always tomorrow.

Upcoming Ryder Cup Competitions

2008: Valhalla Golf Club, Louisville, Kentucky, September 16–21
2010: Celtic Manor Golf Club, Newport, South Wales
2012: Medinah Country Club, Medinah, Illinois
2014: PGA Centenary Course, Gleneagles, Scotland
2016: Hazeltine National Golf Club, Chaska, Minnesota

Tiger Woods gets the Green Jacket from Phil Mickelson after blowing away the field in the 2005 Masters at the Augusta National Golf Club.

CHAPTER NINE

2005:
I of the Tiger

PRELUDE

With a growing winless streak in major tournaments and a shrinking aura of invincibility, the hottest hotshot golf has ever seen checked into Augusta National for the 2005 Masters. At just 29 years old, Eldrick "Tiger" Woods was playing in the tournament for the 11th time—the ninth time as a professional. This year, though, seemed a bit different.

Just a couple seasons earlier, all signs pointed to a run of dominance never before seen in the golf world. Having won the Masters three times previously, including back to back in 2001 and 2002, the over/under on career green jackets was what? Ten? Fifteen? However many his closet would hold?

But as he hit town in 2005, he wasn't even the clear-cut favorite. A pre-Masters article written by Leonard Shapiro of *The Washington Post* identified five players—Woods, Phil Mickelson, Ernie Els, Vijay Singh, and reigning U.S. Open champ Retief Goosen—as co-favorites.

The sentiment was that Tiger's days of simply needing to show up and not lose a tournament were over. And many tour players seemed to agree. "When you go back to 2000, 2001, everybody thought that Tiger was so much ahead and it's very difficult to get to that level," Denmark's Thomas Bjorn was quoted as saying. "But now there's five or six of them playing at that level."

"It's a totally different ballgame at the moment," echoed Ernie Els, "with guys playing at a better level than a couple of years ago. Anybody out there who's playing well and believes in himself can win a golf tournament, and this week is no different."

Mickelson went into the Masters sporting the 1-2 perfecta of being both defending champion and the tour's leading money winner. Singh racked up nine victories the previous year and held the number one world ranking; Goosen was the defending U.S. Open champion; Els came in with two early-season European tour victories; and Woods was just getting past the 2004 season, which saw him shut out completely in stroke-play tournaments. Yes, the golf landscape certainly seemed to be shifting.

It had been eight years since Tiger came into the Masters as anything but an overwhelming favorite. The last time was 1997, when he was in the field as a professional for the first time. In his two previous appearances, he had finished tied for 41st in '95 when he was the low amateur, and he missed the cut in '96. He failed to break par in any of his six rounds.

In 1997 he won the season-opening tournament, the Mercedes Championship. After that, though, the road to Augusta was paved with mostly erratic play, culminating with a 31st-place finish at the Players Championship two weeks earlier. His arrival in Georgia was met with mixed feelings—excitement about his long-term potential and cynicism about a 21-year-old kid's chances of beating a field of far more seasoned professionals with far more experience in the world's most prestigious golf tournament.

One Texas newspaper columnist, Kirk Bohls, wrote of Tiger, "He won't win...not this year, because he occasionally has erratic iron play and isn't a terrific lag putter on lightning-fast greens. And because he hasn't suffered enough here to win." The article quoted Sam Snead asking a curious public for patience, saying, "Give him some more time, two or three more years on the Tour."

There were many who joined Snead in his sentiment. In fact, Tiger naysayers barely had the last *o* in "told ya so" out of their mouths on Thursday when things began to change. Woods turned a miserable front nine into a warning shot of a back nine that sent shivers through everything at Augusta National but the early-blooming azaleas.

Two hours after making the turn with a messy 4-over-par 40, Tiger stood on the 18th green, 15 feet away from history. He rolled through the back nine as if it were your local putt-putt course, racking up four pars, four birdies, and an eagle. He missed tying Mark Calcavecchia's back-nine record of 29 by about an inch as he slid his 15-foot birdie try on the final hole just by the cup.

He walked off the course with the unusual combination of a 40 on the front and a 30 on the back for an opening round of 70, good for fourth place behind only John Huston (67), Paul Stankowski (68), and Paul Azinger (69).

First-round leads at the Masters are kind of like first dates with the prom queen; they often don't lead to anything very meaningful. Nineteen ninety-seven was a textbook case.

Huston, you have a problem.

After taking the lead with an eagle on 18 in the opening round, John Huston was still in good position through 12 holes on Friday. Standing in the 13th fairway a single stroke off the pace, the man known as the fastest golfer on tour hit 3 consecutive shots into the water, finally got onto the green, then 2-putted for a quintuple bogey 10. He finished the day with a 77 and was not a factor over the weekend.

Tiger, on the other hand, made his move and took the lead with a solid 6-under-par 66. Averaging an epic 336 yards off the tee, about 40 yards longer than the field, Woods played the four par-5s in a collective 5 under. He finished the day 3 shots ahead of Colin Montgomerie and 4 or more ahead of everybody else.

The next day, it was more of the same. Even better, in fact. The young superstar-in-the-making shot a 7-under-par 65, storming out to an all-time Masters-record third-round lead of a whopping 9 strokes. On the strength of prodigious drives, which took strategically placed bunkers and hazards out of the equation, pin-point accuracy on ever-shortening approach shots, and an ultraconfident putting stroke, Woods was effectively making a joke out of one of the most delicate and sinister courses in all of golf.

After the round, a media member who concluded Tiger would be wearing the prized green jacket the next day, asked Woods what size sport coat he wore. Tiger, always focused on the task at hand, shrugged and answered simply, "I don't know."

The lead was so bulky and the other players so resigned to their sudden demotion to the level of commoners amidst the Royalty of Tiger that Championship Sunday was more of a coronation than a competition. Like a child prodigy setting the curve in a Harvard biophysics class, 21-year-old Tiger Woods ripped apart the very fabric of the PGA Tour, causing every caddie, player, and official to rethink the game they thought they knew so well.

Dressed in his traditional final-day red, a "power color" according to his mother and a shade that has come to symbolize Woods's propensity to go for Sunday blood, he took the first tee to an electric buzz from the gallery. He was as confident and steady during the tournament's final round as he had been in early-week practice sessions. It was all working again, and by the time it ended, there was a new undisputed king of golf.

A stroll-in-the-park Sunday 69 brought his tournament total to 18-under-par 270—the best Masters score ever. He won it by a cool dozen strokes, also a Masters record. He became the youngest player and the first African American ever to win the tournament.

Although the average fan walked away talking about Tiger's incredible power, it was, as much as anything, his surgeonlike touch that allowed him to leave the field in his dust. In a four-day stretch that saw just about every other player frustrated by the fast and tricky greens, Woods expertly worked them without registering a single 3-putt. Not one.

In about 18 hours of golf, the kid laid waste to a reputation the grand course developed over 61 years' worth of silent superiority. Every April, one player won a green jacket, but nobody ever beat Augusta National. Until now.

The Masters doesn't start until the final round on Sunday? Nonsense. In 1997 it was over long before that.

"Tiger is out there playing another game," Jack Nicklaus said after finishing 29 strokes behind, 11 years removed from his own Masters miracle. "He's playing a golf course he'll own for a long time. This young man will win many more of these. It's not my time, anymore, it's his."

1997 Masters, Final Leader Board

1.	Tiger Woods	70–66–65–69	270
2.	Tom Kite	77–69–66–70	282
3.	Tommy Tolles	72–72–72–67	283
4.	Tom Watson	75–68–69–72	284
5.	Paul Stankowski	68–74–69–74	285
	Costantino Rocca	71–69–70–75	285
7.	Jeff Sluman	74–67–72–73	286
	Fred Couples	72–69–73–72	286
	Davis Love III	72–71–72–71	286
	Justin Leonard	76–69–71–70	286
	Bernhard Langer	72–72–74–68	286

THE TOURNAMENT

THE MASTERS, AUGUSTA NATIONAL GOLF CLUB, AUGUSTA, GEORGIA, APRIL 7–10, 2005

The eight years since his breakthrough victory had brought Tiger Woods worldwide fame and more fortune than a kid could realistically hope for. But like early-morning storm clouds collecting over Augusta National before the opening round, a recent rough patch was blocking out the once brilliant sunshine that seemed to illuminate every aspect of his career.

His last major championship, the eighth of his career, came at the 2002 U.S. Open. In the 10 majors since then, he was in final-day contention only once, at the 2003 British. He insisted the down period was due to swing changes he had been implementing for the past couple of years. "Any time you make changes to your game, it's not going to be an immediate success," he said in the days before the Masters. "Did I probably take a step back? Yeah, probably."

But then he reminded everybody about his last "step back."

"I did the same in 1998 and the beginning of 1999, almost two years where I didn't really do anything in the game of golf. But once those changes kicked in," he said. And then with a confident smile, "I had a pretty good little run."

The previous tinkering he spoke of was done with coach Butch Harmon, specifically to get control of his distances with irons. The recent changes were done with Hank Haney and were about finding a new swing plane to attain a consistent trajectory.

"Everybody is trying to say, 'You can get back to [your level of play in] 2000,'" Woods said. "But I don't want to get back to

2000. I want to become better. That's the whole idea of making a change. I'm starting to see results and I've got to continue down that path."

A delay of more than five hours wreaked havoc on the tee sheet and kept players off the course until 1:30 in the afternoon. Tiger went off on the back side and got a little taste of what lay ahead when his approach shot on number 10, his first hole of the day, hit the flagstick a few inches from the bottom and rebounded back into a bunker. Instead of opening with a near-certain birdie, he failed to get up-and-down from the sand and walked away with bogey.

He followed with another bogey on 11, parred the 12th, and was in great position to gain at least a stroke on 13 when he watched in horror as his round just about disappeared before his very eyes.

After reaching the par-5 13th in 2, Woods was looking at a big-bending right-to-left 40-foot putt for eagle. He put a good stroke on the ball, and the gallery began to murmur as it rode its break toward the hole. It slid a few inches by on the high side, and as the crowd groaned, the ball kept rolling. And rolling. And rolling.

The back half of the putt was downhill, not allowing the ball to lose pace at a normal rate. It sped the final 10 to 15 feet past the pin, through a few feet of fringe, and down a back slope. As gravity took over, and the ball began rolling down a steep hill, its eventual stopping point became obvious. Mr. Nike, meet Rae's Creek.

Amazingly, the man who made a mockery of the Augusta greens in his win in '97 had putted completely off the green and into the water. He took a penalty stroke and elected, instead of chipping from the other side of the hazard, to re-putt. The second time he took a lot of steam off and left the ball about three feet away. He knocked it in for the kind of bogey 6 that fans are likely never to see again.

Due to darkness, most of the golfers, including Woods, did not finish the round. Tiger played 12 holes in 2 over par and left the course a half-dozen strokes behind leader Chris DiMarco, who got through 14 holes. Also ahead of Woods were three of the other players considered co-favorites: Vijay Singh, Retief Goosen, and Phil Mickelson were all 2 under par, with none of them playing more than 13 holes. Ernie Els played 11 holes and was a shot behind Tiger at plus 3.

For all the rain and the strange happenings, nothing that happened on Thursday was as notable—or ultimately as forgettable—as the round turned in by 73-year-old Billy Casper.

The 1970 Masters champ, back for a farewell tour, did not, alas, fare well. Casper shot a 34-over-par round of 106, breaking the shit out of the previous record of all-time tournament 95 turned in by Charles Kunkle in 1956. Five double bogeys, two triples, and a 14 on the par-3 16th—an all-time Augusta worst on any hole—combined to vault Casper to his famously infamous round.

Check the Masters record books, though, and you won't find evidence of Billy's day of futility. Next to his name are only the letters *WD* (withdrew) for the 2005 event. He never signed the scorecard, opting instead to bring it home and frame it.

Day 2

Another dreary Georgia morning practically dared fans to enjoy whatever golf would be played on a gray spring Friday. The Augusta National fairways were so wet they hadn't been mowed in 48 hours. And more rain was in the forecast.

Players again went off on both sides of the course, with some starting their second rounds before others had finished their first rounds. Names were stacked on the leader board as usual, but when a player who is through, say, 26 holes is a stroke ahead of a player who has played just 14 holes, who is really ahead? It's like comparing azaleas and oranges.

England's David Howell, fresh off a stellar showing in Europe's 2004 Ryder Cup victory, birdied five of the first eight holes before his round was halted. Playing in his first Masters, Howell packed it in for the day at minus 5, sharing the top spot on the board with Luke Donald, who was through 20 holes, and Chris DiMarco, who had played 19 holes. Vijay Singh was also at 5 under par, but had yet to tee off for his second round.

Tiger played just seven holes on day two, six to finish off his opening round and one to start his second. What he lacked in quantity, though, he made up in drama. Woods put up two birdies, two pars, and two bogeys to finish an erratic 2-over-par 74, making it three straight years in which he failed to break par in the opening round.

He went off on the front to start round two and left himself 30 feet from his second birdie ever on the tough 1st hole. He rapped his putt perfectly on line, but the ball stopped a couple of revolutions short of the cup. He tapped in for par, and a couple of moments later, at 12:40 PM, play was halted for the day.

Nobody in the field played more than nine holes of round two, so not surprisingly, the most notable news came not from the golf course, but from the champions' locker room. The world's top-ranked player, Vijay Singh, playing in the group behind defending champ Phil Mickelson, lodged an official complaint against Mickelson for leaving spike marks on the 12th green.

The complaint itself, though, was not what irked Mickelson. The fact that he overheard Singh talking about him to other players in the locker room angered him. Phil confronted Vijay and said afterward, "He expressed his concerns, and I expressed my disappointment with the way it was handled."

With the wet conditions, nearly half the field was using steel spikes instead of the more popular Soft Spikes. A tournament official explained that some spike marks Singh encountered were far more pronounced than a normal spike mark, as if one of the spikes was frayed, resulting in larger holes on the greens.

Mickelson said, at Singh's request, officials had approached him twice on the back nine. Masters rules chairman Will Nicholson said, "One of our officials talked to Phil to see if there was a burr on the side of one of his spikes. He very generously, as you know he would, said he would change them when he got in if there was any problem. There wasn't. If there were [irregular] spike marks, they were created by a person or persons unknown."

Day 3

Only four players in the history of the Masters led the tournament wire to wire. Chris DiMarco was trying to become the fifth. After making a bogey on the first hole of the first round, the former University of Florida standout rolled through the next 44 with nothing but pars and birdies.

Play was once again halted with players on the course Saturday, but not because of bad weather. They simply ran out of daylight. On a clear and warm day, DiMarco put a pair of loving arms around his lead and hugged it as if it were his child. He ended the day at 13 under par, with a 4-stroke lead through 45 holes and an intact bogey-free stretch just six holes shy of the all-time Masters record.

Despite the relatively comfortable lead, in the rearview mirror, there was trouble. Its name was Tiger.

Looking every bit like the Woods of old, the now 29-year-old star played 26 glorious holes over a span of about 10 hours, chalking up 12 birdies along the way. He finished his second round, playing the final 17 holes in 6 under par, and then smoked the front nine of his third round in 5-under-par 31, with three straight birdies to send him home.

A dawn that saw him take the tee at 2 over par turned into an unwelcome dusk that had him at 9 under. He was having such a great day the other players were resigned to rooting for the earth to spin faster and nightfall to come sooner. The only thing that could seemingly stop Woods's assault on the course and the field was a lack of light. The rest of the field celebrated sunset as if they were at Mallory Square in Key West.

And even then, the halt of play because of darkness actually benefited Tiger. His drive on the 10th hole rolled to a stop in the fairway with a large chunk of mud covering about a quarter of the ball. As he arrived at the ball, officials decided it was too dark to continue. "That was a huge break," Woods said months later, "a huge break. I was tired from the entire day and if I had to hit that [mud-covered] ball right then, I probably would have made bogey."

The day ended with Woods in second place, 4 shots off the lead with 27 holes to play. "All of a sudden," he said afterward, "the momentum started to build."

While one great career was apparently getting back on track, another one was coming to an end. Jack Nicklaus, playing in his 45th Masters, was competing in Augusta for the final time. It was an emotional trek around the grand old course for the grand old champion. "The patrons" (as the Masters association insists fans are referred to on CBS's coverage) had always been behind Jack, but the cheers and shouts had seemingly become more of a collective energy, an urging, in an attempt to pull the 65-year-old legend through a final round.

Finishing on the 9th hole, he boomed a drive about 300 yards, then poured a 6 iron to within five feet. Walking up that final fairway, his eyes welled with tears as he took in the wild applause from the gallery. The noise seemed to build with every step.

"Jackie was saying, 'Come on, Dad, let's make another birdie.' Me, I just wanted to finish without making a fool of myself, but by the time I got to that green I'd already sort of lost it."

The Golden Bear missed his birdie, but knocked in his par putt to finish in style, although his two-day total of 77–76 was not good enough to make the cut.

"It was about as good as I'm going to play on this golf course, with the conditions and the length that it is," he said after the round. "I played more 3 woods, 4 woods, and 5 woods, and if I'd had my 6 and 7 woods in the bag I'd have played them, too. I don't know how in the world I would ever be able to compete doing that.

"You know, it's great and it's fun to play in the Masters, but it's certainly no fun to play that way. It's no fun to go out there and hack it around and struggle and try to figure out some way to break 80. That's never been the way I've operated. This is not a celebrity walk-around—this is a major golf tournament. If you're going to play, you should be competitive."

By the time the final shot of the day landed in the cup, Nicklaus had already made the trip back to his Florida home. The next day was Masters Sunday, a day that had brought out the best in him for so many years, a day that stoked competitive fires that burned as brightly as any human's ever had. This year, though, before he left Augusta he was asked what he would be doing while the final round was being played. He thought for a moment, cracked a satisfied smile, and answered, "I'll probably be fishing."

Play was halted because of darkness Saturday evening with only six of the 50 remaining golfers having completed three rounds. With the leaders through 45 holes, a trip to a department store seemed the best way for all but three players to get a green jacket the following day.

Saturday Night Leader Board

Chris DiMarco	-13
Tiger Woods	-9
Thomas Bjorn	-8
Vijay Singh	-4
Rod Pampling	-4
Mark Hensby	-4
Phil Mickelson	-3

Day 4

What Chris DiMarco had in talent, there was growing evidence he just might have lacked in nerves. For the third time in five years, he had a lead in the late stages of the Masters, but if history was any indication, the lead would not last. In 2001 he led the field by 2 strokes heading to the weekend only to finish tied for 10th, 8 shots behind. In 2004 he shared the lead with Phil Mickelson on the final day but faltered to finish in a tie for sixth, 7 strokes off the pace. He had also seen several other tournaments escape his grasp on the final day or in playoffs.

This time around, DiMarco's lead was 4, and only two players were within 8 shots. That was the good news. The bad news was a hard-charging Tiger Woods was his nearest competitor, and he had a full 27 holes to make up the ground.

Woods was asked whether he thought his very presence in second place might intimidate DiMarco. His answer was not "yes." That would have been a bit arrogant. His answer was not "no." That might have been disingenuous. Instead, Tiger cleverly responded simply, "I'm not in his shoes."

The old saying, "The Masters doesn't start until the back nine on Sunday," took on a new meaning in 2005. Play actually did start on the back nine as the leaders completed their final nine of round three before playing round four. And it didn't take long for the lead to change hands.

Woods walked out to the very spot at which he had marked his muddy ball about 13 hours earlier and placed on the grass a clean, shiny Titleist with dimples as pure and pronounced as Jennifer Garner's. And he picked up right where he left off.

In a span of a mere 32 minutes, with just 4 swings of his clubs and 3 strokes of his putter, Tiger put himself at the top of the board. Birdies on 10, 11, and 12, combined with DiMarco's double bogey at 10, accounted for a 5-stroke swing and, just like that, a new leader. Woods went on to rack up another bird at the 13th, giving him seven straight birdies going back to the previous day, to tie an all-time Masters record.

DiMarco finished the nine in 41 while Woods eventually put up a pair of bogeys to finish in 34. The 7-shot difference gave Tiger a 3-stroke lead with 18 to play. Thomas Bjorn was 4 back but would finish his day with a fourth-round 81 and was not a factor in the afternoon. In fact, other than Woods and DiMarco, not a single player even made a flinch toward the top. It was a two-man battle in the final round.

Wearing his traditional Sunday red, Woods got off to another great start with birdies on each of the first two holes, while DiMarco started par, birdie. Tiger bogeyed the 5th, and both players birdied the 9th to send them to that oft-talked-about back nine with Woods holding a 3-stroke lead.

On 10, the edge was sliced down to 2 when Tiger missed the fairway left and the green right, before settling for bogey. Then on 11, Chris pulled to within a single stroke, drilling a 30-footer for birdie.

DiMarco lost a stroke with a bogey at 12, but then regained it with a birdie at 14. He was a single shot behind, but was quickly running out of holes, and one of the four remaining was the par-5 15th, a clear advantage for Tiger with his superior length.

Woods, as many figured, did reach the 15th green in 2 and 2-putted for birdie. DiMarco, though, hanging tough, birdied it, as well, to stay within 1 shot with just three holes to play.

THE SHOT

The 16th hole at Augusta National is a seemingly simple 170-yard par-3 surrounded by spectacular greenery and the beautiful brilliant glow of blooming azaleas. Focusing only on the green from the tee box can be a bit tricky, especially on Sunday with a tournament on the line. A player who takes his eyes off the target can quickly become a mental mess. There is trouble everywhere.

The Masters website describes 16 this way: "The hole is played entirely over water, and the green is secured by three bunkers. With the green significantly sloping from right to left, an exacting tee shot is required to have a reasonable birdie opportunity."

"Entirely over water and secured by three bunkers" is another way of saying, "There is no room for error." Yes, there is some fringe around the green, but for the most part, any ball not on the putting surface is in trouble.

DiMarco, coming off consecutive birdies, hit first. The safety of his tee shot was never in doubt, landing on the green and stopping about 10 to 15 feet short of the pin. He was not only in birdie range but also was looking at an uphill putt allowing him to take a good run at it.

Woods hit next, pulling out an 8 iron. He later explained, "I wanted to hit it short and right of the hole. I was saying to myself, 'Short and right, short and right, short and right,' and then I came right over the top of it and hit it long and left."

Advantage DiMarco.

Tiger's ball came to rest on a downslope about 20 feet off the putting surface. The pin was cut to the left side of the green about mid-depth. Tiger had plenty of room with which to work—maybe 60 feet between the cup and the edge of the green nearest to him.

Working in his favor was the fact that the ball was on the first cut of fringe allowing clean access. Working against him was the fact that there was only about an inch between the ball and a far thicker cut of rough behind the ball. He approached the area where his ball had landed, took a good look, and then turned his attention to the flag. He walked up the slope and onto the green. He didn't head toward the cup, though. Instead, he moved slowly on a line about 30 to 40 feet above the hole. He was clearly picking a spot to land his upcoming chip shot.

With the rough right behind the ball, he would have to pick the club up almost dead straight on his back swing and effectively chop down on the ball forcing it to come out flat. Flat was far from optimal. A high arc and a soft landing would be best, but with the thick grass certain to impede the path of the club head, the smooth swing that would produce that kind of shot was not a viable option.

Once he identified his landing spot, he walked back to his ball, gripped his wedge, and settled his feet. He stood upright with the ball toward the back of his stance, his front foot on the first cut and his back foot on the second cut. He took three practice swings, looking up to his projected landing spot after each one to compute a bit more data.

"I wanted to get it inside Chris's ball," he reflected. "I found a sliver of light that was coming through the trees and thought, 'If I hit the ball in this area, I can probably get it inside his ball.' That's what I kept focusing on."

The grandstands all around the green and down the fairway were jam-packed with fans. There wasn't an empty spot in the place, but you never heard so many people make so much quiet. *An exacting tee shot is required to have a reasonable birdie opportunity.*

The silence was broken when Woods made contact with the ball, sending it over the slope and up onto the green. It appeared to come out a bit hot at first, but even with its low trajectory, the ball bit hard on its second hop and slowed down nicely. As it moved on a line perpendicular to the hole, it caught the down slope and made a hard right turn, losing what remained of the forward motion from the impact with the club. The ball was now moving down the slope, moving solely by the force of gravity.

The hard right turn it made sent it on a line that would have brought it right at the cup, but as it rode the contour of the green, it began to drift a few inches back to the right. With the crowd growing louder, the ball first flattened out, then coasted back to the left directly at the hole. As it crept to within a couple of feet, it appeared to be on line to drop. A brilliant shot. The question now was the speed. Would it get there?

Each agonizingly slow revolution brought it closer to the pin. "Oh...my...goodness," marveled CBS announcer Verne

Lundquist. Within six inches, it was no longer a matter of line—only strength. Would it get there?

Two inches from dropping, the CBS camera shot was so tight and the ball was moving so slowly, home viewers could actually see the Nike logo printed on the dimples of the golf ball. But...would it get there?

No. It wouldn't. It didn't.

Amazingly, after a grassy and glorious trek over about 80 feet of tradition-soaked terrain, the ball stopped on the lip of the cup—one-eighth of a roll from free-falling a couple of inches into golf legend.

Ohhhhhh! The crowd gasped collectively. The ball was what? Two millimeters from the edge of the cup?

And then...it fell.

The place went nuts. Tiger, who had been crouched over, reacting to his misfortune, sprung upward as if lifted by the roar of the gallery. He leaned back, clenching his fists about chin-high, and he and his caddie, Steve Williams, bungled their way through an awkward-looking pair of high-fives. Then Tiger, holding his wedge low on the shaft, lifted it quickly to acknowledge the cheering fans before walking to the hole to retrieve his ball.

Lundquist shrieked rhetorically, "*Oh, wowwww!* In your *life* have you seen anything like that?"

Nobody had.

"It looked pretty good. All of a sudden, it looked really good," Tiger would recount later. "Then, it looked like, 'How can it not go in?' to 'How did it not go in?' And all of a sudden, it went in. It was pretty sweet."

Tiger pulled his ball from the cup, powerfully punched the air with both fists, and then managed a far-better-orchestrated high-five with Williams, grasping each other's hand for a few seconds on the back end. The crowd continued to cheer raucously with delight.

DiMarco? He wasn't so delighted.

After spending the early part of the morning under a scorching assault from Woods, watching his lead evaporate like water in the desert, DiMarco could only shake his head. The combination of luck and skill that had just played out before his eyes and the sounds of the screaming minions ringing in his ears signified a tremendous shift in fortune. A minute earlier, DiMarco was looking at a possible 2-shot swing and a 1-stroke lead. Now the best he could hope for was status quo—a 1-shot deficit, but with another hole gone.

But that wasn't to be, either. DiMarco missed his birdie putt and found himself 2 down to the flaming-hot, once and (apparently) future king with two holes to play. He moved to the 17th, trying to get a grasp on the events of the past few minutes. DiMarco just played 14, 15, and 16 in 2 under par, seemingly had a huge advantage after their tee shots on the par-3, and amazingly, incredibly, hadn't gained a single shot. How did this kid get the name Tiger? He was more like a snake—slippery, elusive, and dangerous.

With the miracle birdie at 16, Woods had honors on the 17th tee, but he whipped his drive wildly to the right. DiMarco followed, telling himself just to play his game. Tiger ended up with a bogey on the hole while Chris dropped his putt for par. The lead was down to 1 as they went to the final hole.

So often in golf, one great shot leads to another, which leads to another. That was not the case here. Tiger, the great finisher, was stumbling home. His approach on the par-4 18th was nearly as far right as his tee shot on 17 and landed in a green-side bunker. He blasted out and saw his ball come to rest about eight feet from the hole. DiMarco, meantime, after a 5-iron approach shot that landed pin-high but spun back off the green, was in great position to par the hole. A chip and a putt would do it.

But DiMarco wasn't thinking par. With about four feet to the edge of the green and another 15 to 20 feet to the cup, he took dead aim and punched a soft little wedge onto the putting surface. The ball rode a gentle slope to the right and headed directly at the cup for a possible birdie. Problem was, it hadn't checked up as much as he might have expected, and it approached its target with a bit too much pace. It caught a good chunk of the right side of the cup and actually jumped a couple of inches in the air as it carried four to five feet past.

Tiger now was in position to win. All that stood between him and a fourth Masters was eight feet of finely manicured Augusta grass. This was the kind of moment he lived for, right? He had 1 putt to win the most prestigious tournament in golf.

It wasn't to be. His ball drifted left and ran slowly by the hole. He never even gave it a chance. But now the pressure was back on DiMarco, who needed to sink a four-and-a-half-footer to force a playoff. Chris's putt was on a similar line to the one Tiger just missed. Whatever he saw in Woods's run at it served him well. He confidently knocked in his putt, played to the roar of the crowd with a few fist-pumps of his own, and joyously strode from the green with thoughts of taking down Tiger in sudden death.

THE PLAYOFF

The pendulum of good fortune that seemed to linger on Tiger's side, just like that chip shot on 16 lingered on the lip, had swung back to DiMarco. Yes, his chip shot at 18 could have ended it, but given his 2-stroke deficit a half hour earlier, a playoff was more than he could have hoped for. After a back-nine 41 to start the day, he pulled himself together and fired a final-round 68 to chase down Woods, who closed with a 71. With both men at 12 under par, it was back to 18—being used as the first playoff hole for the first time in tournament history. The first to blink would send the other home in a green jacket.

Both men hit good tee shots, Woods with a 3 wood and DiMarco with a driver. Chris was about 15 yards ahead of where he was in regulation and decided to approach with a 6 iron. But like his 5 iron minutes earlier, this shot too rolled back down the front slope of the green leaving him with an almost identical chip.

Tiger hit an 8 iron, about which he would later simply say, "Flushed it. It felt so good." It carried a few yards past the pin and settled less than 15 feet away.

DiMarco hit another good wedge. This one did bite, sending the ball rolling softly toward the cup. The line, though, wasn't quite what the first chip was, and it stopped about six inches left and two inches past the cup for an easy tap-in par.

Now, for the second time in about 20 minutes, Tiger Woods had a chance to win the tournament with a putt. This time he didn't miss. The ball rolled purely into the right-center of the hole, brought out the expected roar from the gallery, and sent Woods scurrying to his left in celebration. He pulled his right arm back behind him like a relay runner reaching for a baton, clenched his fist, and then swung it forward, ripping skyward like a Mike Tyson uppercut.

The green jacket Tiger slipped on with help from his one-time rival, defending champ Phil Mickelson, was the same as the previous three he had won, but something was definitely different. Something was missing. Or more accurately: someone.

Tears were flowing as the man who has become known for his steely nerves, unparalleled mental toughness, and impenetrable concentration allowed his thoughts and emotions to get the better of him.

Missing from the scene was Tiger's father, Earl Woods, the omnipresent figure who instilled and helped develop all those invaluable qualities in his son. This year, though, there were no reassuring looks and no green-side bear hugs. Battling both prostate cancer and heart disease, Earl could only watch on TV.

"My father is not able to be here," Tiger said, holding back tears. "He's struggling. It meant so much to me to win to give him motivation to fight. I can't wait to go home."

When he arrived to see his pops, he did so as one of three men to ever win four Masters, joining Jack (6) and Arnold (4)— two other players identified by a single name. The win was his first at a major since the 2002 U.S. Open and ninth major overall, pulling him even with Ben Hogan and Gary Player, trailing only Walter Hagen (11) and Nicklaus (18).

Tiger also moved back to the once-familiar top spot of the World Golf Rankings—a position he held a record 264 consecutive weeks during the monumental run of his early twenties.

The kid king was back on his rightful throne.

2005 Masters, Final Round

HOLE	1	2	3	4	5	6	7	8	9	OUT	10	11	12	13	14	15	16	17	18	IN	TOTAL
Woods	3	4	4	3	5	3	4	5	3	34	5	4	3	5	4	4	②	5	5	37	71
DiMarco	4	4	4	3	4	3	4	5	3	34	4	3	4	5	3	4	3	4	4	34	68

FINAL LEADER BOARD

Tiger Woods*	74–66–65–71	276
Chris DiMarco	67–67–74–68	276
Retief Goosen	71–75–70–67	283
Luke Donald	68–77–69–69	283
Rod Pampling	73–71–70–70	284
Mike Weir	74–71–68–71	284
Mark Hensby	69–73–70–72	284
Vijay Singh	68–73–71–72	284
Trevor Immelman	73–73–65–73	284
Phil Mickelson	70–72–69–74	285

*Won on first hole of sudden death.

POSTSCRIPT

If golf were a poker game, Chris DiMarco would be forever known as the victim of a bad beat. With all his chips in the pot, Tiger hit his one-outer on 16—catching an inside straight flush on the river to trump DiMarco's figurative four of a kind.

Living to play another hand, DiMarco's own chip shot that lipped out on 18 was also on his mind after the round.

"This is such a game of a missed putt here, a missed thing there," DiMarco said. "If you go back to two really big points in the whole day, it was his chip-in on 16 and my chip on 18 that had every right to go in the hole. I don't know how it didn't go in. But Tiger's was a great chip with great imagination. Actually, I was expecting him to make it. You expect the unexpected and, unfortunately, it's not unexpected when he's doing it.

"I went out and shot 68 around here on Sunday," Chris continued, "which is a very good round, and 12 under is usually good enough to win. I would let it hurt if I gave it away, but I didn't. I really didn't. I just was playing against Tiger Woods."

DiMarco, a likable good guy who hasn't won on tour since 2002, went on to challenge for another major the year after his close call at the Masters, but again came up short. The winner? Who else?

As he did in 2005, DiMarco put constant pressure on Tiger, shooting a final-round 68 at the 2006 British Open. Ultimately, though, he ran out of holes and finished in second place, 2 strokes behind. In the two Masters since his playoff loss, he has failed to make the cut.

Tiger, of course, spoke about his chip-for-the-ages as well. "A lot of it is luck, but I hit it pretty good. I hit it right on my spot. Under the circumstances, it's one of the best I've ever hit."

Woods was asked whether he had ever previously hit a shot, even in practice, from where he was on 16. "Never," he answered. "Never ever. You're not even supposed to be any-where near there."

Interestingly, Tiger himself ranks the shot as the third best of his career. Quoted in a 2007 *Men's Fitness* article, Woods says he hit the ball exactly where he wanted to, but chalks up the shot actually dropping into the cup to a great deal of luck.

His own version of "Tiger's Tops" has two far-less-celebrated shots ranked one and two. The second best, he says, is a shot he hit at the 2000 Canadian Open: a slightly cut 6 iron from a fair-way bunker that rode a prevailing left-to-right wind exactly as he envisioned—over trees, over water, and beyond a green-side bunker. The ball landed on the fringe about 15 feet from the cup. He 2-putted for birdie to preserve a 1-stroke victory.

At the top of his list is, amazingly, another shot from a fair-way bunker: this one a 3 iron from 202 yards in round two of the 2002 PGA Championship at Hazeltine. He was about two feet from the left edge of the left bunker on the 18th fairway, hitting directly into what he estimates was a 30-mile-per-hour wind. With his heels set on the back lip of the trap, he was a bit closer to the ball than he wanted to be and, to make matters worse, had to get the shot up in a hurry to clear some trees in front of him. Unable to use his legs to generate any power, and forced to make a compromised swing because of the unusual stance, he relied solely on feel and instinct. He brought the club through and nailed it in a way he eloquently described as the kind of shot "that goes up the shaft, through your arms, and right into your heart."

"The most solid shot I'd ever hit," he adds. The ball fought through the stiff breeze and onto the green, where a few minutes later, he dropped it into the cup for one of the more satisfying birdies of what has become one of the most impressive careers in the history of sports.

Unlike many others who attain success, there has been no slowing down for Woods. His dedication to the game and preparation for events is the same today, as a husband and father, as it was as a college kid who had not a care in the world. In August of 2007, he won the Bridgestone Invitational in Akron, Ohio. Less than 12 hours later, he was not only a thousand miles away in Tulsa, but also already on the golf course playing a practice round for the PGA Championship. He won that, too—his 13th career major. He entered 2008 just having claimed his third-straight PGA Player of the Year Award, winning it for the ninth time in 11 seasons.

Eldrick "Tiger" Woods was born to play golf just as Mozart was born to compose music, Einstein to think, Brando to act, Streisand to sing, and Clooney to pick up babes. The stories of his sitting in a high chair as an infant and watching his father hit golf balls into a net are widely known. His career in golf has been documented since the age of two, when he appeared on the nationally televised *Mike Douglas Show* to strut his stuff.

His long list of accomplishments could be catalogued here, but for what? Everybody gets it. There's no need to kill trees to offer evidence toward proving a point that is already made.

More intriguing than any documentation of tournaments won or records set is the brilliant way Earl Woods went about raising his son. A former Green Beret who served two tours of duty in Vietnam, Earl was not what has become the caricature of a sports-crazed father. He did not force Tiger into golf. He did not beat the sport into the psyche of an unwilling student. He lovingly guided the kid toward following the passion in the child's heart. He insisted in every interview he ever did that the fact that Tiger has attained the wild success he has in golf is secondary. His only goal, he said, was to raise his boy to be a good man.

On the eve of the final round of that 1997 Masters, with the finish as close to a foregone conclusion as there is in sports, Earl was quoted as saying, "This wasn't my dream. My dream was that Tiger become a good person. And I assure you he's a better person than golfer."

A year earlier, Earl Woods made a prediction that was, by all accounts, absurd. The thing is, that prediction crops up in an article or a news story every now and then, and those who have heard it—as absurd as it is—somehow hold on to it, storing it somewhere in the back of their minds…just in case.

In 1996, when Tiger was just 20 years old, Earl was quoted by *Sports Illustrated* as saying—and remember, this is absurd—that Tiger "will do more than any other man in history to change the course of humanity."

Earl went on, "He's the bridge between the East and the West. There is no limit because he has the guidance. I don't know yet exactly what form this will take, but he is the Chosen

One. He'll have the power to impact nations. Not people. Nations. The world is just getting a taste of his power."

Absurd, right? Right?

It certainly sounds a bit ambitious. A bit grand. Yes, but haven't we seen enough examples of athletes who have obtained a degree of power through their accomplishments and personas to realize that with the right combination of creativity, determination, and focus that anything is possible?

How many millions of dollars has Lance Armstrong helped raise for cancer research? Is there a way to overstate the importance of Jackie Robinson's impact on society? How about the past or future political endeavors of men such as Bill Bradley, Jim Bunning, and Steve Largent? Alan Page is an associate justice of the Minnesota Supreme Court. Byron White sat on the United States Supreme Court. Magic Johnson's foundations help develop inner-city communities and offer scholarships for disadvantaged youth. Tiki Barber, Billie Jean King, Albert Pujols, Mario Lemieux, Andre Agassi...the list is long, the contributions are plentiful.

The Tiger Woods Foundation is partnered with a major corporate player from just about every industry in the world. Woods himself has contact with people of power in just about every walk of life. If funding, access, vision, and determination are the keys to large-scale accomplishment, isn't this man just a decision away from beginning to change the world for the better? If Tiger is clear in his goals and willing to work toward them, doesn't it seem likely he will achieve them? Whatever they may be?

There has never been an athlete with a more complete combination of physical skills, knowledge of his craft, work ethic, and mental toughness than Tiger Woods. He seems to be the kind of man who can achieve...well, whatever he wants.

The amount of good an athlete can do is a function of his popularity multiplied by the level of his on-field accomplishment multiplied by his willingness to work toward the specific goal of his chosen endeavor. Given Tiger's potentially unparalleled status and success in the world of sports, doesn't it make sense that, if his degree of dedication to a cause equals his level of popularity and accomplishment, there is a true possibility for the man to make an impact on a scale never before seen from an athlete? From any human being? Is there not the prospect of a man who could...impact nations?

Fans watch the 16th hole of the FBR Tournament in Phoenix, Arizona, in 2008.

CHAPTER TEN

The Future

All in all, golf is in good shape as it moves toward the second decade of the new century. Television coverage and big-money sponsorships are both at levels never before seen in the sport's history, although that is a statement that probably could have been factually made at any time in the past 50 years.

Developments of the past few years, though, make for an interesting study. In January of 2006, the Golf Channel announced a blockbuster deal in which it had acquired the cable rights to the PGA Tour through 2021. Both NBC and CBS retained rights to the weekend rounds while the Golf Channel televises the opening rounds.

The agreement brought up an existential question that sports fans' viewing habits seem to be begging: if a tree falls in a forest and it is not shown on ESPN, does it make a noise? The PGA is betting that it does.

With Tiger Woods's enormous appeal as an ace in the hole, the sport moves forward with enough megamoney corporate partners to own the entire world, let alone reach it. Companies from Coca-Cola to IBM and from Delta Airlines to MasterCard are part of the modern punch packed by the PGA.

Two thousand seven marked the debut of a sponsored event of a different kind—one that will be woven into the very fabric of the tour. The FedExCup is an ongoing tournament within the tournaments, covering 37 weeks, designed to add meaning to events other than majors. With a small percentage of tour players holding a large percentage of the sport's star power, tournaments in which the big names did not play became effectively meaningless. Further, with the star players making no secret of the importance they themselves put on the majors, it was suddenly *uncool* to even show up for regular PGA tournaments. That is a problem.

The obvious hope of the sport's powers-that-be is, as their website states, "The PGA Tour Playoffs for the FedExCup will change the way you watch golf and produce a true PGA Tour champion."

Whether the intended purpose of the cup actually comes to fruition remains to be seen. There are, undoubtedly, as with any new system, tweaks to be made, but with contracts in place and the core group of leading players in their twenties and thirties, the tour has time on its side. And, of course, money.

The prize for first place in the FedExCup is $10 million, and perhaps a decade ago, that in itself would be enough to draw a great deal of fan interest. Now, though, the American sporting public is so numb to obscene contracts and over-the-top prize money that the sheer dollar amount—as impressive as it may be—doesn't have quite the same impact. And there's this: payment of the money is deferred until the winner is 45 years old and will be doled out in monthly installments over five years. Can't you just see Tiger running out to his mailbox in 2024 and rejoicing at the sight of a check? "Honey! Crank up the grill, we're having steak tonight!"

Whether the idea works or not, golf seems to be positioned well; the people running the sport just have to know when to tinker and when to leave it alone.

One major difference will be the way the sport is presented to its spectators. People who actually attend the events in the future will, of course, get a similar experience to those who have attended in the past. The change comes in mass media, through both television and Internet coverage. "The trend in broadcasting is moving to anywhere, anytime, anyway," says Page Thompson, president of the Golf Channel. "The same will happen for golf. You will see the presentation in a variety of formats. We always want to have the traditional golf broadcast for viewers who wish to watch as they always have, but now there is also the ability to have interactive stats and features that can supplement the broadcast. Interactive TV has been talked about for decades now but…I'm certain that in the next few years it's really going to take off, and golf is ideally suited for that. People can sit at home and hit a button on the remote control to look at a given hole and see exactly how it is laid out. If a player is, say, 120 yards away, viewers will be able to call up stats on how successful that player has been historically in that situation."

There will also be more choices for viewers tuning in to watch a given tournament. Eric Shanks, executive vice president of entertainment for DirecTV, says, "Golf is one of those sports that is inherently designed to be viewed on more than one channel. The television-viewing experience should be more like the in-person experience at the course. The fan in the gallery may sit on one hole for a while, then walk to another hole, or maybe follow a certain group for a few holes. It's really hard for a network to deliver that kind of experience for each individual golf fan."

Now, though, a satellite-television distributor can. With ownership of vast television "real estate," DirecTV can set aside five or six channels of separate coverage. Want to watch your favorite player? Set your box on channel 425—it's all Tiger, all day. If Phil is your guy, go to channel 426. Want to focus on the 18th green? Punch up channel 428. Curious about the course layout? Channel 430 has interactive flyovers.

Think of it as your father's golf coverage on steroids. "I don't just want to see the shots," says Shanks. "I want to see a player walk up to his ball; I want to see him choose his clubs; I want to hear him discuss strategy with his caddie. I want the full experience. Sometimes on the network, you might see one of the big-name players hit most of his shots, but that's all you see— the shot. Our coverage will allow you to see it all."

Thompson also insists golf will benefit from high-definition television. "Like hockey, golf is a sport that is so much better in HD. Say you are watching the Masters; you can see all the subtle contours of Augusta National. People will go to Augusta for the first time and say, 'I didn't realize how hilly it is here....' On HD you can see the hills. You can see the way putts will break; you can see everything."

It is a time in the sport's long and storied history when the spotlight burns brightly on the grand stage of the tee box. It is, at its heart, the same beautiful game that was played centuries ago, but the technologically advanced, modern-day version, with its titanium drivers and new media coverage, has integrated an obvious element of big business. Fairways are lush and kept healthy with fertilizer of gold. Greens are rolling true, well maintained, and manicured with money. Players have omnipresent television cameras behind them and a blank canvas in front of them, primed and ready for the sweet strokes of artistry and drama as an adoring public looks on.

That next great shot is out there, somewhere, just waiting to be hit.

Resources

NEWSPAPERS

Atlanta Journal-Constitution

Boston Globe

Boston Herald

Chicago Tribune

Los Angeles Times

Miami Herald

The New York Times

Palm Beach Post

Philadelphia Inquirer

Virginian-Pilot

BOOKS

Thirty Years of Championship Golf: The Life and Times of Gene Sarazen by Gene Sarazen and Herbert Warren Wind

Ben Hogan: An American Life by James Dodson

The Golden Era of Golf by Al Barkow

My Greatest Shot by Ron Cherney and Michael Arkush

A Golfer's Life by Arnold Palmer (with James Dodson)

The Eternal Summer by Curt Sampson

Golf's Greatest Championship: The 1960 U.S. Open by Julian I. Graubart

The Wicked Game by Howard Sounes

Shark by Lauren St. John

Gary Player, World Golfer: His Autobiography by Gary Player

The Golfer's Guide to the Meaning of Life by Gary Player

Tour '72 by Michael D'Antonio

Jack Nicklaus: My Story by Jack Nicklaus and Ken Bowden

Tom Watson's Strategic Golf by Tom Watson
Pebble Beach: Golf and the Forgotten Men by Jerry Stewart

MAGAZINES
Sports Illustrated
Golf
Golf Digest

VIDEOTAPES
PGA Campionship, 1972
CBS Sports, Masters 1986, 1987, 2005
Ryder Cup Highlites 1999